Muses' Library

★

POEMS BY
JOHN WILMOT
EARL OF ROCHESTER

JOHN WILMOT, EARL OF ROCHESTER

*From the painting attributed to J. Huysmans
in The National Portrait Gallery*

[*Frontispiece*

POEMS

BY

JOHN WILMOT
EARL OF ROCHESTER

edited

with an introduction and notes
by

VIVIAN DE SOLA PINTO

Professor of English
in the University of Nottingham

LONDON
ROUTLEDGE AND KEGAN PAUL

First published in 1953
by Routledge and Kegan Paul Ltd
Broadway House, 68–74 Carter Lane
London E.C.4
Printed in Great Britain
by Butler and Tanner Limited
Frome and London

CONTENTS

ACKNOWLEDGEMENTS

I WISH to acknowledge with gratitude the help and encouragement I have received, in preparing this edition, from friends and colleagues on both sides of the Atlantic, and also the kindness and co-operation of librarians and owners of books and manuscripts in this country and in America. I should like particularly to thank Professor J. H. Wilson of the Ohio State University, Columbus, Ohio, both for the useful advice which he gave me when I enjoyed his hospitality at Columbus and for the very considerable help which I have obtained from his published writings, to Professor James M. Osborn of Yale University for his kind and helpful counsel when I was his guest at New Haven, Connecticut, and for giving me access to the manuscripts in his collection, to Mr. David Vieth for much useful help and information, to Mr. Harold F. Brooks of Birkbeck College, London, for some valuable hints and suggestions, to the Trustees of the Folger Library, Washington, D.C., for making me a grant of dollars which enabled me to study the material connected with Rochester in that magnificent collection and to the Director, Professor Louis B. Wright, for his very great kindness and courtesy while I was there, to His Grace the Duke of Portland for allowing me to use the valuable manuscripts in his collection, to the officials of the British Museum, the Bodleian and the Harvard University Libraries and the Dyce Collection at the Victoria and Albert Museum, and finally to Mr. G. Ellis Flack, our Librarian at the University of Nottingham, and his assistants, who have never failed to respond to my incessant demands concerning Rochester and have done all that librarians can do to make an editor's task pleasant.

ix

ACKNOWLEDGEMENTS

I acknowledge permission granted by the following publishers and owners of copyright to reproduce extracts in the Critical Comments: Macmillan and Co., Ltd., for the passage by the late Sir Edmund Gosse from T. H. Ward's *English Poets* and for the passage by W. J. Courthope from his *History of English Poetry*; The Cambridge University Press for the passage by the late Charles Whibley from Volume VIII of *The Cambridge History of English Literature*; Messrs. Edward Arnold and Co. for the passage from the late Sir Walter Raleigh's *Milton*; Messrs. Chatto and Windus and Dr. F. R. Leavis for the passage from Dr. Leavis's *Revaluation*; Mr. Kenneth Murdock for the passage from *The Sun at Noon*.

NOTES ON THE
ILLUSTRATIONS

THE frontispiece (Plate 1) is the well-known portrait of
Rochester attributed to J. Huysmans in the National
Portrait Gallery; it is reproduced by permission of the
Trustees. It represents the poet in flowing robes with
his pet monkey mentioned in one of his letters to
Henry Savile (The Rochester-Savile Letters, ed. J. H.
Wilson, no. XXIII). Rochester is crowning the monkey
with a laurel wreath with one hand and holding sheets
of manuscript with the other. The monkey is seated on
a pile of books and holds one from which he has
apparently torn a page which he is offering to the Earl.
The picture seems to have been conceived in the mood
of the opening lines of *A Satyr against Mankind*.

Plate 2 (opposite p. xxxviii) is a portrait of Rochester
ascribed to W. Wissing at Hinchingbrooke, Huntingdonshire, reproduced by permission of the Earl of
Sandwich. Rochester's second daughter Elizabeth
married the third Earl of Sandwich and I have the
authority of Lord Sandwich for stating that it was
through her that this picture came into the possession
of his family. Plate 3 (opposite p. 116) is a reproduction
of one of the poems in Rochester's handwriting in the
Portland Collection formerly at Welbeck Abbey and
now in the Library of the University of Nottingham.
It is reproduced by permission of the Duke of Portland
and the University of Nottingham.

INTRODUCTION

INTRODUCTION

OCHESTER'S reputation as a poet has suffered from the legend, or perhaps it would be more accurate to say, the two legends, of his life and character. One legend is that of the Wicked Lord, the arch-debauchee of the Restoration, who, in the words of Dr. Johnson, 'blazed out his youth and health in lavish voluptuousness' and was pictured by Sir Edmund Gosse as 'a petulant and ferocious rake, whose wasting hold on life only increased his malevolent licence'.[1] The other is that of the Noble Convert who atoned for all his misdeeds by a dramatic conversion to Christianity at the end of a misspent life, and became the subject of numerous pious tracts down to the nineteenth century. Neither of these legends will survive a critical examination. The best source of information about Rochester is to be found in his own writings and not in gossip, but modern methods of research now enable the biographer to disengage from the record of his career a considerable amount of untruthful scandal and to piece together a narrative which reveals a much more credible and interesting figure than either Sir Edmund Gosse's 'ferocious rake' or the 'Noble Convert' of the tracts.

John Wilmot was born on 1st April[2] 1647 at Ditchley Manor House in Oxfordshire; he was the son of Henry, Viscount Wilmot, an Oxfordshire landowner and royalist general, and of his wife Anne, daughter of Sir John St. John and a member of a famous Puritan family. The elder Wilmot was a witty and amusing companion as well as an able soldier, and was a favourite of the young Charles II, whom he accompanied on his expedition to Scotland in 1650 and his

---

[1] *Seventeenth Century Studies* (1914), p. 316.
[2] Old style, as all other dates mentioned in this introduction.

invasion of England in the following year. It was largely through his coolness and ingenuity that the King was able to escape after his defeat at Worcester in 1651. He became a prominent member of the exiled court in France, and was created Earl of Rochester on 13th December 1652. He died at Sluys on 19th February 1657/8.

The young John Wilmot thus inherited the earldom of Rochester and his father's not very extensive estate in Oxfordshire in his eleventh year. His mother and Sir Ralph Verney of Claydon, Bucks., were appointed his guardians; he received a good education, at first at home from a clergyman called Francis Giffard, who found him 'very virtuous and good natur'd', and then at Burford Grammar School under John Martin, who had the reputation of a good scholar and teacher. While he was at school he was 'an extraordinary Proficient at his Book' and 'acquired the *Latin* to such perfection, that to his dying-day he retained a great rellish for the fineness and Beauty of that Tongue: and was exactly versed in the incomparable Authors that writ about *Augustus's* time'. On 18th January 1659/60 he entered Wadham College, Oxford, as a Fellow Commoner or 'Nobleman'. Wadham was at that time one of the chief intellectual centres of the University and the cradle of the group that was to form the nucleus of the Royal Society. Rochester's tutor was an amiable mathematician called Phineas Bury, and there can be little doubt that, young as he was, he came into contact with some of the most advanced thought of the day, and especially with the much-discussed philosophy of Thomas Hobbes.

When Rochester came up to Wadham, Monk was leading his army from Scotland to London, and that spring, the University and city of Oxford went mad with excitement and enthusiasm for the restored monarchy. The sudden relaxation of the severe Puritan discipline in the University seems to have produced a kind of saturnalia among dons and undergraduates alike. We are told that the young Earl, who had hitherto been a modest and studious youth, 'began to love these disorders too much', and that he 'broke off the Course of his Studies'. His guide to the night-life of Oxford was a rather disreputable don, Dr. Robert Whitehall, Fellow of Merton, who used to lend him a Master's gown to protect him from the Proctors in his nocturnal rambles. The spectacle of the slender, handsome boy of thirteen being 'debauched' in the Oxford taverns under the expert guidance of the hard-drinking Fellow of Merton, is not a pleasant one. Whitehall is said to have 'doted' on him and to have 'instructed him in the art of poetry'. The earliest verses ascribed to Rochester are some lines to the King on his restoration, and some English and Latin verses on the death of the Princess of Orange, said to have been written when he was at Wadham. It has been alleged that Whitehall was the real author of these lines, but they are not beyond the power of a clever boy of thirteen, though it is likely that Whitehall gave the young poet some help with them. In September 1660 Edward Hyde, Earl of Clarendon and Chancellor of the University, visited Oxford and held a Convocation at which he conferred the degree of M.A. on two young noblemen, one of whom was the Earl of Rochester. This was, doubtless, merely intended as a compliment to the son of an eminent loyalist, but there is irony in the encounter of the chief representative of the old world of stiff ceremonial and conservative legalism with the future author of the *History of Insipids* and the *Satyr against Mankind*.

No one who helped Charles II in his escape from Worcester went unrewarded after the Restoration. Henry Wilmot was dead, but his son was living and Charles II took a personal interest in the young man from the beginning; he granted him an annual pension of £500 in 1661 when he was still at Oxford, and he arranged that his education should be completed in the way considered proper for a gentleman in that period by a tour on the Continent. For this purpose he appointed as his tutor Sir Andrew Balfour, M.D., then a man of thirty, a distinguished Scottish physician and scholar. The choice was an excellent one, and we are told that Sir Andrew 'drew him to read such Books, as were most likely to bring him back to love Learning and Study'. Rochester and Balfour left England on 21st November 1661; they travelled through France and Italy, visiting Milan, Florence, Pisa, Bologna, Venice, Padua, Vicenza, Rome, and Naples. They were at Venice on 1st October 1664, and reached Padua by the end of the month, when Rochester was enrolled as a student in the 'English Nation' at the famous University of that city. Soon after they returned to England.

Rochester seems to have appeared at court in 1665, when he was eighteen. He is described as being at that time 'a graceful and well shaped Person, tall and well made, if not a little too slender'. His conversation was 'easie and obliging', and he had 'a strange Vivacity of Thought and vigour of expression'. His favourite authors, we are told, were '*Boileau* among the *French*, and *Cowley* among the *English* Wits'. He at once became the leader of the set at court which Andrew Marvell called the 'merry gang', the group of Wits[1] in whose conversation the King delighted, but whose opinions and way of life shocked Puritans and old-fashioned cavaliers alike. His friends included George Villiers, Duke of Buckingham (Dryden's *Zimri*), Charles Sackville, Earl of Dorset, Sir Charles Sedley,

---

[1] The best account of this group is to be found in J. H. Wilson's admirable book, *The Court Wits of the Restoration* (Princeton, 1948)

Sir George Etherege, Fleetwood Shepheard, Henry Savile, and Thomas Killigrew. This is the set whose wild doings and 'cursed bawdy talk' are described by Pepys in his diary with a mixture of pious horror and prurient envy.

Lord Hawley, an old cavalier from Somerset, came to London in the spring of 1665 and brought with him his granddaughter Elizabeth Malet, daughter of Sir John Malet, a Somersetshire knight. Elizabeth was beautiful and witty and the heiress to a great estate. Charles II thought she would be a good match for Rochester, but she had many suitors, and her starchy relatives were horrified at the King's suggestion that she should marry a wild young rake who was almost wholly dependent on the King's bounty. On 26th May Rochester made a reckless attempt to abduct her when she was being driven home by her grandfather from a supper party at Whitehall; she was seized by a party of armed men who transferred her to a coach and six where two women were provided to wait on her. Her relatives appealed to the King, who promptly issued a proclamation for a search to be made for the missing heiress. She was soon found and Rochester was arrested and committed to the Tower for his 'high misdemeanour'. He promptly petitioned for his release which was granted on 19th June. He seems to have volunteered at once for service with the navy, then engaged in hostilities with the Dutch, and he was entrusted by the King with a letter to the Earl of Sandwich, who was in command of the fleet in the North Sea. On 17th July Sandwich informed the King in a letter sent from the Yorkshire coast that Rochester had come aboard as a volunteer, and that his vessels were under sail, bound for the coast of Norway in order to intercept the immensely valuable Dutch East India fleet said to be in these waters. When the Norwegian coast was reached, it was learnt that the

Dutch ships had taken refuge in Bergen harbour and Sir Thomas Teddiman was sent with twenty frigates to go in and capture the rich prizes. Rochester volunteered to serve in Teddiman's squadron and took part in the action in Bergen harbour, showing 'as brave and as resolute a Courage as was possible'. It was on this occasion that he entered into an engagement 'not without Ceremonies of Religion' with another gentleman volunteer that 'if either of them died, he should appear and give the other notice of the future State if there was any'. Rochester's friend was killed in the battle, but his spirit did not return to give information about the next world, and, later, Rochester told Burnet that this 'was a great snare to him, during the rest of his life'. However, he was somewhat shaken in his materialism by the fact that both the man with whom he had made the pact and another friend who was killed with him had a presentiment that they would not survive the battle. In a charming letter to his mother Rochester described the action in detail, concluding with a revealing postscript: 'I have bin as good a husband as I could, but in spite of my teeth have been faine to borrow mony.' On 12th September he was sent by Sandwich with despatches to the King, and was described by the Admiral as 'Brave, Industrious, and of parts fitt to be very usefull in yr Maties service'. Soon after he returned to London, but the following summer he slipped away from Whitehall, went on board Sir Edward Spragge's ship on 31st May 1666, and took part in the sanguinary Four Days' Battle in the Channel. He volunteered to take a message from the admiral to one of the captains in a small boat during the action. He set out under heavy fire, delivered the message successfully and returned to his ship, 'which was much commended by all that saw it'. The King was so pleased with Rochester's service in the navy that he made him a gift of £750 on 31st October 1666 and so probably cleared off the debts mentioned in his letter to his mother. Elizabeth Malet, in spite of the fact that she had many suitors at court, surprised everyone by marrying Rochester on 29th January 1666/7. In March the Earl was appointed a gentleman of the Bedchamber with an annual salary of £1,000, and probably about the same time his wife was made Groom of the Stole to the Duchess of York.

There can be no doubt about Rochester's deep and genuine affection for his wife, which finds expression in a number of his extant letters[1] to her, the tone of which is very similar to that of his best love lyrics. One of his letters to her shows that he scrupulously avoided using her fortune for his own purposes and employed it wholly (his own phrase) for her benefit and that of her dependents. She appears to have been a cultivated woman and some transcripts of poems ascribed to Rochester in her handwriting have been preserved. One of these poems may well be her own composition. Rochester had four children by her: Charles, who inherited the title and died at the age of eleven in 1681, Anne, who married first Henry Baynton and then Francis Greville, Elizabeth, who married the third Earl of Sandwich, and Malet, who married Viscount Lisburne.

In the years that followed his marriage, Rochester seems to have led a curious double life, a manifestation of a divided personality. On the one hand, he was an affectionate husband and a good and popular landlord; on the other, he was one of the wildest debauchees at the court of Charles II, 'prince of all the devils of the Town', the hero of scores of escapades, and the lover of a series of mistresses. According to Aubrey he 'was wont to say that when he came to Brentford the devill entred into him and never left him

---

[1] Brit. Mus., Harl. MS. 7003. These letters are printed by Prinz in his *John Wilmot Earl of Rochester*, pp. 253–72.

till he came into the country again at Alderbury or Woodstock'. He told Burnet that 'for five years together he was continually Drunk: not all the while under the visible effect of it, but his blood was so inflamed, that he was not in all that time cool enough to be perfectly Master of himself'. Many stories were told of his wild pranks, some of which, as Professor J. H. Wilson has shown, are certainly apocryphal.[1] Sometimes he went too far even for the easy going Charles II and was frequently banished from Court, but was always recalled by the king, who delighted in his conversation.

At a dinner given to the Dutch Ambassador on 17th February 1668/9, Rochester boxed Tom Killigrew's ears in the royal presence, and Pepys was shocked not only to hear that he was pardoned but to see the King 'publickly walk up and down' with him 'as free as ever'. A little later he insulted Killigrew's father, and this time his offence was not forgiven so easily. He was sent to Paris with a message to the Duchess of Orleans, Charles II's sister, on 12th March, and was present at a riotous scene at the Opera there in July. Besides outrageous conduct of this kind, another way in which Rochester gave offence at court was by means of the 'Libels and Satyrs' in which we are told 'he laid out his Wit very freely'. He told Burnet that he used to employ as his spy a footman who 'knew all the Court', and that he disguised him with 'a red coat and a musket as a sentinel' and 'kept him all the winter long every night at the door of such ladies as he believed might be in intrigues'. By this means he is said to have made 'many discoveries', and, when he had plenty of material, he 'used to retire to the country for a month or two to write libels'.

It was during the fourteen or fifteen years that he spent at Court that Rochester acquired the reputation

---

[1] See, for instance, *The Court Wits of the Restoration*, pp. 44, 45.

for wickedness that hung round him like a sulphurous halo in the eighteenth and nineteenth centuries. He seems to have made an enemy of John Sheffield, Earl of Mulgrave (afterwards Duke of Buckinghamshire), in the late sixteen-sixties. Sheffield was one of the minor Court Wits, a humourless, rather pompous person, not without literary talent, but with an immense opinion of his own importance. He became the friend and patron of Dryden and later of Pope and appears to be one of the chief sources of Rochester's evil reputation. The quarrel between the two men came to a head in November 1669, and Rochester has commonly been accused of cowardice for refusing to fight a duel with 'My Lord All Pride' as he called Sheffield. This was the version of the story given by Mulgrave himself in his *Memoirs*,[1] but entries in the Journals of the House of Lords[2] show that the duel was actually stopped by the personal intervention of the King, at whose request the House sent the Gentleman Usher of the Black Rod to secure the persons of both the peers. Both of them were brought before the House, and made to promise to keep the peace. These entries seem to prove that there is no foundation for the charge of cowardice brought against Rochester on this occasion. When he judged that fighting was necessary, he was quite willing to fight; on 25th March 1673 a duel between him and Lord Dunbar, a notorious bully, was narrowly averted by the Earl-Marshal's intervention, and in December 1674, when Mulgrave challenged Henry Savile, Rochester offered to act as second to his friend.

Another accusation commonly brought against Rochester has been that he behaved in a cruel and capricious way to contemporary writers, and parti-

---

[1] *The Works of John Sheffield* (London, 1723), ii, 9, 10.
[2] *Journals of the House of Lords*, vol. xii (1666–75), pp. 272, 274, 276, 277 *s.d.* 23rd, 24th, 26th Nov. 1669.

cularly to Dryden. The most serious charge is that he not only turned against Dryden after generously helping him but that he was the instigator of the cowardly assault which took place in Rose Alley, Covent Garden, on 18th December 1679, when Dryden was set upon and cudgelled by a gang of ruffians. Actually there is no evidence to show that Rochester treated Dryden badly, or that he had anything to do with the Rose Alley outrage. It is certain that the two poets were on good terms in the spring and summer of 1672, when Dryden dedicated his comedy, *Marriage à la Mode*, to Rochester in very complimentary terms. In the dedication he states that Rochester actually helped him to revise the play for publication. Rochester appears to have written to thank him for the dedication, and Dryden replied in a charming extant[1] letter with which he sent the Earl copies of a prologue and epilogue he had recently written. There seems to be no foundation in fact, for the commonly repeated gossip that Rochester slighted Dryden by patronizing Elkanah Settle, or that he had anything to do with the selection of John Crowne instead of the poet laureate to provide a masque to be acted at Court in the spring of 1675. Much as Rochester admired Dryden's genius, however, there was something tame and prosaic in the elder poet's character that annoyed him, just as somewhat similar aspects of Wordsworth's character annoyed Byron. He criticized him severely but not maliciously or unfairly in his *Allusion to the Tenth Satyr of the First Book of Horace*, probably written in 1675. Dryden took offence and commented somewhat tartly on noble amateurs in poetry who wrote 'malicious satire', almost certainly with reference to Rochester, in the Preface to his *All for Love*, acted in December 1677 and published early in 1678. A passage

---

[1] *The Works of John Dryden*, ed. Sir W. Scott (1808), xviii, 89, 90.

in an undated letter from Rochester to his friend
Henry Savile has been commonly cited as proof that
Rochester was responsible for the Rose Alley outrage.
Professor J. H. Wilson[1] has, however, shown that this
letter was almost certainly written in April 1676,
nearly four years before the attack on Dryden. It is
therefore very unlikely that it had anything to do with
it, and the passage seems to me simply a humorous
reference to Dryden's touchiness.

The assault on Dryden was certainly connected with
the scurrilous lampoon called *An Essay upon Satyr*
written by Mulgrave and probably corrected by
Dryden. This poem was being circulated in manuscript
in the winter of 1679. It contains a violent attack on all
the members of the 'merry gang', including Rochester
(whom Mulgrave has the impudence to blame for his
'meer want of Wit') and the king's mistresses, with a
particularly ferocious onslaught on Louise de Keroualle, Duchess of Portsmouth. There is every reason to
believe the suggestion of Anthony à Wood that this
corrupt and vindictive woman was the real instigator
of the Rose Alley outrage, and it is likely that the
perpetrator of it was the murderous maniac, Philip
Herbert, Earl of Pembroke,[2] brother-in-law of the
Duchess.

Rochester's relationship with Otway seems to have
followed a somewhat similar course to that of his
connection with Dryden. Otway dedicated his tragedy
of *Don Carlos* to the Duke of York in 1676 and boasts
of Rochester's patronage in his dedication. In the
following year he dedicated in fulsome terms his *Titus
and Berenice* to Rochester himself. In the autumn of
the same year a humorous attack on Otway appeared
in the squib called *A Session of Poets* attributed to

[1] See his article in *The Review of English Studies* (July 1939)
xv, 59, and his edition of *The Rochester-Savile Letters* (Columbus,
Ohio, 1940), pp. 87, 88.

[2] See J. H. Wilson, *The Court Wits of the Restoration*, p. 118.

Rochester, and there is also a slighting reference to
him in the *Allusion to the Tenth Satyr of the First
Book of Horace*. Otway, like Dryden, took offence and
described Rochester in his poem, *The Poet's Complaint
to his Muse*, under the name of 'Lord Lampoon' as
one who sought the Muses' favours in vain.

None of Rochester's detractors have been able to
smear the record of his relations with a third contemporary writer outside the Court circle, John
Oldham. This young Oxford graduate's verses
attracted Rochester's attention when he was an usher
at a school at Croydon some time after 1676. He was
apparently fascinated by Rochester's character, and
two of his poems written between 1676 and 1677 are
imaginary monologues put into the Earl's mouth.[1]
Rochester is said to have visited him at Croydon and
to have befriended him generously. Transcripts of two
of Rochester's finest poems in Oldham's hand survives
and one of them was possibly corrected by Rochester
himself.[2]

Rochester plunged into the life of pleasure at Court
with a kind of frenzy, but he was no vulgar sensualist.
We know from Robert Parsons, his mother's chaplain,
that he adopted the fashionable materialism of Hobbes
and he also admired Lucretius. His hedonism seems to
have been a kind of experiment in the life of pure
sensation, an attempt to find the fulfilment of his being
in the moment of sensuous pleasure which is comparable with the experiments of his contemporaries,
George Fox and John Bunyan, who tried to find it in
religious experience. In a fragment of a letter to his
wife, he writes of the 'great disproportion 'twixt our
desires and what is ordained to content them' and of
'those who are soe intirely satisfyed with their shares

---

[1] See Harold F. Brooks, 'A Bibliography of John Oldham',
Proceedings and Papers of the Oxford Bibliographical Society,
vol. v, pt. i.

[2] See below, p. xlvi.

in this world that their wishes nor theire thoughts have not a farther prospect of felicity and glory'. Rochester's mind was fundamentally religious: it was 'felicity and glory' that he was seeking, and he thought he had found it in such moments as that described in the finest of his lyrics:

> *All my past Life is mine no more,*
> *The flying Hours are gone...*

Such fleeting experiences, however, could not ultimately satisfy this ardent seeker for reality, and, as his health declined, he came to realize the truth which Simone Weil has expressed so forcibly:

'La misère humaine contient le secret de la sagesse divine, et non pas le plaisir. Toute recherche d'un plaisir est recherche d'un paradis artificiel, d'une ivresse, d'un accroissement, mais elle ne vous donne rien, sinon l'experience qu'elle est vaine. Seule la contemplation de nos limites et de nos misères nous met un plan au dessus.'[1]

Up to about 1675 Rochester had been living in artificial paradises, but the progressive decline in his health, due apparently to venereal disease contracted early in his career, made it more and more difficult for him to find satisfaction in the life of pleasure. In 1671 we hear of him suddenly walking out of Garraway's Coffee House and posting down to the country as a result of eye trouble. In the summer of 1672 he was with his wife at her estate at Enmore in Somersetshire and apparently enjoying the life of a country gentleman. He took his duties as a landowner seriously and we hear of him championing 'the commoners and cottagers' of certain lands in Gloucestershire. In October 1672 he was appointed Deputy-Lieutenant of Somersetshire and in November 1677 an Alderman of

[1] S. Weil, *La Pesanteur et la Grâce* (Paris, 1948), p. 109.

Taunton. In 1673 and 1674 he had returned to the bohemian life of the London taverns and theatres. It was at this time that he had a liaison with a girl called Elizabeth Barry, who had been a servant to a lady in Norfolk; she was not beautiful, but Rochester saw in her the making of a fine actress. He took immense pains in teaching her 'not only the proper cadence or sounding of the voice, but to seize also the passions, and adapt her whole behaviour, to the situations of the character'. Her first appearance in the Duke's company in 1674 was a complete failure, but Rochester would not admit defeat. Probably through his influence she was re-engaged by the same company in the following year, and won much applause by her acting in the *Alcibiades* of Otway. Her subsequent career was brilliant and she became one of the most celebrated actresses of her day. There appears to be no foundation for the story that she jilted Otway or that Rochester's quarrel with Otway was due to his connection with her. Rochester had a daughter by Mrs. Barry. She is probably the Elizabeth Clerke mentioned in his will, to whom he bequeathed an annuity of £40 secured on one of his manors.[1]

In the spring of 1674/5 he was appointed Ranger of Woodstock Forest in his native county of Oxfordshire. Woodstock was an ancient royal hunting domain; the rangership was in the gift of the King and Rochester had long coveted the office, because it carried with it the right to reside at the Ranger's Lodge, which now became his favourite place of retirement. He seems to have been in London in the spring and summer of 1675 and on the night of 24th June took part in a wild debauch at Whitehall with Buckhurst, Fleetwood Shepheard, and others. In the middle of the great Privy Garden at Whitehall there was an elaborate and expensive set of 'dialls' or chronometers made for the

[1] See J. Prinz, *John Wilmot Earl of Rochester* (1927), p. 300.

King by a learned Jesuit, Franciscus Linus. Rochester
staggered up to the mechanism in the grey light of the
early morning and asked it an amusing but unprint-
able question. Then 'dash they fell to work' and the
glass spheres with the dials enclosed in them were soon
smashed to atoms. The result was another banishment
from the Court. The Earl seems to have gone first to
Tunbridge Wells, where at the end of June he wrote
his amusing satire on the company assembled at that
fashionable watering-place, and then to the Ranger's
Lodge at Oxford, where he composed some of his
most powerful poems, *An Allusion to the Tenth Satire
of the First Book of Horace* and the *Satyr against
Mankind*.

It is difficult to date Rochester's works with any
degree of accuracy, but it is likely that most of his
lyrics are early works. His great satiric poems were
probably all written in the last five years of his life.
These are no mere literary exercises but expressions of
the agony and indignation of a man who had sought
for 'felicity and glory' in the world of pleasure and had
found that it was an illusion concealing ugliness, folly,
hypocrisy and injustice. In the social satires such as
Artemisa's Letter, it is the inanity and hypocrisy of
le monde ou l'on s'amuse that is attacked. In *The Satyr
against Mankind* it is the much-vaunted reason. Man,
the rational creature, is compared to his disadvantage
with the beasts.

> *Be Judge your self, I'le bring it to the test,*
> *Which is the basest Creature, Man or Beast?*
> *Birds, feed on Birds, Beasts, on each other prey;*
> *But Savage Man alone, does Man betray.*

The writer of these lines could no longer be content
with an artificial paradise of pleasure, yet he could not
tear himself away from his old habit of going to
London and plunging recklessly into the vortex of

debauchery. As time went on this life became a kind of phantasmagoria, a dance of death, as he himself seems to describe it in a significant passage in his adaptation of Fletcher's *Valentinian*:

Mishapen Monsters round in Measures went,
Horrid in Form with gestures insolent;
Grinning throu' Goatish beards with half-clos'd eyes.

In the year 1676 the dance reached its climax. In the spring of this year Etherege's brilliant comedy, *The Man of Mode* or *Sir Fopling Flutter*, was produced in London; the central figure of the play was Dorimant, whom everyone recognized as an idealized portrait of Rochester, the type of the court wit, the aesthetic and non-moral hero of the Restoration. It was in that spring too that Rochester carried out one of his most daring and original frolics. Banished again from Court, this time, it is said, on account of an impudent and outspoken satire on the King, he gave out that he was going to France, but instead took lodgings on Tower Hill, and, with the help of his faithful servant Thomas Alcock, disguised himself as an Italian quack doctor and set up in business under the name of Alexander Bendo. In the manner of the mountebanks of the day, he issued a bill to advertise Dr. Bendo, which has been preserved[1] and is a masterpiece of witty, ironic prose; in it Dr. Bendo compares the mountebank with other men and especially with the Politician, who is described as 'a *Mountebank* in State-affairs'. He claims to cure a remarkable variety of diseases as well as to 'practise rare secrets ... for the Help, Conservation and Augmentation of Beauty and Comeliness'. In addition to distributing this bill, he employed a merry andrew to lure customers to Tower

[1] Versions of it are printed in the 1691 and other editions of his poems. A manuscript copy with an account of the escapade prepared by Thomas Alcock himself for Rochester's daughter is now in the Library of the University of Nottingham.

Hill in the approved style, and multitudes, especially of women, came to consult him in his lodgings, where he employed a team of assistants to compound medicaments from soap, ashes, brickdust, and other unpromising materials. When the King decided to revoke the sentence of exile, Dr. Bendo and his assistants suddenly vanished into thin air and 'the very next [night] the Earl was seen in Splendor at Whitehall, dancing in a ball in as great a favour as ever'. That summer he was involved in a drunken affray with the watch at Epsom, in which one of his friends called Downs was killed in a scuffle with the constable and his men. Rochester as usual was blamed for the mishap, but he does not seem to have actually been guilty of anything but drunken folly. After the wild doings of this summer he never seems to have been really well again. He was ill in the spring of 1677, and during his convalescence he was reading Livy and thinking of state affairs. In the following August he was well enough to be in London and to spend at least one very merry evening with the King and Buckingham at his lodgings. The next winter he was seriously ill again and his death was reported in London.

What Rochester needed at this stage in his career was a religion in which he could believe and which would provide him with a positive attitude in place of the nihilism which followed his rejection of the ideal of the court wit or aesthetic hero. His position now closely resembled that of Byron at the time of the composition of the Fourth Canto of *Childe Harold* and *Manfred*. In the last years of his life he was working at the composition of his most romantic poem, an adaptation of Fletcher's tragedy of *Valentinian*, in which the three leading characters all seem to represent aspects of his own personality; Valentinian, the lustful tyrant, is Rochester the reckless debauchee of Whitehall and Covent Garden; Maximus, the upright and wronged husband, is Rochester the fierce and clear-sighted satirist of Restoration morals and manners; Lucina, the ravished wife, who remains pure in spirit, is the *anima* or soul of Rochester bewildered by the phantasmagoria or witches' rout of contemporary life and longing for 'felicity and glory'.

In the winter of 1678/9 he was inquiring in a letter to Charles Blount about the doctrines of the English deists or freethinkers, who rejected revealed religion and accepted the 'five points' of Lord Herbert of Cherbury. Early in 1680 he saw his friend Blount again and talked to him about the soul and immortality. On 6th February 1680 he sent Blount his great poem on Death suggested by the famous chorus in the *Troades* of Seneca, 'Post mortem nihil est ipsaque mors nihil.' On the surface this poem appears to be a rejection of the belief in immortality. Actually it is a hymn to the grandeur of 'impartial Death' and a denial of the conception of immortality in time with the out-worn myths connected with a material hell, 'senseless Stories, idle Tales', which could no longer be accepted by an adult mind.

By this time Rochester was in contact with a type of belief which furnished him with concepts far better calculated to show him a way out of his difficulties than those of the 'natural religion' of the deists. In October 1679 Gilbert Burnet, a Scottish Anglican clergyman who had been one of the King's chaplains and had a great reputation as a preacher, heard that Rochester would like to make his acquaintance. Burnet was an admirer of the famous group of Cambridge Platonists and was a champion of their peculiar type of latitudinarian and philosophic religion which had become the doctrine of a third party in the Church of England, standing apart both from the narrow dogmatism of the Puritans and the rigid conservatism of the high church party. During his illness Rochester had read with enjoyment the first volume of Burnet's *History of the Reformation* which had appeared in the spring of 1677 and had met the author 'accidentally in one or two places'. After Burnet had visited him once or twice a genuine friendship between the two men and Rochester 'grew into that freedom' 'as to open ... all his thoughts, both of Religion and Morality' and give 'a full view of his past life' to his new friend.

They agreed to enter into a regular debate on the subjects of religion and morality, and Burnet continued his visits throughout the winter of 1679 and the early spring of 1680. Their freest conversation took place when they were alone, but on some occasions others were present. Burnet gives a very full and frank account of their conversation in his *Some Passages of the Life and Death of John Earl of Rochester* published shortly after the poet's death in 1680. What is remarkable about the discussions as Burnet reports them is their reasonable tone and freedom from dogmatizing. Rochester's starting-point is that of a sceptical deist, Burnet's that of a liberal Anglican. Burnet's technique in argument is to make religion appear not as a body of doctrine imposed by a supernatural dictator but as an inward spiritual force which grows up in men who had led good lives. He minimizes the dogmatic, historical and ritual elements in Christianity and lays the chief stress on ethics and religious experience. Rochester's most damaging criticisms came under the heading of 'Revealed Religion'. He was sceptical about the 'Prophesies and Miracles' of the Bible, revolted by the moral code of parts of the Old Testament, and could not believe in the first three chapters of Genesis 'unless they were Parables'. Burnet makes a rather half-hearted defence of the historical and ritual elements in Christianity and especially of the historicity of the Old Testament. He lays little stress on 'the

business of the Fall of Man' and contends that
Christianity is to be judged by 'the Rules it gives' and
the 'Methods it prescribes'. It is 'Generous and Great'
to 'supply the Necessities of the Poor and to forgive
Injuries' and the ceremonies of Christianity are said to
be 'few and significant....' In fact, Burnet describes
the Church as it would have been if the latitudinarians
had had their way. Rochester on his side disavowed
the immoralism that had governed much of his life
hitherto, and suggested that he could bring about a
change by the study of philosophy. Burnet argued that
the only really valuable kind of virtue was a positive
force, not a mere negation of sin or restraint of
appetite. The good man must 'feel a Law within himself'. He must be 'internally regenerated and changed
by a higher Principle'. This sounded to Rochester
dangerously 'like *Enthusiasme* or *Canting*' (he was
thinking no doubt about Puritan talk of the 'inner
light'). Burnet tried to show that religious experience
was no mere fantasy but something concrete which
had real effects on the mind comparable to those which
'good nourishment' has on the body. This was his
strongest argument and was 'pursued in many discourses'. Rochester continued to think that 'all was
the effect of Fancy', though he went so far as to admit
that 'he thought they were very happy whose Fancies
were under the Power of such Impressions'. This was
an important point gained by Burnet; it was an
admission not indeed of the absolute 'truth' of religious experience but of the 'suasive' value of a belief
in it, which to seventeenth-century minds was a kind
of 'truth'. This part of the argument made a deep
impression on Rochester: it showed him a possible
avenue of escape from the blind alley of materialism
and scepticism. During his last illness he told Burnet
'He had another sense of what we talked concerning
prayer and inward assistances.' The conference ended

with an admission by Rochester of the anti-social character of libertinism and his acceptance of the arguments in favour of Christian ethics though he had not yet 'a full persuasion of Christianity'. The popular notion that Burnet 'converted' him is quite false; what Burnet did was to put him in touch with a type of Christian doctrine which he could understand and respect, and which suggested a means of release from his spiritual dilemma.

Early in April 1680 Rochester left London; he was still very weak and he told Burnet 'he believed he should never come to Town more'. His health greatly improved once he was in the country, and he was well enough to attend Newmarket races. It is likely that at the time of his departure from London he wrote a draft of the powerful poem called *Rochester's Farewell to the Court* published some years after his death. In this poem (if it be his) he conjures up a pageant of the 'Rogues, Whores and Bawds' among whom he had spent the best years of his life and finally rejects them and all their works. At this point he has come to see that, to adapt a phrase of D. H. Lawrence, 'the whole coinage of valuation' of the world of fashion and pleasure was 'spurious'. After his return from Newmarket he decided to visit his wife's estate in Somersetshire and 'rode thither post'. The exertion was too much for him; he arrived at Enmore in a state of collapse and had to be brought back by coach to the Ranger's Lodge in Woodstock Forest. During the journey the debate between the two halves of his split personality was going on furiously in his mind. He told Robert Parsons that at the time 'he had been arguing with greater vigor against God and Religion than ever he had done in his life time before'. He reached Woodstock in the last week in May, and for the next few weeks he lay at the Ranger's Lodge in physical and mental agony. There seems to be no doubt that he was passing through what mystics call 'the dark night of the soul', which commonly precedes a state of illumination. Later he said that 'the Hand of God touched him ... It was not only a general dark Melancholy over his Mind, such as he formerly felt: but a most penetrating cutting Sorrow ... all the pleasures he had known in Sin were not worth that torture he had felt in his Mind.' He was nursed by his long-suffering wife and his mother, attended by eminent physicians and visited by several of the local clergy. He took most pleasure in the ministrations of Robert Parsons, his mother's chaplain, an Oxford graduate of the same age as himself. Deliverance from his mental agony came to him when Parsons was reading to him, probably on 19th June, the moving poetry of the fifty-third chapter of Isaiah describing the Suffering Servant of Jahweh:

Hee hath no form or comelinesse:
And when we shall see him; there is no beautie that we
*   shall desire him,*
He is despised and rejected of men,
A man of sorrows and acquainted with griefe ...

As he heard these words Rochester had a moment of illumination which can only be described in his own words: 'as he heard it read, he felt an inward Force upon him, which did so enlighten his Mind, and convince him, that he could resist it no longer. For the words had an authority which did shoot like Raies or Beams in his Mind; so that he was not only convinced by the Reasonings he had about it, which satisfied his Understanding, but by a power which did so effectually constrain him, that he did ever after as firmly believe in his Saviour, as if he had seen him in the Clouds.' There is no doubt that this is a record of a genuine and memorable religious experience. The metaphor of an energizing light used to describe the moment of exultation is one commonly used by intellectual mystics whose minds do not work pictorially. Now at last Rochester's personality was integrated, and he knew that 'felicity and glory' which he had sought for so long.

Rochester never did anything by halves and his conversion had to be as dramatic as the events of his unregenerate life. On the day of his illumination, he made a public recantation before his whole household including 'the piggard boy'. He took the sacrament in company with his wife, who, to his great joy, renounced Romanism, to which she had formerly been converted partly at his instigation. It was probably on the same day that he ordered the burning of all 'his profane and lewd writings' and his 'obscene and filthy pictures'. In this holocaust his manuscript 'History of the intrigues of the Court of Charles II in a series of letters to his friend Henry Savile' was apparently overlooked but, unfortunately, was afterwards burnt by his mother.

In the following weeks, except for one interval of delirium, his mind was clear and untroubled and we are told that he 'never dictated or spoke more composed in his life'. He promised Parsons that, if he lived, he would make it his business to try to produce 'an Idea of Divine Poetry', and it is probable that two poems, *Plain Dealings Downfall* and *Consideratus Considerandus*, ascribed to him in one of the collections published soon after his death, represent a first attempt to carry out this resolution. The central image of both poems is that of virtue conceived as poor, homeless, rejected and outcast, yet possessing the secret of happiness and 'sollid good'. Both poems seem to be connected with the description of the Suffering Servant in *Isaiah* liii, which Parsons tells us that the Earl got by heart. He wrote to Burnet on 25th June describing his conversion, and asking him to visit him. Burnet, not realizing the seriousness of his condition and not liking to appear to compete with the local clergy, delayed for nearly a month, and finally reached Woodstock on 20th July. Rochester told him about his experience when he heard Parsons read the fifty-third chapter of Isaiah and laid particular stress on the second verse, which he paraphrased as follows: 'The meanness of his appearance and Person has made vain and foolish people disparage Him, because he came not in such a Fools-Coat as they delight in.' The sensuous beauty which was the dress of the Aesthetic Hero deified by the young Rochester has now become a 'Fools-Coat' rejected by the Religious Hero of whose reality he had become convinced on 29th June.

In these last days of his life he often sent for his children, his son Charles now nine years old and his three daughters, and spoke to them 'with a sense and feeling that cannot be expressed in Writing'. Burnet left him early on 24th July without taking leave, as he feared the parting might upset him. Some hours later Rochester asked for him and was told he was gone. He said, 'Has my friend left me, then I shall die shortly.' After that he spoke very little, but once was heard praying very devoutly. He died at two o'clock in the morning of Monday, 26th July, 'without any *Convulsion*, or so much as a groan'. He was buried in the north aisle of Spelsbury Church and a plain stone with no inscription was placed on his grave.

Voltaire rightly called Rochester 'homme de génie et . . . grand poète'. He is not a great poet in the sense in which the term is applied to Milton, Dryden, Pope, or Wordsworth. Unlike them, he left no monument of his art in the form of a series of masterpieces of poetic construction. His most memorable achievements as an artist are a few exquisite love songs which, as Sir Herbert Grierson has said, 'might have been written by Burns with a difference', and the best of his satires, to which Dr. F. R. Leavis has rightly given a distin-

JOHN WILMOT, EARL OF ROCHESTER

From the painting by W. Wissing
at Hinchingbrooke, Huntingdonshire

[*face page xxxviii*

guished place in the 'line of wit' that leads from Donne to Pope. He is, however, one of these English poets who deserve to be called 'great' as daring and original explorers of reality; his place is with such memorable spiritual adventurers as Marlowe, Blake, Byron, Wilfred Owen and D. H. Lawrence. Like Byron and Lawrence, he was denounced as licentious, because he was a devastating critic of conventional morality. Alone among the English poets of his day, he perceived the full significance of the intellectual and spiritual crisis of that age. His poetry expresses individual experience in a way that no other poetry does till the time of Blake. It makes us feel what it was like to live in a world which had been suddenly transformed by the scientists into a vast machine governed by mathematical laws, where God has become a remote first cause and man an insignificant 'reas'ning Engine'.[1] In his time there was beginning the great Augustan attempt to found a new orthodoxy on the Cartesian-Newtonian world-picture, a civilized city of good taste, common sense and reason. Rochester's achievement was to reject this new orthodoxy at the very outset. He made three attempts to solve the problem of man's position in the new mathematical universe. The first was the adoption of the ideal of the purely aesthetic hero, the 'Strephon' of his lyrics and the brilliant and fascinating Dorimant of Etherege's comedy. It was a purely selfish ideal which bore no relation to truth. The second was the ideal of the ethical hero, the disillusioned and penetrating observer of the satires. This ideal was related to truth, but its relationship was purely negative. The third was the ideal of the religious hero, who bore a positive relation to truth. This was the hero who rejected the 'Fools-Coat' of the world and lived by an absolute passion for reality. In his short life Rochester may be said to have anticipated

[1] See *A Satyr Against Mankind*, l. 29 (p. 119) and note (p. 216).

the Augustan Age and the Romantic Movement and passed beyond both. In the history of English thought his poetry is an event of the highest significance. Much of it remains alive in its own right in the twentieth century, because it is what D. H. Lawrence called 'poetry of this immediate present, instant poetry... the soul and the mind and body surging at once, nothing left out'.

FORMER EDITIONS OF ROCHESTER'S WRITINGS

During Rochester's life-time only a few of his writings were printed as broadsides or in miscellanies, but many of his works were known widely from manuscript copies, a considerable number of which seem to have existed. In the late summer of 1680, very soon after his death, there appeared in London a badly printed little book called *Poems on Several Occasions by the Right Honourable the E. of R.* which professed on its title-page to be published at Antwerp. This book was obviously produced for readers interested in pornography. It was widely read (no less than ten editions are recorded), but there is evidence that it was handled surreptitiously. It contains sixty-one poems, thirteen of which are certainly not by Rochester, while another eleven are of uncertain authorship; the remainder include some of Rochester's best known poems, but the text is suspect and it is likely that it has been tampered with in order to attract the amateur in pornography. Rochester's friends offered a reward of £5 for the discovery of the printer of the book, which they described in an advertisement in the *London Gazette* as 'a Libel of lewd scandalous Poems'. In 1685 Robert Wolseley published Rochester's tragedy *Valentinian* with a long introduction and the prologues and epilogues spoken at the recent production of the play.

In the same year Andrew Thorncome, a London bookseller, probably taking advantage of the interest aroused by the production of *Valentinian*, produced an edition of Rochester's poem entitled *Poems on Several Occasions written by a late Person of Honour*, from which he omits nine poems included in the 'Antwerp' editions and adds five new ones, two of which are by Thomas Randolph and another two the very interesting poems which may have been written by Rochester on his death-bed (see above, p. xxxvii). Thorncome's text is perhaps a little better than that of the 'Antwerp' editions, but his book is very carelessly printed. It was reprinted with two interesting additional poems in 1701.

On 19th November 1690 Francis Saunders obtained a licence from the Stationers' Company to publish an edition of Rochester's poems, but this projected edition never appeared. Four months later, in February 1690/91, Jacob Tonson, the most reputable publisher of the day, produced a volume entitled *Poems on Several Occasions: with Valentinian; a Tragedy written by the Right Honourable John Late Earl of Rochester*. The appearance of the author's name and title on the title-page is significant. It may indicate that this edition was produced with the approval of the Earl's family and friends, and it is possible that they may have intervened to prevent the publication of Saunders's projected edition. Tonson's edition is introduced by a laudatory preface written by Thomas Rymer which states that the book contains 'such Pieces only, as may be receiv'd in a vertuous Court' and is therefore to be regarded only as a selection of Rochester's writings. Nevertheless it contains, in addition to twenty-three genuine poems which had appeared in the 'Antwerp' editions, sixteen others, including some of Rochester's best lyrics. No spurious material[1] seems to have been admitted to this collection, but there is a possibility that salacious passages may have been toned down to suit the taste of a 'virtuous Court'. Tonson's edition was reprinted in 1696, 1701 and 1713. The 1713 edition contains important additional matter, all of which is undoubtedly genuine.

Meanwhile a group of Rochester's poems had been printed in the collections of Whig satires, commonly called *Poems on Affairs of State*, which began to appear shortly after the Revolution in the volumes called *A Collection of the Newest and Most Ingenious Poems, Songs, Catches &c Against Poetry* (1689), *Poems on Affairs of State* (1697), and *State Poems Continued* (1697). It is tempting to connect this group of poems with Andrew Marvell's praise of Rochester as a satirist as recorded by Aubrey (see p. liii), and it is significant that they include the admirable satire *Tunbridge Wells* which contains Rochester's only allusion to Marvell. These collections contain much of Marvell's own satiric poetry and may well have been printed from manuscript copies belonging to members of Marvell's circle.

In 1707 Benjamin Bragge published a book entitled *The Miscellaneous Works of the Right Honourable the Late Earls of Rochester and Roscommon*. This is a thoroughly dishonest production, continuing on a large scale the pornographic tradition of the 'Antwerp' and Thorncome editions. Indeed, there was probably a link between these editions and Bragge's volume in the form of an edition of 1702, no copy of which appears to have survived (see no. xvi in Prinz's bibliography). In Bragge's edition appeared for the first time *The Memoirs of the Life of John Wilmot Earl of Rochester*, falsely ascribed to Saint-Evremond, an im-

[1] With one possible exception; see note to no. xxv of this edition, p. 173.

pudent eighteenth-century forgery. Unsold sheets of this book seem to have been taken over by the notorious Edmund Curll, who reissued it in 1707 with a cancel title-page as *The Works of the Right Honourable the late Earls of Rochester and Roscommon ... The Second Edition*. In 1709 Curll produced a 'third edition' of the 'Works' of Rochester and Roscommon with a little additional matter. The Bragge-Curll editions include a few additional poems which may be by Rochester, the most interesting of which is the famous *pastiche* based on two poems of Quarles called *To his Mistress*. This may well have been printed from an unfinished draft by Rochester (similar to the drafts in the Portland MS., see below, p. xlv), but like everything else in these editions must be regarded with suspicion. In 1711 Curll published a separate edition of Rochester's poem *Upon Nothing*, 'Now first Correctly printed'. It includes a Preface in which he announces that he plans 'with convenient speed, to give the World a Genuine Edition of his Lordship's Works' and states that he begins 'with this *Poem*, to show with what Disingenuity his Lordship's Memory has been treated by Such Paltry Scriblers, as did not in the least understand what they presum'd to Publish'. He makes a violent attack on the editor of the Tonson editions, obviously referring to Rymer, whom he describes sarcastically as 'this Nice Critic' and blames him for 'leaving out whole *Stanza's* in many of them' (i.e. the poems), and especially for printing bad texts of *A Satyr Against Mankind* and *Upon Nothing*. The text of *Upon Nothing* which he himself prints does not, however, inspire confidence in him as a potential editor of Rochester. It is simply a reprint of one of the broadside versions of the poem reproducing an absurd misprint in the first line. Curll did not proceed with his plan of a separate edition of Rochester's works, but in 1714 he produced a 'Fourth

Edition' of *The Works of the Earls of Rochester, Roscommon, Dorset, etc.*, in two volumes with illustrations and an appendix of indecent poems called *The Cabinet of Love.* This edition formed the basis of the majority of about thirty subsequent editions which appeared in the eighteenth and early nineteenth centuries, none of which can be regarded as having the slightest claim to authenticity.[1]

John Hayward's edition of *The Collected Works of John Wilmot Earl of Rochester* published by the Nonesuch Press in 1926 is a useful but uncritical collection of almost every scrap of verse and prose rightly or wrongly attributed to Rochester. *The Poetical Works of John Wilmot Earl of Rochester*, edited by Quilter Johns, published by the Haworth Press in 1933, professes to be based on 'the editions of 1685, 1696, 1739 and 1757'. It has no textual value and contains much spurious material, including the forged memoir ascribed to Saint-Evremond.

In 1950 the Princeton University Press published a facsimile reprint of the copy of one of the 'Antwerp' editions in the Henry E. Huntington Library, with a very valuable introduction and commentary (chiefly textual) by James Thorpe. In my opinion, Mr. Thorpe attaches too much importance to the text of the 'Antwerp' editions and is unduly distrustful of the authority of those published by Tonson. Nevertheless, his introduction and critical apparatus constitute by far the most scholarly and best informed study of the text and canon of Rochester's works hitherto published, and I gladly acknowledge my indebtedness to them.

---

[1] See J. Prinz's useful and fairly exhaustive bibliography in his *John Wilmot Earl of Rochester His Life and Writings* (Leipzig, 1927), pp. 313–83.

MANUSCRIPTS [1]

The most important manuscript source for the text of Rochester's poems is a finely bound album in which there have been inserted drafts of a number of poems, some of which are in the autographs of Rochester and his wife. This book is in the Duke of Portland's Collection formerly at Welbeck Abbey and now deposited in the Library of the University of Nottingham. Attention was first drawn to it by Mr. Francis Needham, formerly Librarian at Welbeck Abbey, who published two poems from it in The Welbeck Miscellany, no. 2, 1934. Mr. Needham informs me that it was once the property of Edward Harley, Earl of Oxford, and he suggests that it may have come into his possession with the Rochester correspondence (Brit. Mus., Add. MS. 7003), now in the British Museum. It contains drafts of poems (and one fragment of prose) in three hands, one of which is certainly Rochester's, another that of Lady Rochester, and a third which has not been identified.

Many transcripts of poems by or attributed to Rochester are to be found in the numerous extant

---

[1] Since this edition went to press Mr. David Vieth has drawn my attention to a manuscript miscellany in the Harleian collection in the British Museum (Harl. 7316) containing on ff. 20–3v. transcripts of several of the poems in Rochester's autograph and one in Lady Rochester's in the Portland MS. The poems are nos. XXXV, LXII, XIII (version given in note pp. 167, 168), XXIX, XXX and LXXVII. The last fifteen lines of no. LXII are omitted and the others arranged in a different order from that of the Portland MS. No author's names are given. After no. LXXVII on f. 23v. the following doggerel lines occur in the same hand. I have never seen them in print:

Under King Charles II's Picture,
By Wilmot Earl of Rochester

I John Roberts writ This same,
I pasted it, & plaister'd it, and put it in a Frame:
In Honor of my Master's Master, King Charles the Second by Name.

xlv

manuscript miscellanies of the Restoration period. The largest known collection is in a manuscript miscellany apparently made about 1680, now in the Houghton Library at Harvard University (MS. Eng. 636F). This volume contains transcripts of seventy-nine poems, thirty-three of which are ascribed to Rochester. Another important collection is in a folio volume, which apparently was once the property of the First Earl of Pomfret and is now in the collection of the Duke of Portland. It contains, along with poems by Dryden, Marvell, Oldham and others, texts of thirty authentic poems of Rochester. Interesting transcripts of Rochester's *A Letter from Artemisa in the Town to Cloe in the Country* and *A Satyr against Mankind* in the autograph of John Oldham are contained in a commonplace book which once belonged to Oldham and is now in the Bodleian Library, Oxford (Rawl. Eng. Poet. 123).

SPURIOUS AND DOUBTFUL POEMS

A substantial volume could be filled with poems wrongly fathered on Rochester or attributed to him without convincing evidence of his authorship. Anthony à Wood in his Life of Rochester in *Athenae Oxonienses* states that 'most of this kind' (i.e. the obscene kind) were 'fathered upon the Earl', 'right or wrong, which came out at any time, after he had obtained the Names of an excellent smooth, but withall a most lewd poet'. The obscene farce in rhyming verse called *Sodom* or *The Destruction of Sodom*,[1] to which Wood is particularly referring in the passage just quoted, exists in several manuscript copies and was printed at Amsterdam in 1904. It was commonly

[1] For an account of the various manuscripts and editions of *Sodom*, see J. Prinz, *John Wilmot Earl of Rochester*, pp. 390–400. There is a transcript of a version of the play, called *The Destruction of Sodom*, in the Portland Miscellany, see below, p. 163.

attributed to Rochester, but there are strong reasons for believing that he had nothing to do with it, and that it is the work of a certain Christopher Fishbourne (see 'Rochester or Fishbourne, a Question of Authorship', by R. M. Baine, R.E.S., vol. 23, pp. 201–6). Among the numerous satiric and indecent poems attributed to Rochester in manuscript and printed miscellanies of the late seventeenth and early eighteenth centuries the following are examples of poems which have often been reprinted as his but which are almost certainly by other authors. The poem called *A Satyr which the King took Out of his Pocket* beginning with the line 'Preserved by Wonder in the Oak, O Charles' is headed in a transcript in Brit. Mus., Harl. MS. 7139, f. 26, 'Satyr Mr Lacy 1677'. 'Mr Lacy' is probably John Lacy, the well-known Restoration actor and dramatist, and there is no reason to doubt the correctness of the attribution of the poem to him. The satire on the Duchess of Portsmouth called *Portsmouth's Looking Glass*, first attributed to Rochester in *Poems on Affairs of State*, 1697, contains an allusion to the trial of Philip Doughty, an event which took place in July or August, 1680,[1] and to the scandal of the delay in his pardon, which was the common talk of the town in the winter of 1680. As Rochester died on 26th July 1680 it can be confidently asserted that he had nothing to do with this poem. Similarly, the satire called *The Royal Angler* or *Windsor* attributed to Rochester in the Bragge-Curll edition of 1707 certainly contains allusions to the intrigues at Court when Charles II was at Windsor in June and July 1680. It must have been written by someone who was with the Court at Windsor and not by Rochester who was lying on his death-bed at Woodstock at that time. The powerful poem called *A Satyr against Marriage*, first attributed to Rochester in the Addenda printed

[1] See *Judge Jeffreys*, by H. B. Irving (London, 1898), pp. 115–17.

at the end of *Poems on Affairs of State*, 1697, is probably by Oldham. There is a transcript of it in the Portland Miscellany, where it is followed by some lines entitled 'An Apology to ye foregoing Satyr by way of Epilogue'. These are identical with a poem by Oldham printed in 1679 with his burlesque Ode entitled *A Satyr against Vertue*, and there called 'An Apologie for the preceeding Poem by way of Epilogue'. According to a note in Brit. Mus., Add. MS. 14047, f. 112,[1] *A Satyr against Vertue* was supposed to be placed in the mouth of 'ye Court Hector', who is identified with 'Ld Roch^r'. It seems likely therefore that *A Satyr against Marriage* is another burlesque monologue in which Oldham was impersonating a 'Court Hector' and for which he used as an 'Apology' a draft of the same lines employed by him for this purpose in connection with *A Satyr against Vertue*. A number of other satires on marriage are attributed to Rochester in contemporary manuscript miscellanies, probably merely because he was regarded as the typical 'Court Hector' and enemy of matrimony.

THE PRESENT EDITION

The present edition is designed to provide reliable texts of the poems which can be attributed to Rochester with a reasonable degree of certainty. The text of Tonson's edition of 1691 has been used for all the poems which appear in that collection with the following exceptions: the Prologue to *The Empress of Morocco* and the Epilogue to *Love in the Dark*, which are given in the texts that appear in the first quarto editions of those plays, *A Satyr against Mankind*, in the extended text that appears in the 1680 editions, and a lyric and two dramatic passages from Rochester's

---

[1] See 'A Bibliography of John Oldham the Restoration Satirist', by Harold F. Brooks, *Proceedings and Papers of the Oxford Bibliographical Society*, vol. v, pt. i.

alteration of *Valentinian*, in the text of the quarto edition of that play published in 1685. Other poems are given in the texts of the 1680 editions (the copy in the Folger Library, Washington, has been used by kind permission of the Librarian), the Thorncome edition of 1865, the 'State Poems', the Portland MS. and other sources indicated in the notes.

The notes are partly textual, partly explanatory. No attempt has been made to provide a 'variorum' edition giving all the extant readings of every poem, but some of the more interesting and significant variants have been recorded.

Original spellings, capitalizations and punctuation of copy texts have been retained and their use of italics has also been reproduced, except where the copy text is, according to seventeenth-century usage in certain conditions, printed entirely in italics with proper names, etc., in roman type. In these instances the position of the two founts has been reversed and roman type has been substituted for the italics of the copy text, and *vice versa*. The modern *s* has been substituted for the old long *ſ* throughout, and contractions have been expanded. Obvious printer's errors have been corrected, but where these corrections involve the insertion of a different reading from that of the copy text, the word or letters inserted are enclosed in pointed brackets.[1]

A selection of poems ascribed to Rochester on doubtful authority has been printed as an appendix.

Two poems (n. XXXVII and LIX) have had to be omitted at the request of the publishers owing to the risk of prosecution in this country under the existing law. Under each title page references have been given to Thorpe's edition, where the texts of the excluded poems will be found.

[1] Pointed brackets have not, however, been used where punctuation only has been inserted.

BIOGRAPHY

The earliest biography of Rochester is Gilbert Burnet's *Some Passages of the Life and Death of the Right Honourable John Earl of Rochester* published soon after his death in 1680. There is important biographical information also in Robert Parsons's *A Sermon Preached at the Funeral of the Rt. Honorable John Earl of Rochester* (Oxford, 1680), in Aubrey's *Brief Lives* compiled between 1669 and 1696 (ed. A. Clark, 1898) and in the life by Anthony à Wood in *Athenae Oxonienses* (1699). The memoir falsely attributed to Saint Evremond, first published in the Bragge-Curll edition of 1707 and often reprinted in the eighteenth century is a fabrication of no value. Dr. Johnson included a short account of Rochester in his *Lives of the Most Eminent Poets* (1781). The chief modern studies are *John Wilmot Earl of Rochester his Life and Writings* by J. Prinz (Leipzig, 1927) with its very full and valuable bibliography, and *Rochesteriana* by the same author (Privately Printed, Leipzig 1926), *Rochester Portrait of a Restoration Poet* by V. de S. Pinto (London, 1935), *Rochester* by Charles Williams (London, 1935) and 'A very Profane Wit' in *The Sun at Noon* by Kenneth Murdock (New York, 1939).

CRITICAL COMMENTS

CRITICAL COMMENTS

I

ANDREW MARVELL

Mr ANDREW MARVELL, who was a good judge of witt, was wont to say that he [Rochester] was the best English satyrist and had the right veine

AUBREY, Brief Lives, ed. Clark, ii, 304

II

SIR FRANCIS FANE

WHAT was favourably said of my Lord *Bacon* in his time, may much more justly be affirmed of your Lordship, in yours; That if ever there were a beam of Knowledge, immediately deriv'd from God, upon any Man, since the Creation, there is one upon your self. Others, by wearisome steps, and regular gradations, climb up to knowledge; your Lordship is flown up to the top of the Hill: you are an Enthusiast in Wit; a Poet and Philosopher by Revelation; and have already in your tender Age, set out such new and glorious Lights in Poetry, yet these so orthodox and Unquestionable, that all the Heroes of Antiquity, must submit, or *Homer* and *Virgil* be judg'd Nonconformists. For my part, I account it one of the great felicities of my life, to have liv'd in your age; but so much greater, to have had access to your Person, and to have been cherish'd and enlighten'd by the influences, and irradations of so great a Luminary. For I must confess, I never return from you Lordships most Charming and Instructive Conversation, but I am inspir'd with a new Genius, and improv'd in all those Sciences I ever coveted the knowledge of: I find my self not only a better Poet, a better Philosopher; but much more than these, a better Christian: your Lordship's miraculous Wit, and intellectual pow'rs being the greatest Argument that I ever could meet with, for the immateriality of the Soul, they being the highest exaltation of humane Nature; and, under Divine Authority, much more convincing to suspicious Reason, than all the Pedantick proofs of the most Learnedly peevish Disputants; so that, I hope, I shall be oblig'd to your Lordship, not only for my Reputation in this World, but my future Happiness in the next.

Dedicatory Epistle to the Right Honourable John, Earl of Rochester prefixed to *Love in the Dark*, Written by Sir Francis Fane, Junior, Knight of the Bath, London, 1675. Sigg. A2v, A3

III

ROBERT PARSONS

A WIT he had so rare and fruitful in its invention, and withall so choice and delicate in its judgment, that there is nothing wanting in his composures to give a full answer to that question, what and where Wit is? except the purity and choice of subject: for had such excellent seeds but fallen upon good ground, and instead of pitching upon a Beast or a Lust, been raised up on high, to celebrate the mysteries of the Divine love, in Psalms, and Hymns, and Spiritual songs; I perswade my self we might by this time have receiv'd from his pen as excellent an Idea of Divine Poetry, under the Gospel, useful to the teaching of virtue, especially in this generation, as his profane Verses have been to destroy it. And I am confident, had God spared him a longer life, this would have been the whole business of it, as I know it was the vow and purpose of his sickness.

> *A Sermon preached at the Funeral of the Rt. Honorable John Earl of Rochester*, by Robert Parsons, M.A. (Oxford, 1680), p. 7

IV

GILBERT BURNET

HE came from his travels in the 18th Year of his Age, and appeared at Court with as great Advantages as most ever had. He was a Graceful and well shaped Person, tall and well made, if not a little too slender: He was exactly well bred, and what by a modest behaviour natural to him, what by a Civility become almost as natural, his Conversation was easie and obliging. He had a strange Vivacity of thought, and vigour of expression: His Wit had a subtility and sublimity both, that were scarce imitable. His Style was clear and strong: When he used Figures they were very lively, and yet far enough out of the Common Road: he had made himself Master of the Ancient and Modern Wit, and of the Modern *French* and *Italian* as well as the *English*. He loved to talk and write of Speculative Matters, and did it with so fine a thread, that even those who hated the Subjects that his Fancy ran upon, yet could not but be charmed with his way of treating of them. *Boileau* among the *French*, and *Cowley* among the English Wits were those he admired most. Sometimes other mens thoughts mixed with his Composures, but that flowed rather from the Impressions they made on him when he read them, by which they came to return upon him as his own thoughts, than that he servilely copied from any. For few men ever had a bolder flight of fancy, more steddily governed by Judgment than he had ...

He said to me, He never improved his Interest at Court to do a premeditate Mischief to other persons. Yet he laid out his Wit very freely in *Libels* and *Satyrs*, in which he had a peculiar Talent of mixing his Wit with his Malice, and fitting both with such apt words, that Men were tempted to be pleased with them: from thence his Composures came to be easily known, for few had such a way of tempering these together as he had; So that when any thing extraordinary that way came out, as a Child is fathered sometimes by its Resemblance, so was it laid at his Door as its Parent and Author.

Some Passages of the Life and Death of the Right Honourable John Earl of Rochester (1680), pp. 6–14

V

SAMUEL PEPYS

As he [Rochester] is past writing any more [poems] so bad in one sense, so I despair of any man surviving him to write so good in another.

S. PEPYS to W. Hewer, 4th November, 1680, q. A. Bryant in *Pepys The Years of Peril*, p. 340

VI

ROBERT WOLSELEY

HE had a Wit that was accompanied with an unaffected greatness of Mind, and a natural Love to Justice and

Truth; a Wit that was in perpetual War with Knavery, and ever attacking those kind of Vices most, whose malignity was likely to be most diffusive, such as tended most immediately to the prejudice of publick Bodies, and were of a common Nusance to the happiness of humane kind. Never was his Pen drawn but on the side of good Sence and usually imploy'd, like the Arms of the ancient Heroes, to stop the progress of arbitrary Oppression, and beat down the Bruitishness of head-strong Will ... Add to this, the generousness of his Temper and the affability of his good Sence; the willingness he still show'd to raise the oppress'd, and the pleasure he took to humble the proud; the constant readiness of his Parts, and that great presence of Mind, which never let him want a fit and pertinent Answer to the most sudden and unexpected Question ... the strong facility he had to talk to all Capacities in their own Dialect, and make himself good Company to all kind of People at all times ... What last, and most of all, deserves admiration in my Lord, was his Poetry, which alone is Subject enough for perpetual Panegyrick. But the Character of it is so generally known; it has so eminently distinguish'd it self from that of other men by a thousand irresistible Beauties; every Body is so well acquainted with it, by the effect it has had upon 'em, that to trace and single out the Several Graces may seem a Task as superfluous as to describe to a Lover the Lines and Features of his Mistress's Face. 'Tis sufficient to observe that his Poetry, like himself was all Original, and has a stamp so particular, so unlike any thing that has been written before, that, as it disdained all servile imitation, and copying from others, so neither is it capable... of being copy'd.... His Poetry has every where a Tincture of that unaccountable Charm in his Fashion and Conversation, that peculiar Becomingness in all he said, and did, that drew the Eyes and won the Hearts of all who came near him.

> *Preface to Valentinian: A Tragedy, as 'tis Alter'd by the Late Earl of Rochester* (1685)

VII

SAINT-EVREMOND

THE late Earl of *Rochester*, who was my *Lady Sandwich*'s Father, had more wit than any man in England ...

> Letter to Ninon de Lanclos, 1698, in *The letters of Saint-Evremond*, edited by John Hayward (1930), pp. 322, 323

VIII

JOSEPH SPENCE

CETTE Periode fut três feconde en Satire. Outre le grande Dryden, elle produisit Dorset, Rochester, Oldham, Buckingam, et Butler ... *Oldham*, ecrivit d'une maniere três forte & três severe. *Rochester*, fut plus clairvoyant sur les caractéres des hommes; il eût une force plus penetrante et plus polië.

> 'Quelques Remarques Hist. sur les Poetes Anglois' (about 1732–3). Text printed by James M. Osborn in *The First History of English poetry* contributed to *Pope and His Contemporaries*, Essays presented to George Sherburn (Oxford, 1949), p. 248

IX

VOLTAIRE

Toute le monde connoit de réputation le Comte de Rochester. Mr. de Saint-Evremont en a beaucoup parlé; mais il ne nous a fait connoître du fameux Rochester, que l'homme de plaisir, l'homme à bonnes fortunes. Je voudrois faire connoître en lui l'homme de génie & le grand poëte. Entr' autres ouvrages qui brilloient de cette imagination ardente qui n'appartenoit qu'à lui, il a fait quelques satires sur les mêmes sujets que notre célèbre Despreaux avoit choisis. Je ne scai rien de plus utile pour çe perfectionner le goût que la comparaison des grands génies qui se sont exercés sur les mêmes matieres.

> *Lettres Philosophiques*, Vingt et Uniéme Lettre, Sur le comte de Rochester et Mr Waller, 1734. (Text: Voltaire, *Lettres Philosophiques*, ed. G. Lanson, 1924, ii, 124)

X

ALEXANDER POPE

Oldham is a very indelicate writer: he has strong rage, but it is too much like Billingsgate—Lord Rochester has much more delicacy and more knowledge of mankind ... Horace's Supper, Boileau's Festin, and Lord Rochester's Feast, all very good.— Rochester, in his Satire on Man, very much improves on his pattern in Boileau.

> Conversation recorded by Joseph Spence in Spence's *Anecdotes*, ed. by S. W. Singer (1858), pp. 14, 15, 50

XI

HORACE WALPOLE

A Man, whom the Muses were fond to inspire, and ashamed to avow, and who practiced without the least reserve that secret which can make verses more read for their defects than their merits. The art is neither commendable nor difficult. Moralists proclaim loudly that there is no wit in indecency: It is very true: Indecency is far from conferring wit; but it does not destroy it neither. Lord Rochester's poems have much more obscenity than wit, more wit than poetry, more poetry than politeness.

> *A Catalogue of the Royal and Noble Authors of England.* Printed at Strawberry Hill. MDCCLVIII

XII

SAMUEL JOHNSON

Lord Rochester was eminent for the vigour of his colloquial wit, and remarkable for many wild pranks and sallies of extravagance. The glare of his general character diffused itself upon his writings; the compositions of a man whose name was heard often, were certain of attention, and from many readers certain of applause . . .

His songs have no particular character; they tell, like other songs, in smooth and easy language, of scorn and kindness, dismission and desertion, absence and inconstancy, with the commonplaces of artificial courtship. They are commonly smooth and easy; but have little nature, and little sentiment.

His Imitation of Horace on Lucilius is not inelegant or unhappy. In the reign of Charles the second began that adaptation, which has since been very frequent, of ancient poetry to present times; and perhaps few will be found where the parallelism is better preserved than in this. The versification is, indeed, sometimes careless, but it is sometimes vigorous and weighty.

The strongest effort of his muse is his poem on Nothing ... In all his works there is sprightliness and vigour, and everywhere may be found tokens of a mind, which study might have carried to excellence.

Life of Rochester in *Lives of the Poets*
(1783)

XIII

E. D. FORGUES

Non: Rochester fut autre chose qu'un courtisan vicieux et un poéte ça et là vraiment inspiré... Il a rampé dans cette fange dont l'avant-dernier Stuart avait rempli White-Hall, et sous laquelle semblent disparaître les traces du sang de Charles Ier, mais il n'a pas succombé, débauché vulgaire, sous le poids abrutissant de l'ivresse, sous l'écrasement des voluptés. Il avait naturellement le cœur assez haut et l'esprit assez subtil pour n'être dominé qu'à demi par les influences énervantes auxquelles sa jeunesse fut exposée. Un secret ressort, même en ses plus mauvais jours, le fait réagir contre elles. Il ne s'assimile pas le poison, il le vomit, à la face des empoisonneurs. Ce n'est pas un sceptique avili qui doute de tout et méprise tout, même la vertu, même la justice; j'aime mieux voir en lui un croyant désesperé, qui débordé par la corruption universelle et mêlé par un caprice du sort, au cortége triomphal du mal victorieux, jette de temps en temps, comme une imprécation involontaire, une malédiction spontanée au milieu des chants de fête, des refrains bachiques, des hymnes serviles.

La Revue de Deux Mondes, August 1857, p. 826

XIV

SIR EDMUND GOSSE

WITH Rochester the power of writing songs died in England until the age of Blake and Burns. He was the last of the cavalier lyrists, and in some respects the best. In the qualities that a song demands, simplicity, brevity, pathos and tenderness, he arrives nearer to pure excellence than any one between Carew and Burns. His style is without adornment, and, save in this one matter of song-writing, he is weighed down by the dryness and inefficiency of his age. But by the side of Sedley and Congreve he seems as fresh as by the side of Dryden he seems light and flowing, turning his trill of song brightly and sweetly with the consummate artlessness of true art. Occasionally, as in the piece ... called *The Mistress*, he is surprisingly like Donne in the quaint force and ingenuity of his images. But the fact is that the muse of Rochester resembles nothing so much as a beautiful child which has wantonly rolled itself in the mud, and which has grown so dirty that the ordinary wayfarer would rather pass it hurriedly by, than do justice to its native charms.

The English Poets, Selections with Critical Introductions, edited by T. H. Ward (1899), ii, 425

XV

SIR WALTER RALEIGH

THEN there was John Wilmot, Earl of Rochester. He was drunk for five years on end,—so his biographer, who had it from his own lips, alleges—and he died at the age of thirty-two. Like Sedley, he professes no virtues, and holds no far-reaching views. But what a delicate turn of personal affection he gives to the expression of his careless creed:—

> The time that is to come is not,
>   How can it then be mine?
> The present moment's all my lot,
> And that, as fast as it is got,
>   Phyllis, is only thine.
>
> Then talk not of inconstancy,
>   False hearts, and broken vows
> If I by miracle can be
> This live-long minute true to thee,
>   'Tis all that Heaven allows.

Rochester's best love-poetry reaches the topmost pinnacle of achievement in that kind. None has ever been written more movingly beautiful than this:—

> When, wearied with a world of woe,
>   To thy safe bosom I retire,
> Where love and peace and truth does flow,
>   May I contented there expire!
>
> Lest, once more wandering from that heaven,
>   I fall on some base heart unblest—
> Faithless to thee, false, unforgiven—
>   And lose my everlasting rest!

Or than that other piece (too beautiful and too intense

to be cited as a sudden illustration of a thesis)
beginning—

> Why does thou shade thy lovely face? O why
> Does that eclipsing hand of thine deny
> The sunshine of the Sun's enlivening eye?
>
> *Milton* (1900), pp. 261–2

XVI

WILLIAM JOHN COURTHOPE

ROCHESTER tried several styles of poetical composition, and up to the point at which he aimed, proven himself a master in each. From very early days he showed that he possessed the power of writing well in verse. Like Buckingham he was an excellent critic. Some of his verdicts on the writers of his time became proverbial and his *Allusion to the Tenth Satire of the First Book of Horace* shows his penetrating judgment ...

His best literary work is to be found in his more general satires. Andrew Marvell, a good judge, thought him the greatest master of satirical style in his day, and with the exception of Dryden, Pope and Byron, no man, perhaps, has possessed an equal command over that peculiar English metrical idiom which is 'fittest for discourse and nearest prose'. He puts forward his principles moral and religious, such as they were, with living force and pungency, showing in every line how eagerly he had imbibed the opinions of Hobbes ...

When he chose to be decent, Rochester could write with elegance in the lyric style. Amid floods of indescribable filth, assigned to him in a volume of his collected poems (for much of which he may not be really responsible), there are to be found songs like the following on love and life, in which, whatever may be said of the sentiment, the form is above criticism.

A History of English Poetry (1911) iii, 464–8

XVII

CHARLES WHIBLEY

SUCH was the life and death of one who set forth his character in his writings with the utmost candour. Though he was never at the pains to gather together his flying sheets, though he is said on his deathbed, one hopes falsely, to have desired the destruction of his poems, it is his poems which still gives us the true measure of his genius. Yet, even here, misunderstanding has pursued him. The worst that he wrote has been acclaimed to be the best. Johnson declares that the strongest effort of his muse is his poem entitled *Nothing*, a piece of ingenuity, unworthy his talent. Still more foolish has been the common assumption that Rochester's poems are unfit to be read. In some few, he reached a height of outspoken cynicism rarely scaled by an English poet. But the most of his works may be studied without fear, and judged upon their very high merits. Tonson's collection contains more than 200 pages, and amply justifies the claims, made for it by Rymer, that it consists 'of such pieces only as may be received in a virtuous court, and not unbecome the Cabinet of the severest Matron'.

It was in satire above all that Rochester excelled. For this kind, he was richly endowed by nature and art. He had studied the ancient models with constancy and understanding. The quenchless vigour of his mind found its best expression in castigating the vices and foibles of humankind, which he knew so well. His daring and malice equalled his vigour, and he attacked Charles II, the Royal Angler, or Nelly, the reigning favourite, with as light a heart as he brought to the demolition of Sir Car Scroop, the purblind knight. He wrote the heroic couplet with a life and freedom that few have excelled, and the most that can be said in his dispraise is that, like the rest of the courtiers, he knew not the use of the file. 'Rochester', said Andrew Marvell, with the voice not of flattery but of criticism, 'is the only man in England who has the true vein of Satire,' and Marvell, in speaking of satire, spoke of an art which he himself had practised with success. And that Rochester looked upon satire as an art is evident from the answer, which he gave to Burnet, who objected that revenge and falsehood were its blemishes.

'A man,' said he, 'could not write with life, unless he were heated with Revenge, for to make a Satire without Resentments, upon the cold Notions of Philosophy, was as if a man would in cold blood cut men's throats, who had never offended him. And he said, the lyes in these Libels came often as in ornaments that could not be spared without spoiling the beauty of the Poem.'

His masterpiece, without doubt, is *A Satire against Mankind*. Imitated from Boileau, it bears in every line the impress of Rochester's mind. The energy of its thought and style separates it sharply from its original, and, if you compare the two works, you may find a clue to the difference between French and English. The one is marked by order, moderation, and good sense. The other moves impetuous like a torrent, and sweeps out of its way the prejudices of all time. In cynical, closely argued contempt of man this satire is unmatched; in expression, it surpasses the most vivid of Rochester's works. The denunciation of reason,

<blockquote>
an ignis fatuus of the mind,
Which leaves the light of Nature, Sense, behind,
</blockquote>

is a purple passage of English poetry, in which the optimist can take no delight. Its conclusion is the very quintessence of hopelessness ...

It was Rochester's added distinction that almost alone in his age, he wrote lyrics touched with feeling, even with passion ... Nor should ever be forgotten that masterpiece of heroic irony *The Maimed Debauchee*, who like a brave admiral, crawling to the top of an adjacent hill, beholds the battle maintained, 'when fleets of glasses sail around the board'. You can but say of it, that it bears the stamp of Rochester's vigour and sincerity in every line, and that he alone could have written it.

> *The Cambridge History of English Literature* (1912), vol. 8, chapter viii ('The Court Poets'), pp. 213–15

XVIII

OLIVER ELTON

Do we not sometimes hear in Byron an echo of Rochester? I have often thought that Byron, at his best, might have written some of Rochester's best things; although, it is true, Rochester had more to repent of than Byron, and repented more deeply, and his few singing arrows go home more surely than anything of Byron's.

> 'The Present Value of Byron', *Review of English Studies*, vol. 1, no. 1, January 1925

F. R. LEAVIS

WE are given a good view of this background in Professor Pinto's book on Rochester,[1] and the background explains, perhaps, why we have to disagree with Professor Pinto's estimate of Rochester as a poet: 'If Milton is the great poet of belief in the seventeenth century, Rochester is the great poet of unbelief.' Rochester is not a great poet of any kind; yet he certainly had uncommon natural endowments, which, it is reasonable to suggest, he might have done much more with had he been born thirty years earlier. As it is, his few best lyrics are peculiarly individual utterances, with no such relation to convention or tradition as is represented by Carew or Marvell—a point that Professor Grierson makes in his introduction to *Metaphysical Lyrics and Poems of the Seventeenth Century* when he says (p. xxxviii).

'When wearied with a world of woe,

might have been written by Burns with some differences.' It is in his satires that Rochester belongs decidedly to a tradition; they are very striking at their best and plainly stand on a line leading from the Metaphysicals to Pope.

Revaluation (1936), p. 35.

XX

KENNETH B. MURDOCK

HIS dissatisfaction with himself and his unhappiness show that, base as he was, he groped romantically for something beyond baseness. He had read widely. He

[1] *Rochester: Portrait of a Restoration Poet*, by V. de Sola Pinto.

had written a few lovely songs. His satire was compact and tense; its fury gave it weight, and even when it was most extravagant, its energy bordered on magnificence. His skill in conversation was celebrated, and he had humor as well as wit, revealed, for example, in the inspired refrain of his song of a young lady to her elderly lover: 'Ancient person of my heart'. He was a court celebrity, flattered and feared, but he called himself a fool, boasted of his idleness, seldom troubled to print his verses, and included himself in his derision of mankind. Behind this there must have been thought, some sense of values that transcended those that his professed materialism allowed. If his satire came from desire for revenge, as he said it did, on what was he eager to revenge himself? If he was an unthinking sinner, with no abstract conception of virtue, why was he enraged at the very follies he permitted himself. To rail as he did at the men who revelled with him, or at Charles II or Edward Hyde, he must have put them and himself into comparison with some vision of excellence not realised in his little world. His disillusionment and his indecent rioting were of a piece with his elaborate efforts to behave as if there were no laws human or divine, and yet his patent disgust with himself implied a suspicion that there were.

'A Very Profane Wit' in *The Sun at Noon*
(New York, 1939), pp. 298, 299

JUVENILIA

JUVENILIA

I

To His Sacred Majesty
On His Restoration.
In the Year 1660

(*Written at* 12 *Years old*)

VIRTUE's Triumphant Shrine! who do'st engage
At once three Kingdoms in a Pilgrimage;
Which in extatick duty strive to come
Out of themselves, as well as from their home:
Whilst *England* grows one Camp, and *London* is 5
It self the Nation, not Metropolis;
And Loyal *Kent* renews her Arts agen,
Fencing her ways with moving Groves of Men;
Forgive this distant homage, which does meet
Your blest approach on sedentary feet: 10
And though my youth, not patient yet to bear
The weight of Arms, denies me to appear
In Steel before you; yet, Great Sir, approve
My manly wishes, and more vigorous Love;
In whom a cold Respect were Treason to   15
A Fathers Ashes, greater than to you;
Whose one Ambition 'tis for to be known,
By daring Loyalty your *Wilmot's* Son.

ROCHESTER.
Wadh. Coll.

II

In obit. Seren. Mariae
Princip. Auran.

IMPIA blasphemi sileant concilia vulgi:
  Absolvo medicos, innocuamque manum.
Curassent alios facili medicamine Morbos:
  Ulcera cum veniunt, Ars nihil ipsa valet.
Vultu femineo quaevis vel pustula vulnus   5
  Lethale est, pulchras certior ense necat.
Mollia vel temeret si quando mitior ora,
  Evadat forsan femina, Diva nequat.
Cui par est Animae Corpus, quae tota venustas,
  Formae qui potis est, haec superesse suae?   10

JOHAN COMES ROFFEN.
è Coll. Wadh.

III

To Her Sacred Majesty,
The Queen-Mother,
On the Death of Mary,
Princess of Orange

(*Written at 12 Years old*)

RESPITE, great Queen, your just and hasty fears!
There's no infection lodges in our tears.
Though our unhappy air be arm'd with death,
Yet sighs have an untainted guiltless Breath.
Oh! stay a while, and teach your equal skill   5
To understand, and to support our ill.
You that in Mighty Wrongs an Age have spent,
And seem'd to have out-liv'd ev'n Banishment:
Whom traiterous Mischief sought its earliest prey,

When to most Sacred Blood it made its way;   10
And did thereby its black Design impart,
To take his Head, that wounded first his Heart:
You that unmov'd Great *Charles* his ruine stood,
When three Great Nations sunk beneath the Load:
Then a young Daughter lost, yet Balsom found   15
To stanch that new and freshly-bleeding wound:
And, after this with fixt and steddy Eyes
Beheld your Noble *Glocester's* Obsequies:
And then sustain'd the Royal *Princess* Fall;
You only can lament her Funeral.   20
But you will hence remove, and leave behind
Our sad Complaints lost in the empty wind;
Those winds that bid you stay, and loudly rore
Destruction, and drive back to the firm shore:
Shipwrack to safety, and the envy fly,   25
Of sharing in this Scene of Tragedy.
While sickness, from whose rage you post away,
Relents, and only now contrives your stay:
The lately fatal and infectious ill
Courts the fair Princess, and forgets to kill.   30
In vain on Fevers Curses we dispence,
And vent our Passions angry Eloquence:
In vain we blast the Ministers of Fate,
And the forlorn Physicians imprecate;
Say they to Death new Poisons add and fire;   35
Murder securely for reward and hire;
Art's Basilisks, that kill whom e're they see,
And truly write Bills of Mortality:
Who, lest the bleeding Corps shou'd them betray,
First drain those vital speaking Streams away.   40
And will you, by your flight, take part with these?
Become your self a third, and new Disease?
If they have caus'd our loss, then so have you,
Who take your self and the fair *Princess* too.
For we depriv'd, an equal damage have   45
When *France* doth ravish hence, as when the Grave.

5

But that your choice th' unkindness doth improve,
And dereliction adds to your remove.

ROCHESTER.
of Wadham College.

LYRICS, LOVE-EPISTLES
AND ELEGIES

LYRICS, LOVE-EPISTLES
AND ELEGIES

IV

A *Dialogue between* Strephon *and* Daphne

Strephon

PRITHEE now, fond Fool, give o're;
Since my heart is gone before,
To what purpose shou'd I stay?
Love Commands another way.

Daphne

Perjur'd Swain, I knew the time   5
When Dissembling was your Crime.
In pity now employ that Art
Which first betray'd, to ease my heart.

Strephon

Women can with pleasure feign:
Men dissemble still with pain.   10
What advantage will it prove,
If I lye, who cannot love?

Daphne

Tell me then the Reason why,
Love from Hearts in love does flye?
Why the Bird will build a Nest,   15
Where he ne're intends to rest?

Strephon

Love, like other little Boys,
Cries for Hearts, as they for Toys:

9

Which, when gain'd, in Childish Play,
Wantonly are thrown away.   20

Daphne

Still on Wing, or on his Knees,
Love does nothing by degrees;
Basely flying when most priz'd,
Meanly fawning when despis'd.
Flatt'ring or insulting ever,   25
Generous and grateful never:
All his Joys are fleeting Dreams,
All his Woes severe Extreams.

Strephon

Nimph, unjustly you inveigh;
Love, like us, must Fate obey.   30
Since 'tis Nature's Law to Change,
Constancy alone is strange.
See the Heav'ns in Lightnings break,
Next in Storms of Thunder speak;
'Till a kind Rain from above   35
Makes a Calm,—so 'tis in love.
Flames begin our first Address,
Like meeting Thunder we embrace;
Then you know the Show'rs that fall
Quench the fire, and quiet all.   40

Daphne

How shou'd I these Show'rs forget,
'Twas so pleasant to be wet?
They kill'd Love, I knew it well,
I dy'd all the while they fell.
Say at least what *Nimph* it is   45
Robs my Breast of so much Bliss?
If she is Fair, I shall be eas'd,
Thro' my Ruine you'll be pleas'd.

10

Strephon

Daphne never was so Fair:
Strephon, scarcely, so sincere.　　　　　50
Gentle, innocent, and Free,
Ever pleas'd with only me.
Many Charms my Heart enthral,
But there's one above 'em all:
With aversion she does flye　　　　　55
Tedious, trading, Constancy.

Daphne

Cruel Shepherd! I submit;
Do what Love and you think fit:
Change is Fate, and not Design,
Say you wou'd have still been mine.　　　　　60

Strephon

Nymph I cannot: 'tis too true,
Change has greater Charms than you.
Be, by my Example, wise,
Faith to Pleasure sacrifice.

Daphne

Silly *Swain*, I'll have you know,　　　　　65
'Twas my practice long ago:
Whilst you Vainly thought me true,
I was false in scorn of you.
By my Tears, my Heart's Disguise,
I thy Love and thee despise.　　　　　70
Womankind more Joy discovers
Making Fools, than keeping Lovers.

V

A Pastoral Dialogue between Alexis *and* Strephon

Written at the *Bath*, in the Year, 1674

Alexis

THERE sighs not on the Plain
   So lost a Swain as I;
Scorch'd up with Love, Froz'n with disdain,
Of killing Sweetness I complain.

Strephon

  If 'tis *Corrinna*, die.   5
Since first my dazled Eyes were thrown
   On that bewitching Face,
Like ruin'd Birds rob'd of their Young,
Lamenting, frighted, and undone,
   I fly from place to place.   10
Fram'd by some Cruel Pow'rs above,
   So nice she is, and fair;
None from undoing can remove,
Since all, who are not Blind, must Love;
   Who are not vain, Despair.   15

Alexis

The Gods no sooner give a Grace,
   But, fond of their own Art,
Severely Jealous, ever place
To guard the Glories of a Face,
   A Dragon in the Heart.   20
Proud and Ill-natur'd Pow'rs they are,
   Who, peevish to Mankind,
For their own Honour's sake, with care,
Make a sweet Form divinely fair,
   Then add a cruel Mind.   25

Strephon

Since she's insensible of Love,
 By Honour taught to hate,
If we, forc'd by Decrees above,
Must sensible to Beauty prove,
 Now Tyrannous is Fate?   30

Alexis

I to the *Nymph* have never nam'd
 The Cause of all my pain.

Strephon

Such bashfulness may well be blam'd,
For since to serve we're not asham'd,
 Why should she blush to Reign? 35

Alexis

But if her haughty Heart despise
 My humble proffer'd one;
The Just Compassion she denies,
I may obtain from others Eyes;
 Hers are not fair alone.   40
Devouring Flames require new Food;
 My Heart's consum'd almost:
New Fires must kindle in her Blood,
Or Mine go out, and that's as good.

Strephon

Would'st live, when Love is lost? 45
Be dead before thy Passion dies;
 For if thou should'st survive,
What Anguish would the Heart surprize,
To see her Flames begin to rise,
 And Thine no more Alive.   50

13

Alexis

Rather what Pleasure shou'd I meet
  In my Tryumphant Scorn,
To see my Tyrant at my Feet;
While taught by her, unmov'd I sit
  A Tyrant in my Turn.   55

Strephon

Ungentle Shepherd! Cease, for shame;
  Which way can you pretend
To merit so Divine a Flame,
Who to dull Life make a mean Claim,
  When Love is at an end?   60
As Trees are by their Bark embrac'd,
  Love to my Soul doth cling;
When torn by the Herd's greedy Taste,
The injur'd Plants feel they're defac't,
  They wither in the Spring.   65
My rifled Love would soon retire,
  Dissolving into Air,
Shou'd I that Nymph cease to admire,
Bless'd in whose Arms I will expire,
  Or at her Feet despair.   70

VI

Womans Honour

A Song

1

LOVE bid me hope, and I obey'd;
  Phillis continu'd still unkind:

14

Then you may e'en despair, He said,
  In vain I strive to change her Mind.

2

Honour's got in, and keeps her Heart,   5
  Durst he but venture once abroad,
In my own right I'de take your part,
  And shew my self a Mightier *God*.

3

This Huffing *Honour* domineers
  In Breasts, where he alone has place: 10
But if true Gen'rous *Love* appears,
  The Hector dares not shew his Face.

4

Let me still languish, and complain,
  Be most inhumanely deny'd:
I have some Pleasure in my pain,   15
  She can have none with all her Pride.

5

I fall a Sacrifice to *Love*,
  She lives a Wretch for *Honour's* sake;
Whose Tyrant does most cruel prove,
  The difference is not hard to make.   20

6

Consider *Real Honour* then,
  You'l find *Hers* cannot be the same;
'Tis noble Confidence in Men,
  In Women mean mistrustful Shame.

VII

Grecian Kindness

A Song

1

THE utmost Grace the *Greeks* could shew,
   When to the *Trojans* they grew kind,
Was with their Arms to let 'em go,
   And leave their lingring Wives behind.
They beat the Men, and burnt the Town,   5
Then all the Baggage was their own.

2

There the kind Deity of Wine
   Kiss'd the soft wanton God of Love;
This clapp'd his Wings, that press'd his Vine,
   And their best Pow'rs united move.   10
While each brave *Greek* embrac'd his Punk,
Lull'd her asleep, and then grew drunk.

VIII

The Mistress

A Song

1

AN Age, in her Embraces past,
   Would seem a Winters Day;
Where Life and Light, with envious hast,
   Are torn and snatch'd away.

16

2

But, oh! how slowly Minutes rowl,   5
    When absent from her Eyes;
That feed my Love, which is my Soul,
    It languishes and dyes.

3

For then no more a Soul but shade,
    It mournfully does move;   10
And haunts my Breast, by Absence made
    The living Tomb of Love.

4

You Wiser Men despise me not;
    Whose Love-sick Fancy raves,
On Shades of Souls, and Heav'n knows what; 15
    Short Ages live in Graves.

5

When e're those wounding Eyes, so full
    Of Sweetness, you did see;
Had you not been profoundly dull,
    You had gone mad like me.   20

6

Nor Censure us, You who perceive
    My best belov'd and me,
Sigh and lament, Complain and grieve,
    You think we disagree.

7

Alas! 'tis Sacred Jealousie,   25
    Love rais'd to an Extream;
The only Proof 'twixt her and me,
    We love, and do not dream.

8

Fantastick Fancies fondly move;
　　And in frail Joys believe;　　　　　　　30
Taking false Pleasure for true Love;
　　But Pain can ne're deceive.

9

Kind Jealous Doubts, tormenting Fears,
　　And Anxious Cares, when past,
Prove our Hearts Treasure fixt and dear,　　35
　　And make us blest at last.

IX

A Song

1

Absent from thee I languish still,
　　Then ask me not, when I return?
The straying Fool t'will plainly kill,
　　To wish all Day, all Night to Mourn.

2

Dear; from thine Arms then let me flie,　　5
　　That my Fantastick Mind may prove
The Torments it deserves to try,
　　That tears my fixt Heart from my Love.

3

When wearied with a world of Woe
　　To thy safe Bosom I retire,　　　　　　10
Where Love, and Peace, and Truth does flow,
　　May I contented there expire.

4

Lest once more wand'ring from that Heav'n,
   I fall on some base heart unblest;
Faithless to thee, False, unforgiv'n,   15
   And lose my Everlasting rest.

X

To Corinna

A Song

1

WHAT Cruel Pains *Corinna* takes,
   To force that harmless frown;
When not one Charm her Face forsakes,
   Love cannot lose his own.

2

So sweet a Face, so soft a Heart,   5
   Such Eyes so very kind,
Betray, alas! the silly Art
   Virtue had ill design'd.

3

Poor feeble Tyrant! who in vain
   Would proudly take upon her,   10
Against kind Nature to maintain,
   Affected Rules of Honour.

4

The Scorn she bears so helpless proves,
   When I plead Passion to her,
That much she fears, (but more she loves,)   15
   Her Vassal should undo her.

XI

A Song of a Young Lady
To her Ancient Lover

1

ANCIENT Person, for whom I,
All the flatt'ring Youth defy;
Long be it e're thou grow Old,
Aking, shaking, Crazy Cold.
But still continue as thou art,   5
Ancient Person of My Heart.

2

On thy wither'd Lips and dry,
Which like barren Furrows lye,
Brooding Kisses I will pour,
Shall thy youthful Heart restore.   10
Such kind Show'rs in Autumn fall,
And a second Spring recall:
Nor from thee will ever part,
Antient Person of my Heart.

3

Thy Nobler Part⟨s⟩, which but to name,   15
In our Sex wou'd be counted shame,
By Ages frozen grasp possest,
From their Ice shall be releast:
And, sooth'd by my reviving Hand,
In former Warmth and Vigor stand.   20
All a Lover's Wish can reach,
For thy Joy my Love shall teach:
And for thy Pleasure shall improve,
All that Art can add to Love.
Yet still I love thee without Art,   25
Antient Person of my Heart.

20

XII

A Song

1

PHILLIS, be gentler, I advise;
 Make up for time mispent,
When Beauty on its Death-bed lyes,
 'Tis high time to repent.

2

Such is the Malice of your Fate,   5
 That makes you old so soon;
Your Pleasure ever comes too late,
 How early e're begun.

3

Think what a wretched thing is she,
 Whose Stars contrive, in spight,   10
The Morning of her love should be
 Her fading Beauties Night.

4

Then if, to make your ruine more,
 You'll peevishly be coy,
Dye with the Scandal of a Whore,   15
 And never know the Joy.

XIII

To a Lady,
in a Letter

1

SUCH perfect Bliss, fair *Cloris*, we
    In our Enjoyment prove:
'Tis pity restless Jealousie
    Should mingle with our Love.

2

Let us, since Wit has taught us how,   5
    Raise Pleasure to the Top:
You Rival Bottle must allow,
    I'le suffer Rival Fop.

3

Think not in this that I design
    A Treason 'gainst Love's Charms,   10
When following the God of Wine,
    I leave my *Cloris* Arms.

4

Since you have that, for all your haste,
    At which I'll ne'er repine,
Its Pleasure can repeat as fast,   15
    As I the Joys of Wine.

5

There's not a brisk insipid Spark,
    That flutters in the Town;
But with your wanton Eyes you mark
    Him out to be your own.   20

6

Nor do you think it worth your care,
    How empty, and how dull,
The Heads of your Admirers are,
    So that their Veins be full.

7

All this you freely may confess,   25
    Yet we ne'er disagree:
For did you love your Pleasure less,
    You were no Match for me.

XIV

The Fall

A Song

1

How blest was the Created State
    Of Man and Woman, e're they fell,
Compar'd to our unhappy Fate,
    We need not fear another Hell!

2

Naked, beneath cool Shades, they lay,   5
    Enjoyment waited on Desire:
Each Member did their Wills obey,
    Nor could a Wish set Pleasure higher.

3

But we, poor Slaves to Hope and Fear,
    Are never of our Joys secure: 10
They lessen still as they draw near,
    And none but dull Delights endure.

4

Then, *Cloris*, while I Duty pay,
   The Nobler Tribute of my Heart,
Be not You so severe to say,   15
   You love me for a frailer Part.

XV

Love and Life
A Song

1

ALL my past Life is mine no more,
   The flying hours are gone:
Like transitory Dreams giv'n o're,
Whose Images are kept in store,
   By Memory alone.   5

2

The Time that is to come is not,
   How can it then be mine?
The present Moment's all my Lot,
And that, as fast as it is got,
   Phillis, is only thine.   10

3

Then talk not of Inconstancy,
   False Hearts, and broken Vows;
If I, by Miracle, can be
This live-long Minute true to thee,
   'Tis all that Heav'n allows.   15

XVI

A Song

1

WHILE on those lovely looks I gaze,
  To see a Wretch persuing,
In Raptures of a blest amaze,
  His pleasing happy Ruine:
'Tis not for pity that I move;   5
  His Fate is too aspiring,
Whose Heart, broke with a load of Love,
  Dies wishing and admiring.

2

But if this Murder you'd forego,
  Your Slave from Death removing;   10
Let me your Art of Charming know,
  Or learn you mine of Loving.
But whether Life, or Death, betide,
  In Love 'tis equal Measure;
The Victor lives with empty Pride;   15
  The Vanquish'd die with Pleasure.

XVII

A Song

1

LOVE a Woman! you're an Ass,
  'Tis a most insipid Passion;
To chuse out for your happiness
  The silliest part of God's Creation.

2

Let the Porter, and the Groom,   5
   Things design'd for dirty Slaves;
Drudge in fair *Aurelia's* Womb,
   To get Supplies for Age and Graves.

3

Farewell Woman, I intend,
   Henceforth, ev'ry night to sit   10
With my lewd well-natur'd Friend,
   Drinking to engender Wit.

XVIII

A Song

1

To this Moment a Rebel, I throw down my Arms,
Great *Love*, at first sight of *Olinda's* bright Charms:
Made proud, and secure by such Forces as these,
You may now play the Tyrant as soon as you please.

2

When Innocence, Beauty, and Wit do conspire   5
To betray, and engage, and inflame my Desire;
Why should I decline what I cannot avoid?
And let pleasing Hope by base Fear be destroy'd?

3

Her innocence cannot contrive to undo me,
Her Beauty's inclin'd, or why shou'd it pursue me? 10
And Wit has to Pleasure been ever a Friend,
Then what room for Despair, since Delight is *Love's*
    End?

26

4

There can be no Danger in sweetness and youth,
Where Love is secur'd by Good Nature and Truth;
On her Beauty I'le gaze, and of Pleasure complain; 15
While ev'ry kind look adds a link to my Chain.

5

'Tis more to maintain, than it was to surprise;
But her Wit leads in Triumph the Slave of her Eyes;
I beheld, with the loss of my Freedom before,
But hearing, for ever must serve and adore. 20

6

Too bright is my Goddess, her Temple too weak:
Retire, Divine Image! I feel my Heart break.
Help, *Love*, I dissolve in a Rapture of Charms;
At the thought of those Joys I shou'd meet in her
Arms.

XIX

Upon his Leaving his Mistress

1

'TIS not that I'm weary grown
Of being yours, and yours alone:
But with what Face can I incline,
To damn you to be only mine?
You, whom some kinder Pow'r did fashion, 5
By merit, and by inclination,
The Joy at least of a whole Nation.

2

Let meaner Spirits of your Sex,
With humbler Aims their thoughts perplex:

And boast, if, by their Arts, they can   10
Contrive to make *one* happy Man.
While, mov'd by an impartial Sense, ⎤
Favours, like Nature, you dispence, ⎬
With Universal Influence.   ⎦

3

See the kind Seed-receiving Earth,   15
To ev'ry Grain affords a Birth:
On her no Show'rs unwelcome fall,
Her willing Womb retains 'em all.
And shall my *Celia* be confin'd?   ⎤
No, live up to thy mighty Mind;   ⎬   20
And be the Mistress of Mankind.   ⎦

XX

Upon Drinking in a Bowl

1

VULCAN, contrive me such a Cup
    As *Nestor* us'd of old;
Shew all thy Skill to trim it up,
    Damask it round with Gold.

2

Make it so large, that, fill'd with Sack   5
    Up to the swelling Brim,
Vast Toasts, on the delicious Lake,
    Like Ships at Sea, may swim.

3

Engrave not Battel on his Cheek;
    With War I've nought to do: 10

28

I'm none of those that took *Mastrick*;
   Nor *Yarmouth* Leaguer knew.

4

Let it no name of Planets tell,
   Fix'd Stars, or Constellations:
For I am no Sir *Sindrophel*,   15
   Nor none of his Relations.

5

But carve thereon a spreading Vine;
   Then add two lovely Boys;
Their Limbs in amorous Folds intwine,
   The Type of future Joys.   20

6

Cupid and *Bacchus* my Saints are;
   May Drink and Love still reign:
With Wine I wash away my Cares,
   And then to Love again.

XXI

A Song

1

As *Cloris* full of harmless thoughts
   Beneath a Willow lay,
Kind Love a Youthful Shepherd brought,
   To pass the time away.

2

She blusht to be encounter'd so,   5
   And chid the amorous Swain:

29

But as she strove to rise and go,
   He pull'd her down again.

3

A sudden passion seiz'd her Heart,
   In spite of her disdain;   10
She found a Pulse in ev'ry part,
   And Love in every Vein.

4

Ah, Youth! (said she) what Charms are these,
   That conquer and surprise?
Ah! let me—for unless you please,   15
   I have no power to rise.

5

She fainting spoke, and trembling lay,
   For fear he should comply:
Her lovely Eyes her Heart betray,
   And give her Tongue the lye.   20

6

Thus she who Princes had deny'd,
   With all their Pomp and Train;
Was, in the lucky Minute, try'd,
   And yielded to a Swain.

XXII

A Song

1

Give me leave to rail at you,
   I ask nothing but my due;
30

To call you false, and then to say
You shall not keep my Heart a day:
But; alas! against my will,   5
I must be your Captive still.
Ah! be kinder then, for I
Cannot change, and would not dye.

2

Kindness has resistless Charms,
All besides but weakly move;   10
Fiercest Anger it disarms,
And clips the Wings of flying Love.
Beauty does the Heart invade,
Kindness only can perswade;
It gilds the Lover's servile Chain,   15
And makes the Slaves grow pleas'd again.

XXIII

The Answer

1

NOTHING adds to your fond Fire
   More than Scorn, and cold disdain:
I, to cherish your desire,
   Kindness us'd, but t'was in vain.

2

You insulted o're your Slave,   5
   Humble Love you soon refus'd:
Hope not then a Pow'r to have,
   Which ingloriously you us'd.

31

3

Think not, *Thirsis*, I will e're,
   By my Love my Empire lose: 10
You grow constant through Despair,
   Love return'd you wou'd abuse.

4

Though you still possess my Heart,
   Scorn and Rigour I must feign:
Ah! forgive that only Art,   15
   Love has left, your Love to gain.

5

You that could my heart subdue,
   To new Conquests ne're pretend:
Let the Example make me true,
   And of a conquer'd Foe a Friend.   20

6

Then, if e're I should complain
Of your Empire, or my Chain,
Summon all the pow'rful Charms,
And kill the Rebel in your Arms.

XXIV

A Song

To Chloris

1

FAIR *Cloris* in a Pig-Stye lay,
   Her tender Herd lay by her:

32

She slept, in murmuring gruntlings they,
Complaining of the scorching Day,
   Her slumbers thus inspire.

2

She dreamt, while she with careful pains
   Her Snowy Arms employ'd,
In Ivory Pails, to fill out Grains,
One of her Love-convicted Swains,
   Thus hasting to her cry'd: 10

3

Flie, Nymph, oh! flie, e're 'tis too late,
   A dear-lov'd life to save:
Rescue your Bosom Pig from Fate,
Who now expires, hung in the Gate
   That leads to yonder Cave.   15

4

My self had try'd to set him free,
   Rather than brought the News:
But I am so abhor'd by thee,
That ev'n thy Darlings life from me,
   I know thou wou'dst refuse.   20

5

Struck with the News, as quick she flies
   As blushes to her Face:
Not the bright Lightning from the Skies,
Nor Love, shot from her brighter Eyes,
   Move half so swift a Pace.   25

6

This Plot, it seems, the lustful Slave
   Had laid against her Honour:
Which not one God took care to save;

For he persues her to the Cave,
   And throws himself upon her.   30

7

Now pierced is her Virgin Zone,
   She feels the Foe within it;
She hears a broken amorous Groan,
The panting Lover's fainting moan,
   Just in the happy Minute.   35

XXV

Constancy

A Song

1

I CANNOT change, as others do,
   Though you unjustly scorn;
Since that poor Swain that sighs for you,
   For you alone was born.
No, *Phillis*, no, your Heart to move   5
   A surer way I'le try:
And to revenge my slighted Love,
   Will still love on, will still love on, and dye.

2

When, kill'd with Grief, *Amintas* lies;
   And you to mind shall call,   10
The sighs that now unpitied rise,
   The Tears that vainly fall.
That welcome Hour that ends this smart,
   Will then begin your pain;
For such a faithful tender Heart   15
   Can never break, can never break in Vain.

XXVI

A Song

1

MY dear Mistress has a Heart
    Soft as those kind looks she gave me;
When with Love's resistless Art,
    And her Eyes she did enslave me.
But her Constancy's so weak,   5
    She's so wild, and apt to wander;
That my jealous Heart wou'd break,
    Should we live one day asunder.

2

Melting Joys about her move,
    Killing Pleasures, wounding Blisses;   10
She can dress her Eyes in Love,
    And her Lips can arm with Kisses.
Angels listen when she speaks,
    She's my delight, all Mankinds wonder:
But my jealous Heart would break,   15
    Should we live one day asunder.

XXVII

A Song

INSULTING *Beauty*, you mispend
    Those Frowns upon your Slave;
Your Scorn against such Rebels bend,
Who dare with confidence pretend,
That other Eyes their Hearts defend,   5
    From all the Charms you have.

Your conquering Eyes so partial are,
　　Or Mankind is so dull,
That while I languish in Despair,
Many proud senseless Hearts declare,　　10
They find you not so killing Fair,
　　To wish you merciful.

They an Inglorious Freedom boast,
　　I triumph in my Chain;
Nor am I unreveng'd, though lost;　　15
Nor you unpunish'd, though unjust,
When I alone, who love you most,
　　Am kill'd with your Disdain.

XXVIII

A Song

⟨From *Valentinian*⟩

Nymph

INJURIOUS **Charmer** of my vanquisht Heart,
　　Canst thou feel Love, and yet no pity know?
Since of my self from thee I cannot part,
　　Invent some gentle Way to let me go.
　　　　For what with Joy thou didst obtain,　　5
　　　　　　And I with more did give;
　　　　In time shall make thee false and vain,
　　　　　　And me unfit to live.

Shepherd

Frail Angel, that wou'dst leave a Heart forlorn,
　　With vain pretence, falsehood therein might lye;
Seek not to cast wild shadows o're your scorn,　　11
　　You cannot sooner change than I can dye.

To tedious life I'le never fall,
   Thrown from thy dear lov'd Breast;
He merits not to live at all,   15
   Who cares to live unblest.

Chor.

Then let our flaming Hearts be joyn'd,
   While in that sacred fire;
E'er thou prove false, or I unkind,
   Together both expire.   20

XXIX

⟨Song⟩

'TWAS a dispute 'twixt heav'n and Earth
Which had produc't the Nobler birth:
For Heav'n, Appear'd Cynthya with all her
   Trayne,
  Till you came forth
  More glorious and more Worth,   5
Than shee with all those trembling imps of Light
  With which This Envious Queene of night
Had Proudly deck't her Conquer'd selfe in Vaine.

I must have perrisht in that first surprize,
   Had I beheld your Eyes,   10
Love, like Appollo when he would inspire
  Some holy brest, laide all his gloryes by.
Els The God cloath'd in his heavnly fire
Would have possest too powerfully,
And making of his Preist A sacrifize   15
Had soe return'd unhallow'd to the Skyes.

XXX

Song

ATT Last you'l force mee to confess
    You need no arts to vanquish:
Such charmes from Nature you posses,
    'Twere dullness, not to Languish;
Yett spare A heart you may surprize   5
    And give my Tongue the glory
To scorne, while my unfaithfull eyes
    Betray a kinder story.

XXXI

⟨*Song*⟩

LEAVE this gawdy guilded Stage
From custome more than use frequented;
Where fooles of either sex and age
Crowd to see themselves presented.
To loves Theatre the Bed   5
youth and beauty fly together,
And Act soe well it may be said
The Lawrell there was due to either:
Twixt strifes of Love and war the difference Lies
    in this
when neither overcomes Loves triumph greater
    is.   10

XXXII

Impromptus

(i)

HERE'S *Monmouth* the witty,
Laurendine the pritty,
 And *Frazier* the great physitian;
But as for the rest,
Take *York* for a jest,   5
 And yourself for a great politician.

(ii)

We have a pretty witty king
 And whose word no man relys on:
He never said a foolish thing,
 And never did a wise one.   10

XXXIII

The Advice

ALL Things submit themselves to your Command,
Fair *Cælia*, when it does not Love withstand:
The Pow'r it borrows from your Eyes alone;
All but the God must yield to, who has none.
Were he not blind, such are the Charms you have, 5
He'd quit his Godhead to become your Slave:
Be Proud to act a Mortal Hero's Part,
And throw himself for Fame on his own Dart.
But Fate has otherwise dispos'd of things,
In diff'rent Bands subjected Slaves, and Kings: 10
Fetter'd in Forms of Royal State are they,
While we enjoy the Freedom to Obey.
That Fate like you resistless does ordain,
To Love, that over Beauty he shall Reign.

By Harmony the Universe does move,   15
And what is Harmony but Mutual Love?
Who would resist an Empire so Divine,
Which Universal Nature does enjoyn?
See Gentle Brooks, how quietly they glide,
Kissing the rugged Banks on either side.   20
While in their Crystal Streams at once they show,
And with them feed the Flow'rs which they bestow:
Tho' rudely throng'd by a too near Embrace,
In gentle Murmurs they keep on their Pace
To the lov'd Sea; for Streams have their desires;   25
Cool as they are, they feel Love's pow'rful Fires;
And with such Passion, that if any Force
Stop or molest them in their Amorous Course;
They swell, break down with Rage, and ravage o're
The Banks they kiss'd, and Flow'rs they fed before.
Submit then, *Cælia*, e're you be reduc'd;   31
For Rebels, vanquish'd once, are vilely us'd.
Beauty's no more but the dead Soil, which Love
Manures, and does by wise Commerce improve:
Sailing by Sighs, through Seas of Tears, he sends 35
Courtships from foreign Hearts, for your own
    ends:
Cherish the Trade, for as with *Indians* we
Get Gold, and Jewels, for our Trumpery:
So to each other, for their useless Toys,
Lovers afford whole Magazins of Joys.   40
But if you are fond of Bawbles, be, and starve,
Your Guegaw Reputation still preserve:
Live upon Modesty and empty Fame,
Foregoing Sense for a Fantastick Name.

XXXIV

The Discovery

C Æ*LIA*, that faithful Servant you disown,
Would in Obedience keep his Love his own:
But bright Ideas, such as you inspire,
We can no more conceal, than not admire.
My Heart at home in my own Breast did dwell,   5
Like humble Hermit in a Peaceful Cell:
Unknown and undisturb'd it rested there,
Stranger alike to Hope and to Despair.
Now Love with a tumultuous Train invades
The Sacred Quiet of those Hallow'd Shades: 10
His fatal Flames shine out to ev'ry Eye,
Like blazing Commets in a Winter Skie.
How can my Passion merit your Offence,
That challenges so little Recompence:
For I am one, born only to admire;   15
Too humble e're to hope, scarce to desire.
A Thing, whose Bliss depends upon your Will;
Who would be proud you'd deign to use him ill.
Then give me leave to glory in my Chain,
My fruitless Sighs, and my unpitied Pain.   20
Let me but ever love, and ever be
Th' Example of your Pow'r and Cruelty.
Since so much Scorn does in your Breast reside,
Be more indulgent to its Mother Pride.
Kill all you strike, and trample on their Graves;
But own the Fates of your neglected Slaves: 26
When in the Croud yours undistinguish'd lies,
You give away the Triumph of your Eyes.
Perhaps (obtaining this) you'll think I find
More Mercy, than your Anger has design'd: 30
But *Love* has carefully design'd for me,
The last Perfection of Misery.
For to my State the Hopes of Common Peace,
Which ev'ry Wretch enjoys in Death, must cease:

My worst of Fates attend me in my Grave, 35
Since, dying, I must be no more your Slave.

XXXV

⟨*Epistle*⟩

COULD I but make my wishes insolent
And force some image of a false content!
But they like mee bashfull and humble growne
Hover att distance about Beautyes throne;
There worship and admire and then they dye, 5
Daring noe more Lay Hold of her than I.
Reason to worth beares a submissive spirritt
But Fooles can be familliar with merritt.
Who but that blund'ring blockhead Phaeton
Could e're have thought to drive about the Sun?
That such another durst make love to you 11
Whom not ambition led but dullness drew,
Noe Am'rous thought would his dull heart incline
But he would have a passion, for 'twas fine.
That, a new suite, and what hee next must say, 15
Runs in his Idle head the live Long day.
Hard hearted saint, since 'tis your will to Bee
Soe unrelenting pittiless to mee,
Regardlesse of A Love soe many yeares 19
Preserv'd twix't Ling'ring hopes in awfull feares,
Such feares in Lovers Breasts high vallue claimes
And such expiring martyrs feele in flames.
my hopes your selfe contriv'd with cruell care
Through gentle smiles to leade mee to despaire.
Tis some releife in my extreame distress 25
My rivall is Below your power to Bless.

XXXVI

A very Heroical Epistle
in Answer to Ephelia

MADAM,

If your deceiv'd, it is not by my Cheat,
For all disguises, are below the Great.
What *Man*, or *Woman*, upon *Earth* can say,
I ever us'd 'em well above a Day?
How is it then, that I inconstant am?   5
He changes not, who always is the same.
In my dear self, I center ev'ry thing,
My *Servants*, *Friends*, My *Mrs.*, and my *King*.
Nay Heav'n, and *Earth*, to that one poynt I bring.
Well manner'd, honest, generous, and stout,   10
Names by dull *Fools*, to plague Mankind found
          out;
Shou'd I regard I must myself constrain,
And 'tis my *Maxim*, to avoid all pain.
You fondly look for what none e're cou'd find,
Deceive your self, and then call me unkind,   15
And by false Reasons, wou'd my falshood prove,
For 'tis as natural to change, as love:
You may as justly at the *Sun*, repine,
Because alike it does not always shine:
No glorious thing, was ever made to stay,   20
My blazing *Star*, but visits and away.
As fatal to it shines, as those 'ith' *Skyes*,
'Tis never seen, but some great *Lady* dyes.
The boasted favor, you so precious hold,
To me's no more than changing of my Gold   25
What e're you gave, I paid you back in Bliss,
Then where's the Obligation pray of this?
If heretofore you found grace in my *Eyes*,
Be thankful for it, and let that suffice,
But *Woman*, *Beggar-like*, still haunt⟨s⟩ the Door, 30
Where they've receiv'd a *Charity* before.

Oh happy *Sultan*! whom we barb'rous call,
How much refin'd art thou above us all:
Who envys not the joys of thy *Serail*?   34
Thee like some God! the trembling Crowd adore,
Each Man's thy *Slave*, and *Woman kind*, thy *Whore*.
Methinks I see thee underneath the Shade, .
Of Golden Canopy, supinely laid,
Thy crowding *Slaves*, all silent as the Night.
But at thy nod, all active, as the light!   40
Secure in solid Sloth, thou there dost reign,
And feel'st the joys of Love, without the pain.
Each *Female*, courts thee with a wishing Eye,
While thou with awful pride, walk'st careless by;
Till thy kind Pledge, at last, marks out the *Dame*,45
Thou fancy'st most, to quench thy present flame.
Then from thy Bed, submissive she retires,
And thankful for the grace, no more requires
No loud reproach, nor fond unwelcome sound,
Of *Womens* Tongues, thy sacred Ear does wound;
If any do, a nimble *Mute*, strait tyes   51
The *True-loves-knot*, and stops her foolish cryes.
Thou fear'st no injur'd *Kinsmans* threatning Blade,
Nor Mid-night Ambushes, by *Rivals* laid;
While here with aking Hearts, our joys we tast,   55
Disturb'd by Swords, like *Damocles* his Feast.

XXXVII

The Imperfect Enjoyment

THIS poem has been excluded from the present
edition at the request of the publishers. The text will
be found in Thorpe, pp. 14–19. See Introduction,
p. xlix.

TRANSLATIONS

TRANSLATIONS

XXXVIII

The Ninth Elegy
in the
second Book of Ovid's Amours,
Translated
To Love

O LOVE! how cold and slow to take my part?
Thou Idle Wanderer about my Heart:
Why, thy old faithful Souldier wilt thou see
Opprest in thy own Tents? They murther me.
Thy *Flames* consume, thy *Arrows* pierce thy Friends:
Rather on Foes pursue more Noble Ends.   6
Achilles Sword would certainly bestow
A Cure, as certain as it gave the Blow.
Hunters, who follow flying Game, give o're
When the Prey's caught, hopes still lead on before. 10
We thine own Slaves feel thy Tyrannick blows,
Whilst thy tame hand's unmov'd against thy Foes.
On Men disarm'd, how can you gallant prove?
And I was long ago disarm'd by Love.
Millions of dull Men live, and scornful Maids: 15
We'll own Love valiant when he these invades.
Rome from each corner of the wide World snatch'd
A Laurel, or't had been to this Day thatch'd.
But the old Souldier has his resting place;
And the good batter'd Horse is turn'd to Grass: 20
The harrast Whore, who liv'd a Wretch to please;
Has leave to be a Bawd, and take her ease.
For me then, who have truly spent my blood
(Love) in thy Service; and so boldly stood
In *Celia's* Trenches; were't not wisely done,   25
E'en to retire, and live in peace at home?

No—might I gain a *Godhead* to disclaim
My glorious Title to my endless Flame:
Divinity with Scorn I would forswear:
Such sweet, dear, tempting, Devils *Women* are.   30
Whene're those flames grow faint, I quickly find
A fierce, black, storm, pour down upon my mind:
Headlong I'm hurl'd, like Horsemen, who, in vain,
Their (fury-flaming) Coursers would restrain.
As Ships, just when the Harbour they attain,   35
Are snatch'd by sudden blasts to Sea again:
So Love's fantastick storms reduce my heart
Half rescu'd, and the God resumes his dart.
Strike here, this undefended bosom wound,
And for so brave a Conquest be renown'd.   40
Shafts fly so fast to me from every part,
You'l scarce discern the Quiver from my heart.
What Wretch can bear a live-long night's dull rest,
Or think himself in lazy slumbers blest?
Fool—is not sleep the Image of pale Death?   45
There's time for rest, when Fate has stopt your
          Breath.
Me may my soft deluding Dear deceive;
I'm happy in my hopes while I believe.
Now let her flatter, then as fondly chide:
Often may I enjoy; oft be deny'd.   50
With doubtful Steps the God of War does move
By thy Example, in Ambiguous Love.
Blown to and fro like Down from thy own Wing;
Who knows when Joy or Anguish thou wilt bring,
Yet at thy Mother's and thy Slaves Request,   55
Fix an eternal Empire in my Breast:
And let th'inconstant, charming, Sex,
Whose wilful scorn does Lovers vex,
Submit their hearts before thy Throne:
The Vassal World is then thy own.   60

48

XXXIX

The latter End of the Chorus of the second Act of Seneca's Troas, translated

AFTER Death nothing is, and nothing Death;
The utmost Limits of a gasp of Breath.
Let the ambitious Zealot lay aside
His hopes of Heav'n; (whose Faith is but his Pride)
Let slavish Souls lay by their Fear,   5
Nor be concern'd which way or where,
After this life they shall be hurl'd:
Dead, we become the Lumber of the World;
And to that Mass of Matter shall be swept,
Where things destroy'd, with things unborn are kept;
Devouring time swallows us whole,   11
Impartial Death confounds Body and Soul.
For Hell, and the foul Fiend that rules
   The everlasting fiery G⟨ao⟩ls,
Devis'd by Rogues, dreaded by Fools   15
With his grim griesly Dog that keeps the Door,
   Are senseless Stories, idle Tales,
Dreams, Whimseys, and no more.

XL

Lucretius, *in his First Book, has these Lines*

*O MNIS enim per se Divum Natura necesse est
Immortali ævo summa cum pace fruatur,
Semota ab nostris rebus, sejunctaque longe.
Nam privata dolore omni, privata periclis,
Ipsa suis pollens opibus, nihil indiga nostri,
Nec bene pro meritis capitur, nec tangitur Ira.*

Thus Translated

The *Gods*, by right of Nature, must possess
An Everlasting Age of Perfect Peace:
Far off remov'd from us and our Affairs;
Neither approach'd by *Dangers*, or by *Cares*:
Rich in themselves, to whom we cannot add: 5
Not pleas'd by *Good* Deeds; nor provok'd by *Bad*.

XLI

⟨*Draft of Translation from Lucretius*⟩

GREATE Mother of Eneas and of Love
Delight of Mankinde, and those powers above,
Who all beneathe those sprinkl'd dropps of light
Which slide upon the face of gloomy night
Whither vast regions of that liquid world   5
Where groves of shipps on watry hills are hurl'd
Or fruitfull earth, do'st bless, sinc 'tis by thee
That all things live, which the bright sun does see.

PROLOGUES AND
EPILOGUES

PROLOGUES AND EPILOGUES
XLII

A Prologue spoken at
the Court at White-Hall
before King Charles the Second,
by the Lady Elizabeth Howard

WIT has of late took up a Trick t'appear,
Unmannerly, or at the best severe.
And Poets share the Fate by which we fall,
When kindly we attempt to please you all.
'Tis hard, your scorn should against such prevail,   5
Whose ends are to divert you, tho' they fail.
You Men would think it an il⟨l⟩natur'd Jest,
Should we laugh at you when you did your best.
Then rail not here, though you see reason for't.⎫
If Wit can find it self no better sport;   ⎬10
Wit is a very foolish thing at Court.   ⎭
Wit's bus'ness is to please, and not to fright,⎫
'Tis no Wit to be always in the right: ⎬
You'll find it none, who dare be so to Night,   ⎭
Few so ill-bred will venture to a Play,   15
To spy out Faults, in what we Women say.
For us no matter what we speak, but how:
How kindly can we say—I hate you now?
And for the Men, if you'l laugh at 'em, do;
They mind themselves so much they'l ne're mind
        you.   20
But why do I descend to lose a Prayer
On those small Saints in Wit, the God sits there.

53

⟨To the King⟩

To you (Great Sir) my Message hither tends,
From Youth and Beauty your Allies and Friends.
See my Credentials written in my Face.   25
They challenge your Protection in this place,
And hither come with such a Force of Charms,
As may give check ev'n to your prosp'rous Armes.
Millions of *Cupids* hovering in the Rear,
Like Eagles following fatal Troops, appear: 30
All waiting for the slaughter, which draws nigh,
Of those bold Gazers, who this Night must dye.
Nor can you 'scape our soft Captivitie,
From which old Age alone must set you free.
Then tremble at the fatal Consequence . . .   35
Since, 'tis well known, for your own part. (Great
    Prince)
'Gainst us you still have made a weak Defence . . .
Be generous, and wise, and take our part;
Remember we have Eyes, and you a Heart;
Else you may find, too late, that we are things   40
Born to kill Vassals, and to conquer Kings.
But oh! to what vain Conquest I pretend,
While *Love* is our Commander, and your Friend.
Our Victory your Empire more assures;
For *Love* will ever make the Triumph yours.   45

XLIII

Prologue

GENTLE Reproofs have long been try'd in vain,
Men but despise us while we but complain:
Such numbers are concern'd for the wrong side;
A weak resistance still provokes their Pride,
And cannot stem the fierceness of the Tide.   5

Laughers, Buffoons, with an unthinking Crowd
Of gaudy Fools, impertinent and loud,
Insult in every Corner: Want of Sense,
Confirm'd with an outlandish Impudence,
Among the rude Disturbers of the Pit,   10
Have introduc't ill Breeding, and false Wit;
To boast their Lewdness here young Scourers meet,
And all the vile Companions of a Street;
Keep a perpetual bawling near that Door   14
Who beat the Bawd last night, who bilk't the Whore:
They snarle, but neither Fight nor pay a Farthing,
A Play-house is become a mear Bear-Garden;
Where every one with Insolence enjoys
His Liberty and Property of Noise.
Should true Sense, with revengeful Fire, come down,
Our *Sodom* wants Ten Men to save the Town: 21
Each Parish is infected, to be clear
We must loose more than when the Plague was here;
While every little Thing perks up so soon,   ⎫
That at Fourteen it hectors up and down,   ⎬ 25
With the best Cheats and the worst Whores i'   ⎭
    th' Town;
Swears at a Play, who should be whipt at School, ⎫
The Foplings must in time grow up to rule,   ⎬
The Fashion must prevail to be a Fool.   ⎭
Some powerful Muse, inspir'd for our defence,   30
Arise, and save a little common Sense:
In such a Cause let thy keen Satyr bite,
Where Indignation bids thy Genius write:
Mark a bold leading Coxcomb of the Town,
And single out the Beast and hunt him down;   35
Hang up his mangl'd Carcass on the Stage,
To fright away the Vermin of the Age.

XLIV

Epilogue ⟨to Circe⟩

SOME few, from Wit, have this true Maxime got,
That 'tis still better to be pleas'd, then not,
And therefore never their own Torment plot.
While the Malitious Criticks still agree;
To loath each Play they come and pay to see;   5
The first know 'tis a Meaner part of sence
To finde a fault, then taste an Excellence,
Therefore they praise, and strive to like, while these
Are dully vain of being hard to please.
Poets and Women have an Equal Right   10
To hate the Dull, who Dead to all Delight
Feel pain alone, and have no Joy but spite.
'Twas Impotence did first this Vice begin,
Fooles censure Wit, as Old men raile of Sin,
Who Envy Pleasure which they cannot tast,   15
And good for nothing, wou'd be wise at last.
Since therefore to the Women it appears,
That all these Enemies of Wit are theirs,
Our Poet the Dull Herd no longer fears.
What e're his fate may prove, 'twill be his pride   20
To stand, or fall, with Beauty on his side.

XLV

Epilogue ⟨to Love in the Dark⟩

As Charms are Nonsense, Nonsense seems a Charm,
Which hearers of all Judgment does disarm;
For Songs, and Scenes, a double Audience bring,
And Doggrel takes, which Smiths in Sattin sing.
Now to Machines, and a dull Mask you run,   5
We find that Wit's the Monster you would shun,
And by my Troth 'tis most discreetly done.

For since with Vice and Folly, Wit is fed,
Through Mercy 'tis most of you are not dead.
Players turn Puppets now at your Desire,　　　　10
In their Mouth's Nonsence, in their Tails a Wire,
They fly through Clouds of Clouts, and show'rs
　　of Fire.
A kind of losing *Loadum* in their Game,
Where the worst Writer has the greatest Fame.
To get vile Plays like theirs, shall be our care:　　15
But of such *awkard* Actors we *despair*.
False taught at first—
Like Bowls ill byass'd, still the more they run,
They're further off, than when they first begun.
In Comedy their unweigh'd Action mark,　　　　20
There's one is such a dear familiar spark,
He yawns, as if he were but half awake;
And fribling for free speaking, does *mistake*;
False Accent, and neglectful Action too.
They have both so nigh good, yet neither true,　　25
That both together, like an Ape's Mock-face
By near resembling Man, do Man disgrace.
Through pac'd ill Actors, may, perhaps be cur'd;
Half Players, like half Wits, can't be endur'd.
Yet these are they, who durst expose the Age　　30
Of the great *Wonder* of the English Stage.
Whom Nature seem'd to form for your delight,
And bid him speak, as she bid *Shakespeare* write.
Those Blades indeed are Cripples in their Art
Mimmick his Foot, but not his speaking part.　　35
Let them the *Traytor*, or *Volpone* try;
Could they—
Rage like *Cethegus*, or like *Cassius* die,
They ne'er, had sent to *Paris* for such Fancies,
As Monster's Heads and Merry-*Andrew's* Dances.　40
Wither'd, perhaps, not perish'd we appear,
But they were blighted, and ne'er came to bear.

Th' old Poets dress'd your Mistress Wit before,
These draw you on with an old Painted Whore,
And sell, like Bawds, patch'd Plays for Maids
   twice o'er. 45
Yet they may scorn our House and Actors too,
Since they have swell'd so high to hector you
They cry, Pox o' these *Covent-Garden* Men,
Dam 'em, not one of them but keeps out Ten.
Were they once gone, we for those thund'ring Blades,
Should have an Audience of substantial Trades, 51
Who love our muzzled Boys, and tearing Fellows,
My Lord, great Neptune, *and great Nephew* Eolus.
O how the merry Citizen's in Love
With— 55
Psyche, *the Goddess of each Field and Grove,*
He cryes i'faith, methinks 'tis well enough,
But you roar out and cry, 'Tis all damn'd stuff.
So to their House the graver Fops repair,
While Men of Wit, find one another here. 60

DRAMATIC POETRY

DRAMATIC POETRY

XLVI

Sab: Lost

Blac: 1
Page: Shee yeilds, she yeilds, Pale Envy said Amen
   The first of woemen to the Last of men
Coach: Just soe those frailer beings Angells fell
Will: Ther's no mid way (it seemes) twix't heav'n and
    hell,   5
Ja: Was it your end in making her to show
Post: Things must bee rais'd soe high to fall soe low?
Gill: Since her nor Angells their owne worth secures
   Looke to it gods! the next turne must bee yours
Gard: You who in careles scorne Laught at the   10
    wayes
But: Of Humble Love and call'd 'em rude Essayes
Upholst:
Cooke: could you submit to Lett this Heavy thing
Doll: Artless and witless, noe way merriting
CK: 15
J.B.:
Gar:
Fr:
Hm:
Dick: 20

XLVII

A Scaen of Sir Robert Hoard's Play,
written by The Earl of Rochester

The Army appeares drawn up in three Battalions
The Empresse Leading the maine Body, on the right
hand Hyachian, on the left Lycungus.

Emp: Lead faster on why creep you thus to fight
　　Faintly to charge is shamefuller than flight.
　　Your Emperour Deify'd hovers in the aire ⎫
　　Commands revenge and does rewards prepare ⎬
　　For the brave Glory, for the base despaire. ⎭　　5
　　Perhaps they think or would perswade the Foe,
　　Warr led by women must be cold or slow.
　　This day I'le prove the Injustice of that scorne
　　Men treat our Sex withall, Woman is borne
　　With equall thirst of Honour and of Fame　　10
　　But treacherous man misguides her in her aime
　　Makes her believe that all her Glories lye
　　In dull obedience, Truth and Modesty,
　　That to bee Beautifull is to bee Brave
　　And calls her Conquerer when she's most his Slave
　　Forbidding her those noble Paths to tread,　　16
　　Which through bold daring deeds to Glory lead
　　With the poore Hypocriticall pretence
　　That Womans merit is her Innocence,
　　Who, treacherously advis'd Retaining thus ⎫　　20
　　The sole Ambition to be vertuous ⎬
　　Thinks 'tis enough if she's not Infamous ⎭
　　On these false grounds is mans stol'n Triumph laid
　　Through Craft alone the Nobler Creature made;
　　Women henceforth by my Example taught　　25
　　To vaster heights of vertue shall bee wrought,
　　Train'd up in Warre and Armes she shall despise
　　The mean pretended Conquests of her Eyes
　　Nor be contented with the low applause
　　Left to her Sex, by mans tyrannique Lawes.　　30
　　Glory was never got by sitting still,
　　The Lazy merits of not doing ill,
　　Who e're aspires to reach a Glorious name ⎫
　　By Acting greatly must lay in their Claime ⎬
　　Storm, tear, and fight with all the world for Fame. ⎭
Hyach: Now all the powers of Warre and Victory　36
　　Forever to your Armes propitious bee,

62

And may that Fame they for your sword reserve
Equall the Glory wee obtain to serve.

Lycun: I will not mingle wishes with the Crowd   40
  Nor till my service pleases you bee proud,
  But, if revenge through conquest you designe
  For that depend on this Sole Arme of mine
  Guarded by this, Danger you may despise
  And finde your Sword as powerfull as your Eyes 45
  Whose brightness shoud the God of Battel see
  As full of Charmes as they appeare to mee
  Hee'd think his Venus were grown young againe
  Leap down from Heaven and Resume his Chaine
  Nor though a God shou'd hee your fetters weare
  Without the hazzard of a Rivall here;   51

Emp: That Prince who to my Aide his Army brings
  I doe expect shall fight not say fine things
  If his presuming Vanity bee such
  Let him take care his Courage bee as much,   55
  And with his daring hand build a pretence
  To bee forgiv'n his Tongues Impertinence.

Lycun: Pride and contempt that often blinde the faire
  Make them least pertinent when most severe
  From unaffected Truths noe Errours flow   60
  I thinke you Lovely and I hold you soe.
  What of my selfe I said I shall make good
  And when I fight bee better understood.

Emp: Fighting indeed your Riddle will explaine
. Distinguishing the Valiant from the Vaine.   65

Hyach: And that distinction quickly will be made
  For I perceive from yonder gloomy shade
  Which those tall woods doe o're the Valleys throw
  Like swelling Tides the numerous Tarters flow,
  Their glittering Helmets force a brighter day 70
  And moving Shields
  Like dancing Billows in the sunbeames Play.

Emp: They meet my just Revenge and their own Fate
  And have the manners not to make mee waite.

To Hyac: But you, brave Prince, whose deeds advance
    your name   75
  Even with the foremost in the mouth of Fame
  Who, wheresoe e're you come, bring Victory
  Blush not this day to leave a part to mee.
  I to your conduct will the trust afford
  Of the first blooming Honour of my Sword.   80
  All here to your unequall'd worth must yield
  This day I make you Generall of the field.
Hyach: Few conquests yet my feeble hand has wrought
  But, were my deeds as humble as my thought
  Rank't with the meanest slave that does pursue 85
  The matchless Glory here to fight for you,
  Since on my Arme you place such confidence
  To think it worthy of your Fames defence
  The sole Ambition not to prove unjust
  May raise my Merit equall to my trust.   90
Emp: My judgement I but weakly shoud expresse
  To value you soe much and trust you lesse
  But in what order will you now bestow
  The Bold Chinesses to receive the Foe?
  Whose discipline as well as ours you know; 95
Hyach: Fiercely the Tartars with confusion Charge
  In broken order here and there at Large
  With wilde Excursions to and fro they bound
  And if not well observ'd will charge you round
  But a large front shall hinder that designe   100
  Half the first Legion draw into a line
  Let the other halfe the two extreames inforce
  And let the point bee wing'd with all the horse
  I'th middle which the greatest shock must prove
  Let the maine Body of the Army move.   105
Emp: My selfe and guards will at the head be plac't
Hyach: My force may follow next
Emp: Lycungus last
  Now Father draw thy vailing Cloud and see
  Thy vow'd revenge thy daughter pays to thee 110

While from the walls each gazing Slave admires
Thy daring Glory this revenge inspires—

Exit Emp.

Lycun: Lycungus last! Empresse I thank your Care
    Tis for Hyachian then that wee **make** warre.
    You who Create what difference can you see   115
    Twixt this admir'd Hyachian and mee
    Woman! ah worthlesse woman! erring still
    In the wilde maze of thy fantastick Will
    Equally shar'd betwixt thy Pride and Lust
    Averse to all that's good and blinde to all that's
      just   120
    For ever is that man of worth undone,
    Whom Fate into thy Barb'rous pow'r hath thrown
    Who in the dumb green sickness of her minde
    Still hungers for the trash of all mankinde
    Not an insipid Fopp on Earth does move   125
    For whom some woman does not die in Love.

Enter an Officer.

Officer: Both Armies Sir by this time are so neare
    They'l bee engag'd ere you can reach the Reare.
Lycun: Bid my advancing Troops with speed bee gone
    Bid em stand still be quiet and look on.   130

Exit off

    Eternall God, but sure there can be none
    To see injustice and looke Idly on
    But if there bee,
    Which of you all below or in the skies
    Is not in debt to mee for Sacrifice?   135
    To the bright shining God some prayers I make
    Some to the Hurtfull grim Bloudthirsty Black,
    Where either hope or fear points out the way
    With Equall zeal, I sacrifice, and Pray.
    If all my Prayers cannot these Blessings raise   140
    Have you the Conscience to expect my Praise
    Though hitherto
    My Innocent desires success doe want?

But I'le ask favours, you'l not stick to grant
When wee for Blessings shue, you stop your Eares
But if wee curse there's not one God but heares. 146
Assist mee then to bring full ruine downe
On this insulting Woman and her Crowne.
Are yee not scorn'd, blasphem'd, deny'd each day
For letting Chance in mortall Actions sway?   150
You'll mend the matter well, if you permit
The Rule of things to woman's Will, or Wit.
Woman of all the Creatures you did make
The only signe and profe you cou'd mistake
That heap of contradictions mass of Lyes   155
Snare of our wishes Bane of all our Joyes
If for a Blessing they were sent us, why
Have you not given them one good quality?
If for a Curse, how are you just or wise
To lend em your own form for a disguise?   160

Enter a Soldier.

Sold: The overpower'd Chinesses give ground,
   The Empress with her Guard's incompass'd round,
   The Prince Hyachians to her rescue fled
   And both by this time taken or else dead
   The wings retire the main battalian's broke.   165
Lycun: No matter, see my men fight not a stroak.

Exit Sold:

Before the sun dip in the azure wave
She shall be Deaths the Tartars or my Slave
My Slave, my wife,
My hated Wife, now my revenge grows strong   170
And may this way bee equall to my wrong,
Thanks to your pow'rs who marriage have allow'd
To make them wretched whom you first made
   proud.
But first Hyachian must in dust be lay'd
The Army next deserted or betray'd.   175
Tis worth the Blackest mischief I can doe
To bee reveng'd and get an Empire too.

If on the Tartars side the day bee lost
I'le take advantage of my noble Post,
When the pursuit most eager does appeare   180
I'le fall on the Chinesses in the reare
If they are put to flight, my forces Lye
Nearest the Towne, and thither first I'le fly
And if mỳ beaten Empress scape the rout
I'le let her in, but shut the Army out   185
Then shall shee from the wall a prospect take
Of the free massacre the Tartars make.
If after she'l consent to marry mee
When she's my Slave, I'le set her Empire free
From my own province call a fresh supply   190
And beat Syunges home with Infamy.
If the proud wretch my proferr'd hand disdaine,
In stead of mee ruine and death shall reigne.
With desolation I'le the City fill
And my fierce Troops shall plunder, fire and kill, 195
When in their bloud the murder'd people swim
And flames for want of more supply grow dim
                              Enter an Officer.
  I'le ravish her and call the Tarters in.
Offic: The China Army Sir has lost the day
  And drivn by conquering Tartars fly this way   200
  Your forces unengag'd your orders waite.
Lycun: Bid em retire and seize the City gate.
  You with some chozen horse must stay behinde
  And if the false Hyachian you can finde
  Among the scatter'd runawayes of the field   205
  Bee it your business Sir to see him kill'd.
  Goe on, Lycungus Murder and betray
  All Acts that lead to thy designes obey
  Noe mischiefe is so Black no crime soe high
  But to the World success will Justify   210
  And you Pale deadly Daemons of the Night
  Whom Altars bath'd in humane Gore delight

Assist my Plots, to make my conquests good
And when I reigne you shall not want for food.

Exit.

A noise of fighting and running Enter Hyachian
Bloudy with his Sword Drawne stopping some who
fly—

Hyach: Stay yee Base wretches, whither would you
    fly?   215
Is it a Race for chaines and Infamy?
Are you such Cowards to hide yourselves in Graves
Or have ye hopes to bee the Tartars Slaves?
In shamefull flight what safety does appeare
Can yee escape a greater Hell than feare?   220

Enter an Officer.

Officer: Ah my deare Lord are you alive and free?
Hyach: Yes and ashamed to see your Infamy.
How durst you bee my friend and run away?
Offic: Where Torrents drive what single force can
    stay?
North Winds broke loose you might assone recall
Fix scatter'd leaves that in the Autumne fall,   226
Resist the Rapid motion of the Spheare
As stop the flowing Tide of Pannique feare.
Through every Rank a swift report was spread
That you were taken and the Empress dead   230
At which they flying cry'd
After such losses twas not worth their Paines
To fight for conquest or decline their Chaines.
Hyach: The Empresse by Rash honour driven on
Into the thickest of the Foe was flowne;   235
I to her rescue ran midst showers of Darts
Cutting my Bloudy way through Tartars hearts
On foot I found her, for her horse was kill'd
Strewing with gasping carcasses the field.
Some drops of Blood   240
Which from her wounds on her faire neck did flow
Like Rubies set in Rocks of Silver show;

Alone she fought expos'd to Vulgar Blowes,
Like a maim'd Eagle in a flock of Crowes,
While I sought death with her I cou'd not Save 245
One more than all the rest generous and Brave
Presses in through the Assassinating Crowd
And with a voice of Terrour cryes alowd,
Desist for shame the Feeble murderers,
Stain not with Womans Bloud your Cymeters 250
Ile lead you on to Nobler Victories.
The Men obey him and away hee flys.
Thus got wee time our Army to regaine
But where's Lycungus taken, fled or slaine?

Officer: Lycungus Sir has never charg'd at all 255
And now stands gazing ore the City Wall.

Hyach: In him the stupid Rage of Envy see
Though Brave turns Coward to be reveng'd on mee.
Enter an Officer.

Officer: The scatter'd Troops
At Amacoa's presence stay their flight 260
And led by her renew a Bloudy fight.

Hyach: Noe more shall Nations in distress and
thrawll
On helpless man for Aid in Battails call:
This Woman's Valour is above us all—
Where ere she fights, Beauty and Ruine joyne 265
Rage on her Arme, While in her Eyes they shine.
With Story and with death the field she fills
Soe thunder led by lightning shines and kills.

Finis

XLVIII

From Valentinian: a Tragedy. As 'tis
Alter'd by the late Earl of Rochester
Act III, Scene 3

Lucina Wakes.

Claudia But see my Lady wakes and comes this way.
  Bless me! how pale and how confus'd she looks!
Lucina In what Fantastique new world have I been?
  What Horrors past? What threatning Visions seen?
  Wrapt as I lay in my amazing Trance,   5
  The Host of Heav'n and Hell did round me Dance:
  Debates arose betwixt the Pow'rs above
  And those below: Methoughts they talkt of Love.
  And nam'd me often; but it could not be
  Of any Love that had to do with me.   10
  For all the while they talk'd and argu'd thus,
  I never heard one word of *Maximus.*
  Discourteous Nymphs! who own these Murmuring
    Floods
  And you unkind Divinities o' th' Woods!
  When to your Banks and Bowers I came distrest 15
  Half dead throu' Absence seeking Peace and Rest.
  Why would you not protect by these your Streams
  A sleeping wretch from such wild dismal Dreams!
  Mishapen Monsters round in Measures went
  Horrid in Form with Gestures insolent;   20
  Grinning throu Goatish Beards with half clos'd Eyes,
  They look'd me in the face frighted to rise!
  In vain I did attempt, methought no Ground
  Was to support my sinking Footsteps! found
  In clammy Fogs like one half choak'd I lay,   25
  Crying for help my Voyce was snatch'd away.
        And when I would have fled,
        My Limbs benumm'd, or dead
  Could not my Will with Terror wing'd obey.

Upon my Absent Lord for help I cry'd   30
But in that Moment when I must have dy'd:
With Anguish of my Fears confusing pains
Relenting Sleep loos'd his Tyrannick Chains.
Claud. Madam, Alas such Accidents as these
    Are not of value to disturb your Peace!   35
    The cold damp-Dews of Night have mixt and
      wrought
    With the dark Melancholy of your Thought.
    And throu' your Fancy these Illusions brought.
    I still have markt your Fondness will afford
    No hour of Joy in th' absence of my Lord.   40

XLIX

⟨*The Soliloquy of Maximus from*⟩
Valentinian: A Tragedy As 'tis Alter'd
by the late Earl of Rochester
Act IV, Scene 3

Max. 'Tis then a certain truth that I am wrong'd,
    Wrong'd in that barb'rous manner I imagin'd:
    Alas, I was in hopes I had been mad,
    And that these Horrors which invade my Heart,
    Were but distracted melancholy Whimseys: 5
    But they are real truths (it seems) and I
    The last of men, and vilest of all Beings.

    Bear me cold Earth who am too weak to move
    Beneath my load of Shame and Misery
    Wrong'd by my lawful Prince, robb'd of my Love,
    Branded with everlasting infamy.   11
    Take pity Fate, and give me leave to die:

Gods! would you be ador'd for being good,
Or only fear'd for proving mischievous?
How would you have your Mercy understood? 15
Who would create a Wretch like *Maximus*,
Ordain'd tho' guiltless to be infamous?

Supream first Causes! you, whence all things flow,
Whose infiniteness does each little fill,
You, who decree each seeming Chance below, 20
(So great in Power) were you as good in Will,
How could you ever have produc'd such ill?

Had your eternal minds been bent to good?
Could humane happiness have prov'd so lame
Rapine, Revenge, Injustice, thirst of Blood, 25
Grief, Anguish, Horror, Want, Despair and Shame,
Had never found a Being nor a Name.

'Tis therefore less impiety to say,
Evil with you has Coeternity,
Than blindly taking it the other way, 30
That merciful and of election free,
You did create the mischiefs you foresee.

Wretch that I am, on Heav'n to exclame,
When this poor tributary Worm below,
More than myself in nothing but in name, 35
Who durst invade me with this fatal Blow,
I dare not crush in the Revenge I owe.
Not all his Power, shall the wild Monster save;
Him and my shame I'le tread into one Grave.

SATIRES

SATIRES

L

The Maim'd Debauchee

1

As some, brave *Admiral*, in former War
  Depriv'd of Force, but prest with Courage still,
Two Rival Fleets appearing from afar,
  Crawls to the top of an adjacent Hill.

2

From whence (with thoughts full of concern) he
     views   5
  The Wise, and daring, Conduct of the Fight:
And each bold Action to his mind renews,
  His present Glory, and his past Delight.

3

From his fierce Eyes flashes of Rage he throws,
  As from black Clouds when Lightning breaks away,
Transported thinks himself amidst his Foes,   11
  And absent, yet enjoys the bloody Day.

4

So when my Days of Impotence approach,
  And I'me by Love and Wines unlucky chance,
Driv'n from the pleasing Billows of Debauch,   15
  On the dull Shore of lazy Temperance.

5

My Pains at last some respite shall afford,
  While I behold the Battels you maintain:
When Fleets of Glasses sail around the Board,   19
  From whose Broad-Sides Volleys of Wit shall rain.

6

Nor shall the sight of Honourable Scars,
 Which my too forward Valour did procure,
Frighten new-listed Souldiers from the Wars,
 Past Joys have more than paid what I endure.

7

Shou'd some brave Youth (worth being drunk) prove
   nice,   25
 And from his fair inviter meanly shrink,
Twould please the Ghost of my departed Vice,
 If, at my Counsel, He repent and drink.

8

Or shou'd some cold-complexion'd Sot forbid,
 With his dull Morals, our Nights brisk Alarms; 30
I'le fire his Blood, by telling what I did,
 When I was strong, and able to bear Arms.

9

I'le tell of Whores attacqu'd their Lords at home,
 Bawds Quarters beaten up, and Fortress won:
Windows demolish'd, Watches overcome,   35
 And handsom Ills by my contrivance done.

10

With Tales like these I will such heat inspire,
 As to important mischief shall incline;
I'le make him long some Ancient Church to fire,
 And fear no lewdness they're call'd to by Wine. 40

11

Thus Statesman-like I'le saucily impose,
 And, safe from Danger, valiantly advise;
Shelter'd in impotence urge you to blows,
 And, being good for nothing else, be wise.

LI

Upon Nothing

1

NOTHING! thou Elder Brother ev'n to Shade,
That hadst a Being e're the World was made,
And (well fixt) art alone, of ending not afraid.

2

E're time and place were, time and place were not,
When Primitive *Nothing* something strait begot,   5
Then all proceeded from the great united—What.

3

Something, the Gen'ral Attribute of all,
Sever'd from thee, it's sole Original,
Into thy boundless self must undistinguish'd fall.

4

Yet something did thy mighty Pow'r command,   10
And from thy fruitful emptiness's hand,
Snatch'd Men, Beasts, Birds, Fire, Air and Land.

5

Matter, the wicked'st off-spring of thy Race,
By Form assisted, flew from thy Embrace,   14
And Rebel Light obscur'd thy reverend dusky Face.

6

With Form, and Matter, Time and Place did joyn,
Body, thy Foe, with thee did Leagues combine,
To spoil thy peaceful Realm, and ruine all thy Line.

7

But turn-Coat Time assists the Foe in vain,
And, brib'd by thee, assists thy short-liv'd Reign,   20
And to thy hungry Womb drives back thy Slaves
    again.

8

Tho' Mysteries are barr'd from Laick Eyes,
And the Divine alone, with Warrant, pryes
Into thy Bosom, where the truth in private lies,

9

Yet this of thee the wise may freely say,   25
Thou from the virtuous nothing tak'st away,
And to be part with thee the Wicked wisely pray.

10

Great Negative, how vainly would the Wise,
Enquire, define, distinguish, teach, devise?   29
Didst thou not stand to point their dull Philosophies.

11

Is, or *is not*, the two great Ends of Fate,
And, true or false, the subject of debate,
That perfect, or destroy, the vast designs of Fate,

12

When they have rack'd the *Politician*'s Breast,
Within thy Bosom most securely rest,   35
And, when reduc'd to thee, are least unsafe and best.

13

But, *Nothing*, why does *Something* still permit,
That Sacred Monarchs should at Council sit,
With Persons highly thought at best for nothing fit,

14

Whilst weighty *Something* modestly abstains,   40
From Princes Coffers, and from States-Men's Brains,
And Nothing there like stately *Nothing* reigns,

15

Nothing who dwell'st with Fools in grave Disguise,
For whom they rev'rend Shapes, and Forms devise,
Lawn Sleeves, and Furs, and Gowns, when they like
   thee look wise.   45

16

French Truth, *Dutch* Prowess, *Brittish* Policy,
Hibernian Learning, *Scotch* Civility,
Spaniards Dispatch, *Danes* Wit, are mainly seen in
   thee.

17

The great Man's Gratitude to his best Friend,
Kings Promises, Whores Vows, tow'rds thee they
   bend,   50
Flow swiftly into thee, and in thee ever end.

LII

A Letter from Artemisa in the Town to Cloe in the Country

CLOE, by your command, in Verse I write:
Shortly you'l bid me ride astride, and fight:
Such Talents better with our Sex agree,
Than lofty flights of dangerous Poetry.
Among the men, I mean the men of Wit,   5
(At least they pass'd for such before they writ)

How many bold Advent'rers for the Bays,
Proudly designing large returns of praise;
Who durst that stormy, pathless World explore; 9⎫
Were soon dasht back, and wreckt on the dull shore, ⎬
Broke of that little stock they had before. ⎭
How wou'd a Womans, tott'ring, Barque be tost,
Where stoutest Ships (the Men of Wit) are lost?
When I reflect on this, I straight grow wise:
And my own self I gravely thus advise: 15

Dear *Artemisa!* Poetry's a Snare:
Bedlam has many Mansions: have a care:
Your Muse diverts you, makes the Reader sad:
You think your self inspir'd; He thinks you mad.
Consider too, 'twill be discreetly done, 20
To make your self the Fiddle of the Town.
To find th'ill-humour'd pleasure at their need:
Curst when you fail, and scorn'd when you succeed.
Thus, like an arrant Woman, as I am, ⎫
No sooner well convinc'd writing's a shame; ⎬ 25
That *Whore* is scarce a more reproachful Name⎭
Than Poetess—
Like Men that marry, or like Maids that woo,
Because 'tis the very worst thing they can do:
Pleas'd with the contradiction, and the sin, 30
Methinks I stand on Thorns till I begin.

Y'expect to hear, at least, what Love has past
In this lewd Town, since you and I saw last;
What Change has happen'd of intrigues, and whether
The old ones last, and who and who's together. 35
But how, my dearest *Cloe*, shou'd I set
My Pen to Write, what I wou'd fain forget?
Or name that lost thing *Love*, without a Tear,
Since so debauch'd by ill-bred-Customs here?
Love, the most gen'rous Passion of the Mind; 40
The softest Refuge Innocence can find:

80

The safe Director of unguided Youth:
Fraught with kind Wishes, and secur'd by Truth:
That Cordial drop Heav'n in our Cup has thrown,
To make the nauseous draught of life go down: 45
On which one only blessing God might raise,
In Lands of Atheists, Subsidies of Praise:
For none did e're so dull, and stupid, prove,
But felt a God, and blest his Pow'r in Love:
This only Joy, for which poor we were made,   50
Is grown, like Play, to be an arrant Trade:
The Rooks creep in, and it has got, of late,
As many little Cheats, and Tricks, as that.
But, what yet more a Woman's Heart wou'd vex,
'Tis chiefly carry'd on by our own Sex: 55
Our silly Sex, who, born like Monarchs, free,
Turn Gipsies for a meaner Liberty;
And hate Restraint, tho' but from Infamy:
That call whatever is not common nice,
And, deaf to Nature's Rule, or Love's advice,   60
Forsake the Pleasure to pursue the Vice.
To an exact Perfection they have brought
The action Love; the passion is forgot.
'Tis below Wit, they tell you, to admire;
And ev'n without approving they desire.   65
Their private Wish obeys the publick Voice,
'Twixt good and bad whimsey decides, not choice.
Fashions grow up for tast, at Forms they strike;
They know what they wou'd have, not what they like.
Bovy's a Beauty, if some few agree   70
To call him so, the rest to that degree
Affected are, that with their Ears they see.
   Where I was visiting the other Night,
Comes a fine Lady, with her humble Knight,   74
Who had prevail'd with her, through her own Skill,
At his Request, though much against his Will,
To come to *London*—

As the Coach stopt, I heard her Voice, more loud
Than a great-bellied Woman's in a Croud;
Telling the Knight that her Affairs require   80
He, for some hours, obsequiously, retire.
I think she was asham'd he shou'd be seen: ⎫
Hard Fate of Husbands! the Gallant had been, ⎬
Though a diseas'd, ill-favour'd Fool, brought in. ⎭
Dispatch, says she, the business you pretend,   85
Your beastly visit to your drunken Friend.
A Bottle ever makes you look so fine;
Methinks I long to smell you stink of Wine.
Your Country drinking Breath's enough to kill:
Sour Ale corrected with a Lemmon Pill.   90
Prithee, farewell: we'll meet again anon.
The necessary Thing bows, and is gone.
She flies up stairs, and all the haste does show
That fifty Antick Postures will allow,
And then burst out—Dear Madam, am not I   95
The strangest, alter'd, Creature: let me dye
I find my self ridiculously grown,
Embarrast with my being out of Town:
Rude and untaught, like any Indian Queen;
My Country Nakedness is strangely seen.   100
How is Love govern'd? Love that rules the state;
And pray who are the men most worn of late?
When I was marri'd, Fools were all-a-mode;
The men of Wit were held then incommode:
Slow of Belief, and fickle in Desire,   ⎫ 105
Who, e're they'll be perswaded, must enquire; ⎬
As if they came to spie, and not to admire.   ⎭
With searching-wisdom, fatal to their ease,
They still find out why, what may, shou'd not please:
Nay, take themselves for injur'd, when we dare   110
Make 'em think better of us than we are:
And, if we hide our Frailties from their sights,
Call us deceitful Jilts, and Hypocrites:

They little guess, who at our Arts are griev'd,
The perfect joy of being well deceiv'd.   115
Inquisitive, as jealous Cuckolds, grow;   ⎫
Rather than not be knowing, they will know,   ⎬
What being known, creates their certain woe.   ⎭
Women should these, of all Mankind, avoid;
For wonder by clear Knowledge, is destroy'd.   120
Woman, who is an arrant Bird of night,   ⎫
Bold in the dusk, before a Fools dull Sight,   ⎬
Must flie, when Reason brings the glaring light. ⎭
But the kind easie Fool, apt to admire   ⎫
Himself, trusts us, his Follies all conspire   ⎬   125
To flatter his, and favour our desire.   ⎭
Vain of his proper Merit, He, with ease,
Believes we love him best, who best can please:
On him our gross, dull, common Flatt'ries pass;
Ever most happy when most made an Ass: 130
Heavy to apprehend; though all Mankind   ⎫
Perceive us false, the Fop, himself, is blind. ⎬
Who, doating on himself,—   ⎬
Thinks every one that sees him of his mind.   ⎭   134
These are true Womens Men—here, forc'd to cease
Through want of Breath, not Will, to hold her peace;
She to the Window runs, where she had spi'd
Her much esteem'd, dear, Friend, the Monkey ty'd:
With forty Smiles, as many antick bows,
As if't had been the Lady of the House: 140
The dirty, chatt'ring Monster she embrac'd;
And made it this fine tender Speech at last.

  Kiss me, thou curious Minature of Man;
How odd thou art, how pretty, how japan:
Oh! I could live and dye with thee: then on,   145
For half an Hour, in Complements she ran.
I took this time to think what Nature meant,   ⎫
When this mixt thing into the world she sent,   ⎬
So very wise, yet so impertinent.   ⎭

One that knows ev'ry thing, that God thought fit   150
Shou'd be an Ass through choice, not want of Wit.
Whose Foppery, without the help of sense,
Cou'd ne're have rose to such an excellence.
Nature's as lame in making a true Fop
As a Philosopher, the very Top,   155
And Dignity of Folly, we attain
By studious search, and labour of the Brain:
By Observation, Counsel, and deep Thought:
God never made a Coxcomb worth a Groat.
We owe that Name to Industry and Arts;   160
An Eminent Fool must be a Fool of parts.
And such a one was she; who had turn'd o're
As many Books as Men; lov'd much, read more:
Had discerning Wit; to her was known
Ev'ry one's Fault, or Merit, but her own.   165
All the good Qualities that ever blest   ⎱
A Woman so distinguish'd from the rest, ⎬
Except Discretion only, she possest   ⎰
And now *Mon Cher* Dear Pug, she cries, adieu;
And the Discourse, broke off, does thus renew.   170
You smile to see me, who the World perchance
Mistakes to have some wit, so far advance
The interest of Fools, that I approve
Their Merit more, than Men of Wit, in love.
But, in our Sex, too many Proofs there are   175
Of such, whom Wits undo, and Fools repair.
This, in my Time, was so observ'd a Rule,
Hardly a Wench in Town but had her Fool.
The meanest, common Slut, who long was grown
The jeast, and scorn, of ev'ry Pit-Buffoon;   180
Had yet left Charms enough to have subdu'd
Some Fop or other; fond to be thought lewd.
Foster could make an *Irish* Lord a *Nokes*;
And *Betty Morris* had her City Cokes.
A Woman's ne're so ruin'd, but she can   185
Be still reveng'd on her undoer, Man:

How lost soe'ere, She'l find some Lover more,
A more abandon'd Fool than she a Whore.
That wretched thing *Corinna*, who has run
Through all the sev'ral ways of being undone: 190
Cozen'd at first by Love, and living then
By turning the too-dear-bought-cheat of Men:
Gay were the hours, and wing'd with joy they flew,
When first the Town her early Beauties knew:
Courted, admir'd, and lov'd, with Presents fed;   195
Youth in her Looks, and Pleasure in her Bed:
'Till Fate, or her ill Angel, thought it fit
To make her doat upon a man of Wit:
Who found 'twas dull to love above a day
Made his ill-natur'd jeast, and went away.   200
Now scorn'd of all, forsaken and opprest,
She's a *Memento Mori* to the rest;
Diseas'd, decay'd, to take up half a Crown
Must Mortgage her Long Scarf, and Manto Gown;
Poor Creature, who unheard of, as a Flie,   205
In some dark hole must all the Winter lye;
And want, and dirt, endure a whole half year,
That, for one month, she Tawdry may appear.
In *Easter* Term she gets her a new Gown;
When my young Master's Worship comes to Town;
From Pedagogue, and Mother, just set free;   211
The Heir and Hopes of a great Family:
Who with strong Beer, and Beef, the Country rules;
And ever since the Conquest, have been Fools;
And now, with careful prospect to maintain   215
This Character, lest crossing of the Strain
Should mend the Booby-breed; his Friends provide
A Cousin of his own to be his Bride;
And thus set out,—
With an Estate, no Wit, and a young Wife: 220
The solid Comforts of a Coxcomb's Life;
Dunghil and Pease forsook, he comes to Town,
Turns Spark, learns to be lewd, and is undone;

Nothing suits worse with Vice than want of sense;
Fools are still wicked at their own expence.   225
This o're-grown School-Boy lost-*Corinna* wins;
At the first dash to make an Ass begins;
Pretends to like a man that has not known
The Vanities or Vices of the Town:
Fresh is the youth, and faithful in his love,   230
Eager of joys which he does seldom prove:
Healthful and strong, he does no pains endure,
But what the Fair One he adores, can cure.
Grateful for favours, does the Sex esteem,
And libels none for being kind to him.   235
Then of the lewdness of the Town complains,
Rails at the Wits, and Atheists, and maintains
'Tis better than good sense, than Pow'r, or Wealth
To have a Blood untainted, youth, and health.
The unbred Puppy, who had never seen   240
A Creature look so gay, or talk so fine,
Believes, then falls in love, and then in debt;
Mortgages all, ev'n to the ancient Seat,
To buy his Mistress a new House for Life;
To give her Plate, and Jewels, robs his Wife.   245
And when to th'height of fondness he is grown,
'Tis time to poyson him, and all's her own.
Thus, meeting in her common Arms his Fate,
He leaves her Bastard Heir to his Estate:
And, as the Race of such an Owl deserves,   250
His own dull, lawful Progeny he starves.
Nature (that never made a thing in vain,
But does each Insect to some end ordain)
Wisely provokes kind-keeping Fools, no doubt,
To patch up Vices, Men of Wit wear out.   255
  Thus she ran on two hours, some grains of sense
Still mixt with vollies of impertinence,
But now 'tis time I shou'd some pity show
To *Cloe*, since I cannot chuse but know,
Readers must reap what dullest Writers sow.   260

86

By the next Post I will such stories tell,
As, joyn'd to these, shall to a Volume swell;
As true as Heav'n, more infamous than Hell.
But you are tir'd, and so am I.

                      Farewel.

LIII

Tunbridge-Wells

At five this Morn, when *Phoebus* rais'd his head
From *Thetis* Lap, I rais'd my self from Bed,
And mounting Steed, I trotted to the Waters,
The Rendevouze of Fools, Buffons and Praters,
Cuckolds, Whores, Citizens, their Wives and
    Daughters.   5
My squemish Stomach, I with Wine had brib'd,
To undertake the Dose, it was prescrib'd:
But turning Head, a cursed suddain Crew,
That innocent Provision overthrew,
And without drinking, made me Purge and Spew. 10
From Coach and Six, a Thing unwealdy roll'd,
Whom lumber Cart more decently, would hold:
As wise as Calf it look'd, as big as Bully,
But handled, prov'd a meer *Sir Nicholas Cully*;
A Bawling Fop, a *Natural Nokes*, and yet   15
He dar'd to Censure, to be thought a Wit.
To make him more Ridiculous in spight,
Nature contriv'd the Fool should be a Knight:
'How wise is Nature when she does dispence
'A large Estate to cover want of Sence?   20
'The Man's a Fool, 'tis true, but that's no matter,
'For He's a mighty Wit, with those that flatter;
'But a *poor Blockhead*, is a wretched Creature.'
Tho' he alone was dismal sight enough,
His Train contributed to set him off;   25

All of his Shape, all of the self-same Stuff.
No Spleen or Malice need on them be thrown,
Nature has done the business of Lampoon,
And in their Looks their Characters are shown.
Endeavouring this irksome sight to baulk,   30
And a more irksom noise, their silly talk;
I silently shrunk down to th'lower Walk.
But often when we would *Charibdis* shun,
Down upon *Scylla* 'tis our fate to run;
For here it was my cursed luck to find   35
As great a Fop, tho' of another kind:
A tall stiff Fool, that walk'd in spanish Guise,
The Buckram Puppet never stir'd his Eyes,
But grave as Owlet look'd, as Woodcock wise.
He scorns the empty talk of this mad Age,   40
And speaks all Proverb, Sentences, adage;
Can with as great Solemnity buy Eggs,
As a Cabal can talk of their Intrigues;
Master o'th'Ceremonies, yet can dispence,
With the formality of talking sence.   45
From hence unto the upper end I ran,
Where a new Scene of Foppery began;
A Tribe of Curates, Priests, Canonical Elves,
Were company for none besides themselves:
They got together, each his Distemper told,   50
Scurvy, Stone, Strangury; and some were bold,
To charge the Spleen to be their Misery,
And on that wise Disease bring Infamy.
But none there were, so modest to complain
Of want of Learning, Honesty or Brain,   55
The general Diseases of that Train.
These call themselves Ambassadors of Heaven,
Saucily pretending a Commission given:
But should an *Indian* King, whose small Command
Seldom extends t'above ten Miles of Land;   60
Send forth such wretched Fools on an Embassage,
He'd find but small effèct, from such a Message.

Listning, I found the Cobb of all the Rabble,
Was pert *Bayes*,* with Importance comfortable:
He being rais'd to an Arch-deaconry,   65
By trampling on Religious Liberty;
Was grown so fat, and look'd so big and jolly,
Not being disturb'd with care and melancholly,
Tho' *Marvel* has enough expos'd his Folly.
He drank to carry off some old Remains,   70
His lazy dull Distemper left in's Veins;
Let him drink on, but 'tis not a whole Flood,
Can give sufficient sweetness to his Blood,
Or make his Nature or his Manners good.
Next after these, a fulsom *Irish* Crew   75
Of silly *Macks* were offer'd to my view;
The Things did talk, but hearing what they said,
I hid my self, the kindness to evade.
Nature has plac'd these Wretches below scorn,
They can't be call'd so vile, as they were born.   80
Amidst the Crowd, next I my self convey'd,
For now there comes (White-wash, and Paint being
    laid,)
Mother and Daughter, Mistress and the Maid,
And Squire with Wig and Pantaloons display'd:
But ne'er could Conventicle, Play, or Fair,   85
For a true Medly, with this Herd compare.
Here Lords, Knights, Squires, Ladies and Countesses,
Chandlers, Mum ⟨-⟩, Bacon ⟨-⟩ Women and
    Sempstresses,
Were mix'd together; nor did they agree
More in their Humours, than their Quality.   90
Here waiting for Gallant, young Damsel stood,
Leaning on Cane, and muffl'd up in Hood;
That would be wit—whose business 'twas to woo,
With Hat remov'd, and solemn scrape of Shooe;
Bowing advanc'd, ⟨and⟩ then he gently shrugs,   95
And ruffled Foretop, he in order tugs;

* *Parker.*
89

And thus accosts her, 'Madam, methinks the Weather,
'Is grown much more serene since you came hither;
'You influence the Heavens; and should the Sun
'Withdraw himself to see his Rays out-done, 100
'Your Luminaries would supply the Morn,
'And make a Day, before the Day be born.'
With Mouth screw'd up, and awkward winking Eyes,
And breast thrust forward; Lord, Sir, she replies:
It is my goodness, and not my deserts, 105
Which makes you shew your Learning, Wit and Parts.
He puzzled, bites his Nails, both to display
The Sparkling Ring, and think what next to say.
And thus breaks out a fresh: Madam, I gad,
Your Luck, last Night, at Cards was mighty bad 110
At Cribbidge; Fifty nine, and the next shew,
To make your Game, and yet to want those Two:
G— d— me, Madam, I'm the Son of a Whore,
If in my Life, I saw the like before.
To Pedler's Hall he drags her soon, and says 115
The same dull stuff a thousand different ways;
And then more smartly to expound the Riddle
Of all his Prattle, gives her a Scotch Fiddle. 118
Quite tir'd with this most dismal Stuff; I ran
Where were two Wives, and Girl just fit for Man,
Short was her Breath, Looks pale, and Visage wan.
Some Curtisy's past, and the old Compliment,
Of being glad to see each other, spent;
With Hand in Hand they lovingly did walk,
And one began thus to renew the Talk. 125
I pray, good Madam, if it may be thought
No Rudeness, what Cause was it hither brought
Your Ladiship? She soon replying, smil'd,
We have a good Estate, but ne're a Child;
And I'm inform'd these Wells will make a barren 130
Woman, as fruitful as a Cony-warren.
The first return'd; for this Cause I am come,
For I can have no Quietness at Home.

My Husband grumbles tho we've gotten one,
This poor young Girl, and mutters for a Son: 135
And this disturb'd with Head ach Pangs and Throws,
Is full Sixteen, and yet had never *Those*.
She answer'd strait, Get her a Husband, Madam;
I Marry'd at that Age, and never had 'em;
Was just like her, Steel Waters let alone,   140
A Back of Steel will bring them better down.
And ten to one, but they themselves will try,
The same way to encrease their Family.
Poor silly Fribble, who by Subtilty
Of Midwife, truest Friend to Letchery;   145
Persuaded art to be at Pains and Charge,
To give thy Wife occasion to enlarge
Thy silly Head. Some here Walk, Cuff and Kick
With brawny Back and Legs and potent—
Who more substantially will cure thy Wife,   150
And to her half Dead-Womb restore new Life.
From these the Waters got their Reputation
Of good Assistance unto Generation.
Some warlike Men were now got to the Throng,
With Hair ty'd back, singing a bawdy Song: 155
Not much afraid, I got a nearer View,
And 'twas my Chance to know the dreadful Crew:
They were Cadets, that seldom did appear,
Damn'd to the stint of Thirty Pounds a Year,
With Hawk on Fist, or Greyhound led in hand,   160
They Dog and Foot-boy sometimes do command;
But now having trim'd a Leash of spavin'd Horse,
With three hard-pincht-for Guineas in their Purse
Two rusty Pistols, scarfe about the Arse—
Coat lin'd with Red, they here presum'd to swell;   165
This goes for Captain, that for Collonel:
Ev'n so Bear-Garden Ape, on his Steed mounted,
No longer is a Jackanapes accounted;
But is, by virtue of his Trumpery, then
Call'd by the Name of the young Gentleman.   170

Bless me! thought I, what Thing is Man, that thus
In all his Shapes, he is ridiculous.
Our selves with noise of Reason we do please
In vain, Humanity's our worst Disease:
Thrice happy Beasts are, who, because they be   175
Of Reason void, are so of Foppery.
[Faith, I was so asham'd, that with Remorse,
I us'd the Insolence to mount my Horse;
For he, doing only Things fit for his Nature,
Did seem to me by much the wiser Creature.]   180

LIV

An Epistolary Essay
From M.G. *to* O.B.
Upon their mutual Poems

Dear Friend,
    I Hear this Town does so abound
    With saucy Censurers, that Faults are found
    With what, of late, We (in Poetick Rage)
    Bestowing, threw away on the dull age.
    But (howsoe're Envy their spleens may raise,   5
    To rob my Brows of the deserved Bays)
    Their thanks, at least, I merit: since through me
    They are partakers of your Poetry:
    And this is all I'le say in my defence   ⎫
    T'obtain one Line of your well-worded sense,   ⎬   10
    I'le be content t'have writ the *British Prince*, ⎭
    I'me none of those who think themselves inspir'd,
    Nor write with the vain hope to be admir'd;
    But from a Rule I have (upon long tryal)
    T'avoid with care all sort of self-denyal.   15
    Which way soe're, desire and fancy lead,
    (Contemning Fame) that Path I boldly tread;

And if exposing what I take for wit,
To my dear self a Pleasure I beget,
No matter though the cens'ring *Criticks* fret.   20
These whom my *Muse* displeases are at strife,
With equal spleen against my course of life,
The least Delight of which I'le not forgo,
For all the flatt'ring praise *Man* can bestow.
If I design'd to please, the way were then,   25
To mend my Manners, rather than my Pen:
The first's unnatural, therefore unfit;
And for the second, I despair of it,
Since Grace is not so hard to get as Wit.
Perhaps ill Verses ought to be confin'd   30
In meer good-breeding, like, unsav'ry Wind.
Were reading forc'd, I should be apt to think,
Men might no more write scurvily than stink:
But 'tis your Choice, whether you'l read, or no.
If likewise of your smelling it were so,   35
I'de fart just as I write for my own ease,
Nor shou'd you be concern'd unless you please.
I'le own, that you write better than I do,
But I have as much need to write as you.
What though the Excrements of my dull Brain,   40
Flows in a harsh and an insipid strain;
While your rich head eases itself of Wit.
Must none but *Civit-Cats* have leave to sh*t?
In all I write, shou'd Sense, and Wit, and Rhyme,
Fail me at once, yet something so sublime   45
Shall stamp my Poem, that the World may see,
It could have been produc'd by none but me.
And that's my End; for Man can wish no more,
Than so to write, as none e're writ before.
Yet why am I no *Poet* of the times?   50
I have *Allusions*, *Similies*, and *Rhymes*,
And *Wit;* or else 'tis hard that I alone,
Of the whole Race of *Mankind*, should have none.

Unequally the partial hand of *Heav'n*,
Has all but this One only Blessing giv'n.   55
The World appears like a great Family,
Whose Lord, opprest with Pride, and Poverty,
(That to a few great bounty, he may show)
Is fain to starve the num'rous Train below.
Just so seems Providence, as poor and vain,   60
Keeping more Creatures than it can maintain :
Here 'tis profuse, and there it meanly saves,
And for one Prince it makes Ten Thousand Slaves.
In *Wit*, alone, 't has been Magnificent,
Of which so just a Share to each is sent,   65
That the most Avaricious are content.
For none e're thought (the due Division's such)
His own too little, or his Friend's too much.
Yet most Men shew, or find, great want of Wit,
Writing themselves, or judging what is writ.   70
But I who am of sprightly Vigour full,
Look on Mankind, as envious, and dull.
Born to my self, I like my self alone;
And must conclude my Judgment good, or, none:
For cou'd my Sense be naught, how shou'd I know
Whether another Man's were good or no.   76
Thus I resolve of my own Poetry,
That 'tis the best; and there's a Fame for me,
If then I'me happy, what does it advance,
Whether to Merit due, or Arrogance?   80
Oh, but the World will take offence hereby!
Why then the World shall suffer for't, not I:
Did e're this saucy World and I agree,
To let it have its beastly Will on me?
Why should my prostituted Sense be drawn,   85
To ev'ry Rule their musty Customs spawn?
But Men may censure you, 'tis two to one
Whene'er they censure they'l be in the wrong.
There's not a thing on Earth, that I can name,
So foolish, and so false, as common Fame: 90

It calls the Courtier Knave; the plain Man rude;
Haughty the Grave; and the Delightful Lewd;
Impertinent the Brisk; Morose the Sad;
Mean the Familiar; the Reserv'd one Mad.
Poor helpless Woman is not favour'd more,   95
She's a slye Hypocrite, or publick Whore.
Then who the Devil would give this—to be free
From th'innocent reproach of Infamy.
These things consider'd, make me (in despight
Of Idle Rumour) keep at home and write.   100

LV

An Allusion to Horace
The 10th Satyr of the 1st Book

Nempe incomposito Dixi pede, &c.

WELL Sir, 'tis granted, I said D[ryden's] Rhimes,
Were stoln, unequal, nay, dull many times:
What foolish *Patron*, is there found of his,
So blindly partial, to deny me this?
But that his *Plays*, embroider'd up and down, } 5
With *Wit* and *Learning*, justly pleas'd the *Town*, }
In the same *Paper*, I as freely own. }
Yet having this allow'd, the heavy *Mass*,
That Stuffs up his loose *Volumns*, must not pass:
For by that Rule, I might as well admit;   10
Crowns, tedious *Scenes*, for *Poetry* and *Wit*.
'Tis therefore not enough, when your false sense,
Hits the false Judgment of an *Audience*:
Of clapping *Fools*, assembled a vast Crowd,
Till the throng'd *Play-house*, crack with the dull
          load;   15
Though ev'n that *Talent*, merits in some sort,
That can divert the *Rabble*, and the *Court*.

Which blund'ring *S[ettle]*, never cou'd attain,
And puzling *O[tway]*, labors at in vain.
But within due proportions circumscribe   20
What e're you write; that with a flowing Tide,
The *Style* may rise, yet in its rise forbear,
With useless words, t'oppress the weary'd Ear.
Here be your Language lofty, there more light,
Your *Rethorick* with your *Poetry* unite: 25
For *Elegance* sake, sometimes allay the force
Of *Epithets*, 'twill soften the discourse;
A jeast in scorn, points out, and hits the thing,
More home, than the *Moros⟨est⟩ Satyrs* sting.
Shake-spear and *Johnson*, did herein excell,   30
And might in this be imitated well;
Whom refin'd *E[therege]*, coppy's not at all,
But is himself, a sheer *Original*.
Nor that slow *Drudge*, in swift *Pindarick* straines,⎫
F[latman], who *C[owley]* imitates with pains,   ⎬35
And rides a jaded *Muse*, whipt with loose Rains.⎭
When *Lee*, makes temp'rate *Scipio*, fret and rave,
And *Hannibal*, a whining Amorous *Slave*,
I laugh, and wish the hot-brain'd *Fustian Fool*,
In *B[usby's]* hands, to be well lasht at *School*.   40
Of all our *Modern Wits* none seems to me,⎫
Once to have toucht upon true *Comedy*,   ⎬
But hasty *Shadwel*, and slow *Wicherley* ⎭
Shadwells unfinished'd works, do yet impart,
Great proofs of force of *Nature*, none of Art;   45
With just bold strokes he dashes here, and there,
Shewing great *Mastery* with little Care;
And scorns to varnish his good Touches o're,
To make the *Fools*, and *Women*, praise 'em more.
But *Wicherley*, earnes hard what e're he gains,   50
He wants no judgment, nor he spares no pains;
He frequently excells, and at the least,
Makes fewer faults, than any of the best.

Waller, by Nature, for the *Bays* design'd,
With force, and fire, and fancy unconfin'd 55
In *Panegyricks*, does excell *Mankind*.
He best can turn, enforce, and soften things,
To praise great *Conquerors*, or to flatter *Kings*.

For pointed *Satyrs*, I wou'd *Buckhurst* choose,
The best good *Man*, with the worst natur'd *Muse*,
For *Songs* and *Verses*, mannerly, obscene, 61
That can stir *Nature* up, by spring unseen,
And without forcing blushes warm the *Queen*,

Sidley, has that prevailing, gentle Art,
That can with a resistless Charm impart, 65
The loosest wishes, to the chastest Heart.
Raise such a conflict, kindle such a *Fire*,
Betwixt declining *Virtue*, and *Desire*;
Till the poor vanquish't *Maid* dissolves away,
In *Dreams* all *Night*, in *Sighs*, and *Tears* all day. 70

D[ryden], in vain try'd this nice way of wit,
For he to be a tearing *Blade*, though fit,
But when he wou'd be sharp; he still was blunt,
To frisk his frollique fancy, he'd cry C**t,
Wou'd give the *Ladies*, a dry *Bawdy* bob, 75
And thus he got the name of *Poet Squab*.
But to be just, 'twill to his praise he found,
His *Excellencies* more than faults abound,
Nor dare I from his sacred Temples tear
That *Lawrel*, which he best deserves to wear, 80
But does not *D[ryden]*, find ev'n *Johnson* dull?
Fletcher and *Beaumont*, uncorrect, and full,
O⟨f⟩ lewd *Lines* as he calls 'em? *Shake-spears* stile
Stiff and affected; to his own the while,
Allowing all the justness, that his Pride 85
So Arrogantly had to these deny'd?
And may not I, have leave impartially,
To search, and censure *D[ryden's]*, *Works*, and try,
If these gross faults, his choice *Pen* does commit,
Proceed from want of Judgment, or of Wit? 90

Or if his lumpish fancy, does refuse,
Spirit and Grace, to his loose slattern *Muse*?
Five hundred Verses ev'ry *Morning* writ,
Proves you no more a *Poet*, than a *Wit*:
Such scribling *Authors*, have been seen before ⎤ 95
Mustapha, the *English Princess*, Forty more, ⎬
Were things perhaps compos'd in half an hour, ⎦
To write what may securely pass the *Test*,
Of being well read over *Thrice* at least;
Compare each *Phrase*, examine ev'ry *Line*,   100
Weigh ev'ry *Word* and ev'ry *Thought* refine;
Scorn all applause the vile *Rout* can bestow,
And be content to please those few who know.
Canst thou be such a vain mistaken Thing,
To wish thy *Works* might make a *Play-house*
      ring.   105
With the unthinking Laughter, and poor praise,
Of *Fops* and *Ladies*, factious for thy *Plays*;
Then send a cunning *Friend* to learn thy doom,
From the shrewd Judges of the *Drawing Room*.
I've no *Ambition* on that idle score,   110 ⎤
But say with *Betty M[orice]*, heretofore,   ⎬
When a *Court Lady* call'd her *B[uckley's] Whore;* ⎦
I please one *Man* of *Wit*, am proud on't too,
Let all the *Coxcombs* dance to *Bed* to you.
 Shou'd I be troubled when the Pur-blind
      Knight,   115 ⎤
Who squints more in his Judgment, than his sight ⎬
Picks silly faults, and censures what I write?   ⎦
Or when the poor-fed *Poets* of the *Town*
For Scraps and Coach-room cry my Verses down?
I loath the *Rabble*, 'tis enough for me,   120
If *S[edley]*, *S[hadwell]*, *S[heppard]*, *W[icherley]*
G[odolphin], *B[utler]*, *B[uckhurst]*, *B[uckingham]*,
And some few more, whom I omit to name,
Approve my sense, I count their censure *Fame*.

LVI

Satyr

‹Commonly called Timon, a Satyr›

A. What *Timon* does old Age begin t'approach
    That thus thou droop'st under a nights debauch?
    Hast thou lost deep to needy *Rogues* on Tick
    Who ne're cou'd pay, and must be paid next *Week*?
Tim. Neither alas, but a dull dining *Sot*,   5
    Seized me i'th 'Mall*, who just my name has got;
    He runs upon me, cries dear *Rogue* I'm thine,
    With me some *Wits*, of thy acquaintance dine.
    I tell him I'm engag'd but as *a Whore*,
    With modesty enslaves her *Spark*, the more,   10
    The longer I deny'd, the more he prest,
    At last I e'ne consent to be his *Guest*.
    He takes me in his *Coach*, and as we go;
    Pulls out a *Libel*, of a Sheet, or two;
    Insipid, as, *The praise of pious Queens*,   15
    Or *S[hadwell's]* unassisted former *Scenes*;
    Which he admir'd, and prais'd at ev'ry *Line*,
    At last it was so sharp, it must be mine.
    I vow'd I was no more a *Wit*, than he,
    Unpractic'd, and unblest in *Poetry*:   20
    A *Song* to *Phillis* I perhaps might make,
    But never Rhym'd, but for my *Pintles* sake:
    I envy'd no *Mans* fortune, nor his fame,
    Nor ever thought of a revenge so tame.
    He knew my *Stile*, he swore, and 'twas in vain,   25
    Thus to deny the Issue of my *Brain*.
    Choak'd with his flatt'ry, I no answer make,
    But silent leave him to his dear mistake.
    Of a well meaning *Fool*, I'm most afraid,
    Who sillily repeats, what was well said.   30
    But this was not the worst, when he came home,
    He askt, are *Sidley, Buc⟨k⟩hurst, Savill*, come?

No, but there were above *Half-wit* and *Huffe*,
Kickum, and *Dingboy*. Oh 'tis well enough,
They're all brave *Fellows*, cries mine *Host*, let's
     Dine,   35
I long to have my *Belly* full of *Wine*,
They'll write, and fight I dare assure you,
They're Men, *Tam Marte quam Mercurio*.
I saw my error, but 'twas now too late,
No means, nor hopes, appears of a retreat.   40
Well we salute, and each *Man* takes his Seat.
Boy (says my *Sot*) is my *Wife* ready yet!
A *Wife*! good *Gods*! a *Fop* and *Bullys* too!
For one poor *Meale* what must I undergo?
In comes my *Lady* strait, and she had been *Fair*.
Fit to give love, and ⟨to⟩ prevent despair;   46
But *Age*, *Beauties* incureable Disease,
Had left her more desire than pow'r to please:
As *Cocks*, will strike, altho' their *Spurrs* be gone,
She with her old bleer *Eyes* to smite begun: 50
Though nothing else, she (in despight of time)
Preserv'd the affectation of her prime;
How ever you begun, she brought in love,
And hardly from that Subject wou'd remove.
We chanc'd to speak of the *French Kings*, success; 55
My *Lady* wonder'd much how *Heav'n* cou'd bless,
A *Man* that lov'd Two *Women* at one time;
But more how he to them excus'd his Crime.
She askt *Huffe*, if *Loves* flame he never felt?
He answer'd bluntly—do you think I'm gelt?   60
She at his plainness smil'd, then turn'd to me,
Love in young *Minds*, proceeds ev'n *Poetry*.
You to that Passion can no *Stranger* be,
But *Wits*, are giv'n to inconstancy.
She had run on I think till now, but *Meat*   65
Came up, and suddenly she took her seat.
I thought the *Dinner* wou'd make some amends,
When my good *Host* cryes out, *Y'are all my Friends*,

Our own plain Fare, *and the best* Terse *the* Bull
Affords, I'll give you, *and your* Bellies *full*:   70
As for French *Kickshaws, Cellery and Champoon,*
Ragous *and* Fricasses, introth we'ave none.
Here's a good *Dinner* towards, thought I, when
 strait
Up comes a piece of Beef full Horsman's weight;
Hard as the *Arse* of M[ordaunt], under which   75
The *Coachman* sweats, as ridden by a *Witch.*
A Dish of *Carrets*, each of 'em as long
As *Tool* that to fair *Countess*, did belong;
Which her small *Pillow*, cou'd not so well hide,
But *Visiters*, his flaming Head espy'd.   80
Pig, Goose and *Capon* follow'd in the *Rear,*
With all that *Country Bumpkins*, call good Cheer,
Serv'd up with Sauces all of *Eighty, Eight,*
When our tough *Youth*, wrestled, and threw the
 Weight.
And now the *Bottle* briskly flyes about,   85
Instead of *Ice,* wrapt in a wet *Clowt,*
A Brimmer follows the Third bit we eat,
Small Bear, becomes our drink, and Wine, our
 Meat.
The *Table* was so large, that in less space,
A Man might save, six old *Italians* place: 90
Each Man had as much room, as *Porter* B[lunt],
Or *Harris* had in *Cullens, Bushel* C**t.
And now the *Wine* began to work, mine *Host*
Had been a *Collonel*, we must hear him boast
Not of *Towns* won, but an *Estate* he lost   95
For the *Kings* Service, which indeed he spent
Whoring, and Drinking, but with good intent.
He talkt much of a Plot, and *Money* lent
In *Cromwell's* time. My *Lady* she
Complain'd our Love was course, our *Poetry*,   100
Unfit for modest Eares, small *Whores*, and *Play'rs.*
Were of our Hair-brain'd *Youth*, the only cares;

Who were too wild for any virtuous *League*,
Too rotten to consummate the Intrigue.
Falkland, she prais'd, and *Sucklings*, easie Pen,   105
And seem'd to taste their former parts again.
Mine *Host*, drinks to the best in *Christendome*,
And decently my *Lady*, quits the Room.
Left to ourselves of several things we prate,
Some regulate the *Stage*, and some the *State*.   110
Halfwit, cries up my Lord of O[*rrery*],
Ah how well *Mustapha*, and *Zanger* dye!
His sense so little forc'd, that by one *Line*,
You may the other easily divine.
 And which is, worse, if any worse can be,   115
 He never said one word of it to me.
There's fine *Poetry*! you'd swear 'twere *Prose*,
So little on the Sense, the Rhymes impose.
Damn me (says *Dingboy*) in my mind *Gods-swounds*
E[*therege*] writes *Airy Songs*, and soft *Lampoons*,
The best of any *Man*; as for your *Nowns*,   121
Grammar, and Rules of Art, he knows 'em not,
Yet writ two talking *Plays* without one *Plot*.
H[*uffe*] was for S[*ettle*], and *Morocco*, prais'd,
Said rumbling words, like Drums his courage ⸜ais'd.
 Whose broad built-bulks, the boystrous Billows,
  bear   126
 Zaphee and *Sally*, *Mugadore*, *Oran*,
 The fam'd Arzile, *Alcazer*, *Tituan*.
Was even braver Language writ by *Man*?
Kickum for *Crown* declar'd, said in *Romance*,   130
He had outdone the very *Wits*, of *France*
Witness *Pandion*, and his *Charles the Eight*,
Where a Young *Monarch*, careless of his Fate,
Though Forreign Troops, and *Rebels*, shock his
 State,
Complains another sight afflicts him more.   135
(*Videl*.) *The Queens Galleys* rowing from the *Shore*.

Fitting, their Oars and Tackling to be gon;
Whilst sporting Waves smil'd on the rising Sun.
Waves smiling on the *Sun*! I am sure that's new,
And 'twas well thought on, give the *Devil* his due,
Mine *Host,* who had said nothing in an hour,   141
Rose up and prais'd the *Indian Emperor.*
 As if our Old World *modestly withdrew,*
 And here in private had brought forth a New.
There are two *Lines*! who but he dare presume   145
To make the old *World*, a new withdrawing Room,
Where of another *World* she's brought to *Bed*!
What a brave *Midwife* is a *Laureats* Head!
But pox of all these *Scriblers*, what do'e think.
Will *Souches* this year any *Champoon* drink?   150
Will Turene fight him? without doubt says *Huffe,*
If they two meet, the meeting will be rough.
Damn me (says *Dingboy*) the *French*, *Cowards* are,
They pay, but, th'*English*, *Scots*, and *Swiss* make
         War;
In gawdy *Troops*, at a review they shine,   155
But dare not with the *Germans*, *Battel* joyn;
What now appears like courage, is not so
'Tis a short pride, which from success does grow;
On their first blow, they'll shrink into those fears,
They shew'd at *Cressy, Agincourt, Poytiers*;   160
Their loss was infamous, *Honor* so stain'd,
Is by a *Nation* not to be regain'd.
What they were then I know not, now th'are brave,
He that denyes it—lyes, and is a *Slave*
(Says *Huffe* and frown'd) says *Dingboy*, that do I,
And at that word, at t'other's *Head* let fly   166
A greasie *Plate*, when suddenly they all,
Together by the Eares in Parties fall.
Halfwit with *Dingboy* joynes, *Kickum* with *Huffe,*
Their Swords were safe, and so we let 'em cuff   170
Till they, mine *Host*, and I, had all enough.

Their rage once over, they begin to treat,
And six fresh *Bottles*, must the peace compleat.
I ran down stairs, with a Vow never more,
To drink Bear Glass, and hear the *Hectors* roar. 175

LVII

A Session of the Poets

SINCE the *Sons* of the *Muses*, grew num'rous, and
  loud,
For th'appeasing so factious, and clam'rous a
  Crowd;
Apollo, thought fit in so weighty a cause,
T'Establish a Government, *Leader*, and *Laws*.
The hopes of the *Bays* at this summoning call,   5
Had drawn 'em together, the *Devil* and all;
All thronging and listening, they gap'd for the
  Blessing,
No *Presbyter Sermon*, had more crowding, and
  pressing.
 In the Head of the Gang *J[ohn] D[ryden]* appear'd,
That Antient grave Wit, so long lov'd, and fear'd; 10
But *Apollo*, had heard a Story ith'Town,
Of his quitting the *Muses*, to wear the Black *Gown*;
And so gave him leave now his *Poetry's* done,
To let him turn *Priest*, now *R[eeve]* is turn'd *Nun*.
 This Reverend Author was no sooner set by,   15
But *Apollo*, had got gentle *George*, in his Eye,
And frankly confest, of all Men that writ,
There's none had more fancy, sense Judgment and
  Wit.
But'th' crying Sin, idleness, he was so harden'd,
That his long Seav'n years silence, was not to be
  pardon'd.   20

Brawny *W[icherley]*, was the next Man shew'd his
    Face,
But *Apollo*, e'ne thought him too good for the Place;
No *Gentleman Writer*, that office shou'd bear
'Twas a *Trader* in *Wit* the *Lawrel* shou'd wear.
As none but a *Citt*, e're makes a *Lord Mayor*.   25

Next into the Crowd, *Tom* S[*hadwell*], does wallow,
And Swears by his *Guts*, his *Paunch*, and his *Tallow*,
'Tis he that alone best pleases the Age,
Himself, and his *Wife* have supported the *Stage*.
Apollo well pleas'd with so bonny a *Lad*,   30
T'oblige him, he told him he shou'd be huge glad,
Had he half so much *Wit*, as he fanc'd he had.
However to please so *Jovial a Wit*,
And to keep him in humor, *Apollo*, thought fit,
To bid him drink on and keep his Old Trick   35
Of railing at *Poets*, and shewing his *Pr**k*.

N[at] L[ee], stept in next in hopes of a Prize,
Apollo, remember'd he had hit once in Thrice;
By the Rubyes in's Face, he cou'd not deny,
But he had as much *Wit*, as *Wine* cou'd supply;   40
Confest that indeed he had a *Musical Note*,
But sometimes strain'd so hard he rattled
    i'th'Throat,
Yet owning he had *Sense*, t'incourage him for't,
He made him his *Ovid* in *Augustus's* Court.

Poet *S[ettle]*, his Tryal, was the next came about, 45
He brought him an *Ibrahim*, with the Preface torn
    out,
And humbly desir'd, he might give no offence;
God damme, cryes *S[hadwell]* he cannot write sense,
And Ballocks cry'd *Newport*, I hate that dull *Rogue*,
Apollo, consid'ring he was not in vogue   50
Wou'd not trust his dear *Bays*, with so modest a *Fool*,
And bid the great *Boy*, shou'd be sent back to *School*.

Tom O[tway] came next, *Tom S[hadwell's]*, dear
    Zany;
And swears for *Heroicks*, he writes best of any;
Don C[arlos] his Pockets so amply hath fill'd,   55
That his *Mange* was quite cur'd, and his *Lice*, were
    all kill'd.
But *Apollo*, had seen his Face on the *Stage*,
And prudently did not think fir to engage,
The scum of a *Play-house*, for the Prop of an *Age*.
In the numerous Herd, that encompast him round 60
Little starcht *Jonny C[rowne]* at his Elbow found,
His *Crevat-string*, new Iron'd, he gently did stretch,
His Lilly white hand out, the *Lawrel* to reach;
Alledging that he had most right to the *Bays*,
For writing *Romances*, and shiting of *Plays*,   65
Apollo, rose up and gravely confest,
Of all *Men* that had writ, his *Tallent* was best:
For since pain, and dishonour, *Mans* life only damn,
The greatest felicity, *Mankind* can claim,
Is to want sense of smart & be past sense of shame: 70
And to perfect his *Bliss*, in *Poetical Rapture*,
He bid him be dull to the end of the *Chapter*.
   The *Poetess Afra*, next shew'd her sweet face,
And swore by her *Poetry*, and her black *Ace*,
The Laurel, by a double right was her own,   75
For the *Plays* she had writ, and the *Conquests* she
    had won:
Apollo acknowledg'd 'twas hard to deny her,
Yet to deal franckly, and ingeniously by her,
He told her ⟨her⟩ *Conquests* and *Charmes* ⟨were⟩
    pretence,
She ought to have pleaded a Dozen years since.   80
⟨At last Mamamouche⟩ put in for a share,
And little *Tom Essences Author*, was there
Nor cou'd *D[urfey]* for bear for the *Lawrel* to stickle,
Protesting he had had the Honor to tickle,   84
The Eares of the *Town*, with his dear *Madam Fickle*.

With other pretenders, whose names I'd rehearse,
But that they're too long to stand in my *Verse*,
Apollo, quite tir'd with their tedious *Harrangue*,
Finds at last *Tom B[etterton's]*, face in the gang,
And since *Poets* with the kind *Play'rs*, may hang, 90
By his own light, he solemnly swore,
That in his search for a *Laureate*, he'd look no more.
A general murmur ran quite through the *Hall*,
To think that the *Bays*, to an *Actor*, shou'd fall,
But *Apollo*, to quiet, and pacifie all; 95
E'ne told 'em to put his desert to the Test,
That he had made Plays aswel as the best;
And was the greatest wonder, the *Age* ever bore
For of all the *Play-Scriblers*, that e're writ before,
His wit had most worthy, and most modesty in't, 100
For he had writ *Plays*, yet ne're came in print.

LVIII

The History of *Insipids*
A LAMPOON 1676

1

CHAST, pious, prudent, *C[harls]* the Second,
The Miracle of thy Restauration,
May like to that of *Quails* be reckon'd
Rain'd on the Israelitick Nation;
The wisht for Blessing from Heav'n sent, 5
Became their Curse and Punishment.

2

The Vertues in thee, *C[harls]* inherent,
Although thy countenance be an odd piece,
Proves thee as true a Gods Vicegerent
As e're was *Harry* with the Codpiece: 10

For Chastity and pious Deeds,
His Grandsire *Harry*, C[*harls*] exceeds.

3

Our *Romish* Bondage breaker *Harry*,
Espoused half a dozen Wives,
C[*harls*] only one resolv'd to marry,   15
And other Mens he never [*swives*]
Yet hath he Sons and Daughters more,
Than e're had *Harry* by threescore.

4

Never was such a Faiths Defender,
He like a politick Prince, and pious,   20
Gives liberty to Conscience tender,
And doth to no Religion tye us.
Jews, *Christians*, *Turks*, *Papists*, he'll please us,
With *Moses*, *Mahomet*, or *J*[*esus*].

5

In all Affairs of Church or State,   25
He very zealous is, and able,
Devout at Prayers, and sits up late
At the Cabal and Council Table.
His very Dog at Council Board,
Sits grave and wise, as any Lord.   30

6

Let C[*harls*] his Policy no Man flout,
The wisest Kings have all some Folly,
Nor let his Piety any doubt;
C[*harls*] like a Sovereign wise and holy,
Makes young Men Judges of the Bench,   35
And B[*ishops*] some that love a Wench.

7

His Fathers Foes he doth reward,
Preserving those that cut off's Head:
Old Cavaliers the Crown's best Guard,
He lets them starve for want of Bread.   40
Never was any King endow'd
With so much Grace and Gratitude.

8

Blood, that wears Treason in his Face,
Villain compleat, in Parson's Gown,
How much is he at Court in Grace   45
For stealing *Ormond*, and the Crown?
Since Loyalty do's no Man good,
Let's steal the King and out-do *Blood*.

9

A Parliament of Knaves and Sots,
Members by name, you must not mention,   50
He keeps in Pay, and buys their Votes,
Here with a Place, there with a Pension
When to give Mony he can't cologue 'um,
He doth with Scorn prorogue, prorogue 'um.

10

But they long since by too much giving,   55
Undid, betray'd, and sold the Nation;
Making their Memberships a Living,
Better than e're was Sequestration.
God give thee C[*harles*] a Resolution
To damn the Knaves by a Dissolution.   60

11

Fame is not grounded on Success,
Though Victories were *Cæsar's* Glory;
Lost Battels make not *Pompey* less,

But left them stiled great in Story.
Malitious Fate doth oft devise   65
To beat the Brave and fool the Wise.

12

C[harls] in the first *Dutch* War stood fair,
To have been Sovereign of the Deep;
When *Opdam* blew up in the Air,
Had not his Highness gone to sleep.   70
Our Fleet slack'd Sails, fearing his waking,
The *Dutch* else had been in sad taking.

13

The *Bergen* Business was well laid,
Though we paid dear for that Design:
Had we not three days parling staid,   75
The *Dutch* Fleet there, C[harls], had been thine.
Though the false Dane agree'd to sell 'um,
He cheated us, and saved *Skellum*.

14

Had not C[harls] sweetly choos'd the States,
By *Bergen* Baffle grown more wise,   80
And made them Sh*t as small as Ratts,
By their rich *Smyrna* Fleets Surprise?
Had haughty *Holms* but call'd in *Spragg*,
Hands had been put into a Bag.

15

Mists, Storms, short Victuals, adverse Winds,   85
And once the Navies wise Division,
Defeated C[harls] his best Designs,
Till he became his Foes Derision.
But he had swing'd the *Dutch* at *Chattam*,
Had he had Ships but to come at 'um.   90

16

Our *Blackheath* Host without dispute,
Rais'd (put on Board, why, no Man knows)
Must C[*harls*] have rendred absolute,
Over his Subjects or his Foes.
Has not the *French* King made us Fools,   95
By taking *Maestricht* with our Tools?

17

But C[*harls*] what could thy Policy be,
To run so many sad Disasters;
To join thy Fleet with false *D'Etrees*,
To make the *French* of *Holland* Masters?   100
Was't *Carewell*, brother *James*, or *Teague*,
That made thee break the Triple League.

18

Could *Robin Vyner* have foreseen
The glorious Triumphs of his Master
The Wool-Church Statue Gold had been,   105
Which now is made of Alabaster:
But Wise Men think had it been Wood,
T'were for a Bankrupt K[*ing*] too good.

19

Those that the Fabrick well consider,
Do of it diversly discourse;   110
Some pass their Censure of the Rider,
Others their Judgment of the Horse:
Must say the *Steed's* a goodly thing,
But all agree 'tis a Lewd K[*ing*].

20

By the Lord Mayor and his grave Coxcombs, 115
Free-man of *London* C[*harls*] is made;
Then to *Whitehall* a Rich Gold Box comes,

Which is bestow'd on the *French* Jade.
But wonder not it should be so, Sirs,   119
When Monarchs rank themselves with Grocers.

21

Cringe, scrape, no more ye City Fopps,
Leave off your Feasting and fine Speeches,
Beat up your Drums, shut up your Shops,
The Courtiers then will kiss your Breeches.
Arm'd, tell the Popish Duke that Rules,   125
You'r Free-born Subjects, not *French* Mules.

22

New upstarts, Pimps, Bastards, Whores,
That Locust like devour the Land,
By shutting up the Exchequer Doors,
When thither our Mony was trapan'd.   130
Have rend'red C[*harls*] his Restauration,
But a small Blessing to the Nation.

23

Then C[*harls*] beware of thy Brother Y[*ork*]
Who to thy Government gives Law;
If once we fall to the old Sport,   135
You must again both to *Breda*:
Where Spight of all that would restore you,
Grown wise by wrongs, we shall abhor you.

24

If of all Christian Blood the Guilt
Cry loud for Vengeance unto Heaven;   140
That Sea by Treacherous *Lewis* spilt,
Can never be by God forgiven.
Worse Scourge unto his Subjects, Lord,
Than Pestilence, Famine, Fire or Sword.

25

That false rapacious Wolf of *France*;   145
The Scourge of *Europe*, and its Curse,
Who at his Subject's cry, does Dance,
And study how to make them worse.
To say such kings, Lord, rule by thee,
Were most prodigious Blasphemy.   150

26

Such know no Law but their own Lust,
Their Subjects' Substance, and their Blood
They count it Tribute, due and just,
Still spent, and spilt, for Subjects good.
If such Kings are by God appointed   155
The D[evil] maybe the L[ord's] Anointed.

27

Such Kings curst be the Power and Name,
Let all the World henceforth abhor'um;
Monsters which Knaves Sacred proclaim,
And then like Slaves fall down before 'um.   160
What can there in Kings Divine?
The most are Wolves, Goats, Sheep, or Swine.

28

Then Farewel Sacred Majesty,
Let's pull all Brutish Tyrants down;
When Men are born, and still live free,   165
Here ev'ry Head doth wear a Crown.
Mankind like miserable Froggs,
Prove wretched, king'd by Storks and Loggs.

LIX

A Ramble in St. James's Park

THIS poem has been excluded from the present edition at the request of the publishers. The text will be found in Thorpe, pp. 28–30. See Introduction, p. xlix.

LX

On Poet Ninny

CRUSHT by that just contempt his *Follys* bring,
On his craz'd *Head*, the Vermin fain wou'd sting.
But never *Satyr*, did so softly bite,
Or gentle *George* himself, more gently write.
Born to no other, but thy own disgrace, 5
Thou art a thing so wretched, and so base,
Thou canst not ev'n offend, but with thy Face.
And dost at once a sad example prove,
Of harmless malice, and of hopeless love.
All pride! and ugliness! oh how we loath, 10
A nauseous Creature, so compos'd of both!
How oft have we thy *Cap'ring Person* seen,
With dismall look, and Melancholly *Meene*,
The just reverse of *Nokes*, when he wou'd be,
Some mighty *Heroe*, and makes love like thee! 15
Thou art below being laught at, out of spight,
Men gaze upon thee as a hideous sight,
And cry, there goes the Melancholly *Knight*.
There are some Modest *Fools*, we dayly see,
Modest, and dull, why they are *Wits*, to thee! 20
For of all Folly, sure the very top,
Is a conceited *Ninny* and a *Fop*.
With Face of *Farce*, joyn'd to a Head *Romancy*,
There's no such Coxcomb as your *Fool* of fancy:

But 'tis too much on so despis'd a *Theam*   25
No *Man* wou'd dabble, in a dirty Stream;
The worst that I cou'd write, wou'd be no more
Than what thy very *Friends*, have said before.

LXI

My Lord All-Pride

BURSTING with *Pride*, the loath'd *Imposthume*
       swells,
Prick him, he sheds his *Venom* strait, and smells;
But 'tis so lewd a *Scribler*, that he writes,
With as much force to *Nature*, as he fights,
Hardned in shame, 'tis such a baffled *Fop*,   5
That ev'ry *School-boy*, whips him like a Top:
And with his *Arme*, and *Head*, his Brain's so weak,
That his starved fancy, is compell'd to take,
Among the *Excrements* of others wit,
To make a stinking *Meal* of what they sh*t.   10
So *Swine*, for nasty *Meat*, the *Dunghil* run
And toss their gruntling *Snowts* up when they've
       done:
Against his *Stars*, the *Coxcomb* ever strives.
And to be something they forbid, contrives.
With a *Red Nose*, *Splay Foot*, and *Goggle Eye*   15
A *Plough Mans*, looby *Meene*, *Face* all a wry,
With stinking Breath, and ev'ry loathsome mark,
The *Punchianello*, sets up for a *Spark*,
With equal self conceit too, he bears Arms,
But with that vile success, his part performs,   20
That he *Burlesques* his Trade, and what is best
In others, turns like *Harlequin*, in jeast.
So have I seen at *Smithfields* wondrous *Fair*,
When all his *Brother Monsters*, florish there;

A *Lubbard Elephant*, divert the *Town*,   25
With making *Legs*, and shooting off a *Gun*.
Go where he will, he never makes a *Friend*,
Shame, and derision, all his steps attend;
Alike abroad, at home, 'ith', *Camp*, and *Court*,
This *Knight*, o'th *Burning Pestle*, make us sport.   30

LXII

⟨Draft of a Satire on Men⟩

WHAT vaine unnecessary things are men
How well we doe with out em, tell me then
Whence comes that meane submissiveness wee finde
This ill bred age has wrought on womankinde
Fall'n from the rights their sex and beautyes gave 5
To make men wish despaire and humbly crave
Now 'twill suffice if they vouchsafe to have,
(To the Pell Mell, Playhous and the drawing roome
Their Woemen Fayres, these Woemen Coursers
        come
To chaffer, chuse, and ride their bargaines home,)
Att the appearance of an unknown face   11
Up steps the Arrogant pretending ass
Pulling by th' elbow his companion Huff.
Cryes Looke, de God that wench is well enough
Faire and well shap't, good lipps and teeth 'twill
        doe   15
Shee shall be Tawdry for a month or two
Att my expence, bee rude and take upon her
Shew her contempt of quallity and honour
And with the generall fate of errant Woman
Bee very proude awhile, then very Common   20
E're beare this scorne I'de bee shutt up at home
Content with humoring my self alone,

DRAFT OF SATIRE IN ROCHESTER'S AUTOGRAPH

*in the Duke of Portland's collection
in Nottingham University Library* (See p. 116)

[face page 116

Force back the Humble Love of former dayes
In pensive madrigalls and ends of playes
When if my Lady frown'd th'unhappy knight   25
was faine to fast and lye alone that night
But whilst th' insulting wife the Breeches wore
The Husband tooke her cloathes and gave his—
Who now maintaines it with a gentler art
Thus Tyrannyes to Commonwealths Convert,   30
(Then) after all you finde what ere we say
Things must goe on in their Lewd naturall way
(Besides the Beastly men wee dayly see
Can Please themselves alone as well as wee)
Therefore Kind Ladyes of the towne to you   35
For our stol'n ravish't men wee (next) sue
By this time you have found out wee suppos⟨e⟩
That they're as errant Tinsell as their Cloath⟨s⟩
Poor broaken Propertyes that cannot serve
To treate such persons soe as they deserv⟨e⟩   40
Mistake us not wee do not heere pretend
That like the young Sparkes you can condescend
to Love a beastly playhous Creature, Foh
Wee dare not thinke soe (hardly) of you, noe
'Tis not the Player pleases but the Part   45
She may like Rollo who despises Hart
To Theaters as Temples you are brought
Where Love is {worshipt / honourd} and his precepts taught
You must goe home and practice, for 'tis here
Just as in other preaching places, where   50
Greate Eloquence is shown gainst sin, and Papists
By men who Live Idolaters and Atheists
(These two were dainty textès indeed could each
Live up to halfe the miracles they teach)
Both are a   55

LXIII

To forme a Plott

THE Illustrius Bard whose rough unruly Rhyme
Gives Plutarch's lives the lie in ev'ry Lyne
Who rapture before nature does preferr
And now himself turn'd his own Imager
Defaceth god's in ev'ry Character.

LXIV

⟨*A Satyr against Mankind*⟩

WERE I (who to my cost already am
One of those strange prodigious Creatures *Man.*)
A Spirit free, to choose for my own share,
What Case of Flesh, and Blood, I pleas'd to weare,
I'd be a *Dog*, a *Monkey*, or a *Bear.*   5
Or any thing but that vain *Animal*,
Who is so proud of being rational.
The senses are too gross, and he'll contrive
A Sixth, to contradict the other Five;
And before certain instinct, will preferr   10
Reason, which Fifty times for one does err.
Reason, an *Ignis fatuus*, in the *Mind*,
Which leaving light of Nature, sense behind;
Pathless and dang'rous wandring ways it takes,
Through errors, Fenny-*Boggs*, and Thorny *Brakes*; 15
Whilst the misguided follower, climbs with pain,
Mountains of Whimseys, heap'd in his own *Brain*:
Stumbling from thought to thought, falls head-long
    down,
Into doubts boundless Sea, where like to drown,
Books bear him up awhile, and makes him try,   20
To swim with Bladders of *Philosophy*;

In hopes still t'oretake the'escaping light,
The *Vapour* dances in his dazl⟨ed⟩ sight,
Till spent, it leaves him to eternal Night.
Then Old Age, and experience, hand in hand,   25
Lead him to death, and make him understand,
After a search so painful, and so long,
That all his Life he has been in the wrong;
Hudled in dirt, the reas'ning *Engine* lyes,
Who was so proud, so witty, and so wise.   30
Pride drew him in, as *Cheats*, their *Bubbles*, catch,
And makes him venture, to be made a *Wre⟨t⟩ch*.
His wisdom did his happiness destroy,
Aiming to know what *World* he shou'd enjoy;
And *Wit*, was his vain frivolous pretence,   35
Of pleasing others, at his own expence.
For *Witts* are treated just like common *Whores*,
First they're enjoy'd, and then kickt out of *Doores*:
The pleasure past, a threatning doubt remains,
That frights th'enjoyer, with succeeding pains: 40
Women and *Men* of *Wit*, are dang'rous Tools,
And ever fatal to admiring *Fools*.
Pleasure allures, and when the *Fopps* escape,
'Tis not that they're belov'd, but fortunate,
And therefore what they fear, at least they hate.   45
    But now methinks some formal Band, and Beard,
Takes me to task, come on Sir I'm prepar'd.
    Then by your favour, any thing that's writ
Against this gibeing jingling knack call'd Wit,
Likes me abundantly, but you take care,   50
Upon this point, not to be too severe.
Perhaps my Muse, *were fitter for this part,*
For I profess, I can be very smart
On Wit, *which I abhor with all my heart:*
I long to lash it in some sharp Essay,   55
But your grand indiscretion bids me stay,
And turns my Tide of Ink another way.

What rage ferments in your degen'rate mind,
To make you rail at Reason, and Mankind?
Blest glorious Man! *to whom alone kind* Heav'n,　60
An everlasting Soul *has freely giv'n;*
Whom his great Maker *took such care to make,*
That from himself he did the Image *take;*
And this fair frame, in shining Reason *drest,*
To dignifie his Nature, *above* Beast.　65
Reason, *by whose aspiring influence,*
We take a flight beyond material sense,
Dive into Mysteries, then soaring pierce,
The flaming limits of the Universe.
Search Heav'n and Hell, find out what's acted there,　70
And give the World true grounds of hope and fear.

　Hold mighty Man, I cry, all this we know,
From the Pathetique Pen of *Ingello*;
from P⟨atrick's⟩ *Pilgrim,* S⟨ibbs'⟩ ⟨soliloquies⟩,
And 'tis this very reason I despise.　75
This supernatural gift, that makes a *Myte*,
Think he is the Image of the Infinite:
Comparing his short life, void of all rest,
To the *Eternal*, and the ever blest.
This busie, puzling, stirrer up of doubt,　80
That frames deep *Mysteries*, then finds 'em out;
Filling with Frantick Crowds of thinking *Fools*,
Those Reverend *Bedlams, Colledges,* and *Schools*
Borne on whose Wings, each heavy *Sot* can pierce,
The limits of the boundless Universe.　85
So charming Oyntments, make an Old *Witch* flie,
And bear a Crippled Carcass through the Skie.
'Tis this exalted Pow'r, whose bus'ness lies,
In *Nonsense*, and impossibilities.
This made a Whimsical *Philosopher*,　90
Before the spacious *World*, his *Tub* prefer,
And we have modern *Cloysterd Coxcombs,* who
Retire to think, cause they have naught to do.

120

But thoughts, are giv'n for Actions government,
Where Action ceases, thoughts impertinent: 95
Our *Sphere* of Action, is lifes happiness,
And he who thinks Beyond, thinks like an *Ass*.
Thus, whilst 'gainst false reas'ning I inveigh,
I own right *Reason*, which I wou'd obey:
That *Reason* that distinguishes by sense, 100
And gives us *Rules*, of good, and ill from thence:
That bounds desires, with a reforming Will,
To keep 'em more in vigour, not to kill.
Your *Reason* hinders, mine helps t'enjoy,
Renewing Appetites, yours wou'd destroy. 105
My Reason is my *Friend*, yours is a *Cheat*,
Hunger call's out, my Reason bids me eat;
Perversely yours, your Appetite does mock,
This asks for Food, that answers what's a Clock?
This plain distinction Sir your doubt secures, 110
'Tis not true Reason I despise but yours.
Thus I think Reason righted, but for *Man*,
I'le nere recant defend him if you can.
For all his Pride, and his Philosophy,
'Tis evident, *Beasts* are in their degree, 115
As wise at least, and better far than he.
Those *Creatures*, are the wisest who attain,
By surest means, the ends at which they aim.
If therefore *Jowler*, finds, and Kills his *Hares*,
Better than M⟨eres⟩, supplyes Committee Chairs; 120
Though one's a *States-man*, th'other but a *Hound*,
Jowler, in Justice, wou'd be wiser found.
You see how far *Mans* wisedom here extends,
Look next, if humane Nature makes amends;
Whose Principles, most gen'rous are, and just, 125
And to whose *Moralls*, you wou'd sooner trust.
Be Judge your self, I'le bring it to the test,
Which is the basest *Creature Man*, or *Beast*?
Birds, feed on *Birds*, *Beasts*, on each other prey,
But Savage *Man* alone, does *Man*, betray: 130

Prest by necessity, they Kill for Food,
Man, undoes *Man*, to do himself no good.
With Teeth, and Claws by Nature arm'd they hunt,
Natures allowances, to supply their want.
But *Man*, with smiles, embraces, Friendships, praise,
Unhumanely his Fellows life betrays;   136
With voluntary pains, works his distress,
Not through necessity, but wantonness.
For hunger, or for Love, they fight, or tear,
Whilst wretched *Man*, is still in Arms for fear;   140
For fear he armes, and is of Armes afraid,
By fear, to fear, successively betray'd
Base fear, the source whence his best passion⟨s⟩ came,
His boasted Honor, and his dear bought Fame.
That lust of Pow'r, to which he's such a *Slave*,   145
And for the which alone he dares be brave:
To which his various Projects are design'd,
Which makes him gen'rous, affable, and kind.
For which he takes such pains to be thought wise,
And screws his actions, in a forc'd disguise: 150
Leading a tedious life in Misery,
Under laborious, mean *Hypocrisie*.
Look to the bottom, of his vast design,
Wherein *Mans* Wisdom, Pow'r, and Glory joyn;
The good he acts, the ill he does endure,   155
'Tis all for fear, to make himself secure.
Meerly for safety, after Fame we thirst,
For all Men, wou'd be *Cowards* if they durst.
And honesty's against all common sense,
Men must be *Knaves*, 'tis in their own defence.   160
Mankind's dishonest, if you think it fair,
Amongst known *Cheats*, to play upon the square,
You'le be undone . . .
Nor can weak truth, your reputation save,
The *Knaves*, will all agree to call you *Knave*.   165
Wrong'd shall he live, insulted o're, opprest,
Who dares be less a *Villain*, than the rest.

Thus Sir you see what humane Nature craves,
Most Men are *Cowards*, all Men shou'd be *Knaves*:
The diff'rence lyes (as far as I can see)   170
Not in the thing it self, but the degree;
And all the subject matter of debate,
Is only who's a *Knave*, of the first *Rate*?

    All this with indignation have I hurl'd,
At the pretending part of the proud World,   175
Who swolne with selfish vanity, devise,
False freedomes, holy Cheats, and formal Lyes
Over their fellow *Slaves* to tyrannize.

    But if in *Court*, so just a Man there be,
(In *Court*, a just Man, yet unknown to me.)   180
Who does his needful flattery direct,
Not to oppress, and ruine, but protect;
Since flattery, which way so ever laid,
Is still a Tax on that unhappy Trade.
If so upright a *States-Man*, you can find,   185
Whose passions bend to his unbyass'd Mind;
Who does his Arts, and *Policies* apply,
To raise his *Country*, not his *Family*;
Nor while his Pride, own'd Avarice withstands,
Receives Aureal Bribes, from *Friends* corrupted
      hands.   190

    Is there a *Church-Man* who on *God* relyes?
Whose Life, his Faith, and Doctrine Justifies?
Not one blown up, with vain Prelatique Pride,
Who for reproof of Sins, does *Man* deride:
Whose envious heart with his obstrep'rous sawcy
      Eloquence,   195
Dares chide at *Kings*, and raile at Men of sense.
Who from his Pulpit, vents more peevish Lyes,
More bitter railings, scandals, Calumnies,
Than at a Gossipping, are thrown about,
When the good *Wives*, get drunk, and then fall out.
None of that sensual *Tribe*, whose Tallents lye,   201
In Avarice, *Pride*, *Sloth*, and *Gluttony*.

Who hunt good Livings, but abhor good Lives,
Whose Lust exalted, to that height arrives,
They act *Adultery* with their own *Wives*.   205
And e're a score of Years compleated be,
Can from the lofty *Pulpit* proudly see,
Half a large *Parish*, their own *Progeny*.
    Nor doating B—— who wou'd be ador'd,
For domineering at the *Councel Board*;   210
A greater *Fop*, in business at Fourscore,
Fonder of serious *Toyes*, affected more,
Than the gay glitt'ring *Fool*, at Twenty proves,
With all his noise, his tawdrey Cloths, and Loves.
    But a meek humble Man, of modest sense,   215
Who Preaching peace, does practice continence;
Whose pious life's a proof he does believe,
Misterious truths, which no *Man* can conceive.
If upon *Earth* there dwell such *God-like Men*,
I'le here recant my *Paradox* to them.   220
Adore those *Shrines* of *Virtue*, *Homage* pay,
And with the *Rabble World*, their *Laws* obey.
If such there are, yet grant me this at least,
Man differs more from *Man*, than *Man* from *Beast*.

LXV

On Rome's Pardons

I F *Rome* can pardon Sins, as *Romans* hold,
And if those *Pardons* can be bought and sold,
It were no Sin t' adore, and worship *Gold*,

If they can purchase *Pardons* with a Sum,
For Sins they may commit in time to come,   5
And for Sins past, 'tis very well for *Rome*.

At this rate, they are happy'st that have most,
They'll purchase *Heav'n* at their own proper cost,
Alas! the Poor! all that are so are lost.

Whence came this knack, or when did it begin? 10
What *Author* have they, or who brought it in?
Did *Christ*, e're keep a *Custom-House* for Sin?

Some subtle *Devil*, without more ado,
Did certainly this sly invention brew,
To gull 'em of their *Souls*, and *Money* too. 15

LXVI

Plain Dealings Downfall

LONG time plain dealing in the Hauty Town,
Wandring about, though in thread-bare Gown,
At last unanimously was cry'd down.

When almost starv'd, she to the Countrey fled,
In hopes, though meanly she shou'd there be fed, 5
And tumble Nightly on a Pea-straw Bed.

But Knav'ry knowing her intent, took post,
And Rumour'd her approach through every Coast,
Vowing his Ruin that shou'd be her host.

Frighted at this, each *Rustick* shut his door, 10
Bid her be gone, and trouble him no more,
For he that entertain'd her must be poor.

At this grief seiz'd her, grief too great to tell,
When weeping, sighing, fainting, down she fell,
Whil's K⟨n⟩avery Laughing, Rung her passing
      Bell. 15

LXVII

Consideratus, Considerandus

WHAT pleasures can the gaudy World afford?
What true delights do's teeming Nature hoard?
In her great Store-house, where she lays her
    treasure,
Alas, 'tis all the shaddow of a pleasure;
No true Content in all her works are found,   5
No sollid Joys in all Earth's spacious round:
For Labouring Man, who toils himself in vain,
Eagerly grasping, what creates his pain.
How false and feeble, nay scarce worth a Name,
Are Riches, Honour, Pow'r, and babling Fame. 10
Yet 'tis, for these Men wade through Seas of Blood
And bold in *Mischief*, Storm to be withstood;
Which when obtain'd, breed but Stupendious Fear,
Strife, Jelousies, and sleep disturbing care,
No beam of comfort, not a Ray of light   15
Shines thence, to guide us through Fates Gloomy
    Night:
But lost in devious Darkness, there we stay,
Bereft of Reason in an endless way;
Vertue's the Sollid good, if any be;
'Tis this Creates our true Felicitie;   20
Though we Despise, Contemn, and cast it by,
As worthless, or our fatal'st Enemy;
Because our darling lusts it dare controule,
And bound the Roveings of the Madding Soul.
Therefore in Garments poor, it still appears, 25
And sometimes (naked) it no Garment wears;
Shun'd by the Great, and worthless thought by
    most,
Urg'd to be gone, or wish'd for ever lost;
Yet is it loath to leave our wretched Coast.
But in disguise do's here and there intrude, 30
Striving to conquer base Ingratitude:

And boldly ventures now and then to Shine,
So to make known it is of Birth divine;
But Clouded oft, it like the Lightning plays,
Loosing as soon as seen, it's pointed Rays.   35
Which Scarceness makes those that are weak in
      wit,
For Virtues self, admire it's counterfeit:
With which dam'd *Hippocrites* the World delude;
As we on *Indians Glass*, for Gems intrude.

APPENDIX

SOME POEMS ASCRIBED TO ROCHESTER ON DOUBTFUL AUTHORITY

LXVIII

As Concerning Man

To what intent or purpose was Man made,
Who is by Birth to misery betray'd?
Man in his tedious course of life runs through
More Plagues that all the Land of *Egypt* knew.
Doctors, Divines, grave Disputations, Puns,   5
Ill looking Citizens, and scurvy Duns;
Insipid Squires, fat Bishops, Deans and Chapters,
Enthusiasts, Prophecies, new Rants and Raptures;
Pox, Gout, Catarrhs, old Sores, Cramps, Rheums
    and Aches;
Half witted Lords, double chinn'd Bawds with
    Patches;   10
Illiterate Courtiers, Chancery Suits for Life,
A teazing Whore, and a more tedious Wife;
Raw Inns of Court men, empty Fops, Buffoons,
Bullies, robust, round Aldermen, and Clowns;
Gown-men which argue, and discuss, and prate   15
And vent dull Notions of a future State;
Sure of another World, yet do not know
Whether they shall be sav'd, or damn'd, or how.
   'Twere better then that Man had never been,
Than thus to be perplex'd: *God Save the Queen.*   20

LXIX

To His Mistress

I

Why do'st thou shade thy lovely face? O why
Does that Eclipsing hand of thine deny
The Sun-shine of the Suns enlivening Eye:

II

Without thy light, what light remains in me
Thou art my Life, my way my Light's in Thee,　5
I Live. I move and by thy beams I see.

III

Thou art my Life, if thou but turn away
My Life's a thousand Deaths, thou art my way
Without Thee (*Love*) I travel not but Stray.

IV

My Light thou art, without thy Glorious sight　10
My Eyes are Darkned with Eternal night
My Love Thou art my way, my Life my light.

V

Thou art my way I wander if thou fly
Thou art my Life, if hid how blind am I
Thou art my Life if thou withdraw'st I Die.　15

VI

My Eyes are dark and blind I cannot see
To whom or whether should my darkness flee
But to that Light, and who's that Light but Thee.

VII

If that be all Shine forth and draw thou nigher
Let me be bold and Dye for my desire　20
A *Phenix* likes to Perish in the Fire.

VIII

If my Puft Light be out give leave to—
My Shameless Snuff at the bright Lamp of thine
Ah! what's thy Light the less for Lighting mine.

IX

If I have lost my Path dear Lover say 25
Shall I still wander in a Doubtful way
Love shall a Lamb of *Israel's* Sheepfold Stray.

X

My Path is lost my wandring Steps does Stray
I cannot go nor safely Stay
Whom should I seek but Thee my Path my Way. 30

XI

And yet thou turn'st thy Face a way and flyest me
And yet I sue for Grace and thou deniest me
Speak art thou angry, Love or tryest me.

XII

Display those Heavenly Lamps, or tell me why
Thou Shad'st my Face perhaps no Eye 35
Can View their Flames and not drop down and
Die.

XIII

Thou art the Pilgrims Path and Blind-Mans Eye
The Dead Mans Life on Thee my hopes rely
If I but them remove I e'er I Die.

XIV

Dissolve thy Sun-Beams close thy Wings and Stay
See See how I am blind and Dead and Stray 41
Oh thou that art my Life my Light my way.

XV

Then work my will if Passion bid me flee
My Reason shall obey my Wings shall be
Streched out no further then from me to thee. 45

LXX

A Satyr

Semper Ego Auditor Tantum, &c.

MUST I with Patience ever silent sit
Perplext with Fools who will believe they've wit?
Must I find every place by *Coxcombs* seiz'd,
Hear their affected Nonsense, and seem pleas'd?
Must I meet *Henningham* where e'er I go   5
Arp, *Arran*, Villain *Frank*, nay *P[oultn]y* too?
Shall *H[ewet]* pertly crawl from place to place
And scabby *Villers* for a Beauty pass?
Shall *H[ow]* and *B[randon]* Politicians prove,
And *S[outherlan]d* presume to be in Love?   10
'Shall pimping *Dencourt* patient Cuckolds Blame
'*Lumley* and *Savage* 'gainst the Pope disclaim,
Who can abstain from Satyr in this Age?
What Nature wants, I find supply'd by Rage.
Some do for Pimping, some for Treach'ry rise,   15
But none's made Great for being good or wise.
Deserve a Dungeon if you would be great,
Rogues always are our Ministers of State.
Mean prostrate Bitches for a *Bridewell* fit,
With *England's* wretched Queen, must equal sit,   20
R[anelagh] and fearful *M[ulgrave]* are preferr'd,
Vertue's commended, but ne'er meets Reward.
'May I ne're be like these I'l ask no more,
'I wou'd not be the Men that have their Pow'r.
Who'd be a Monarch to endure the Prating   25
Of *Nell* and sawcy *Oglethorp* in waiting,
Who would *S[outhampton's]* drivling Cuckold be?
Who would be *Y*——, and bear his infamy?
What wretch would be *Green's* base begotten Son?
Who would be *J[ames]* out-witted and undone?   30
Who would be *S[underland]* a cringing knave
Like *Hallifax* wise, like Boarish *P[embrook]* brave?

134

'Who'd be that patient *Bardash* S[*hrewsbury*]
'Or who wou'd *F——s* chattering *M——* be,
Who'd be a Wit in *Dryden's* cudgel'd Skin?   35
Or who'd be safe and senseless like *Tom Thinn?*

LXXI

Pindarick

LET Antients boast no more,
Their lew'd Imperial Whore,
Whose everlasting Lust
Surviv'd her Body's latest Thrust;
And when that transitory Dust   5
Had no more Vigour left in store,
Was still as fresh and active as before.

2

Her Glory must give place,
To one of Modern *British* Race;
Whose every daily Act exceeds   10
The other's most transcendent Deeds:
She has at length made good,
That there is Humane Flesh and Blood,
Even able to out-do,
All that their loosest Wishes prompt 'em to.   15

3

When she has Jaded quite
Her almost Boundless Appetite;
Cloy'd with the choicest Banquets of Delight,
She'll still drudge on in tastless Vice,
(As if she sinn'd for Exercise)   20
Disabling st⟨out⟩est Stallions every hour:
And when they can perform no more,
She'll rail at 'em, and kick them out of Door.

4

Mon[mou]th and *Ca[ndis]h* droop,
As first did *Henning[ha]m* and *Scrope*:   25
Nay Scabby *Ned* looks Thin and Pale,
And sturdy *Frank* himself begins to fail:
But Wo betide him if he does,
She'll set her *Jockey* on his Toes,
And he shall end the Quarrel without Blows.   30

5

Now tell me all you Pow'rs,
Who e're could equal this Lewd Dame of ours?
Lais her self must yield,
And Vanquish'd *Julia* quit the Field;
Nor can that Princess, one Day fain'd,   35
As wonder of the Earth,
For *Minataurus* glorious Birth,
With Admiration any more be Nam'd.
These Puny Heroins of History,
Eclipst by her, shall all forgotten be   40
Whilst her great Name confronts Eternity.

LXXII

On King Charles *by the Earl of*
Rochester, *For which he was banish'd*
the Court and turn'd Mountebank

In the Isle of Great *Britain* long since famous known,
For breeding the best C[ully] in *Christendom*;
There reigns, and long may he reign and thrive,
The easiest Prince and best bred Man alive:
Him no ambition moves to seek Renown,   5
Like the *French* Fool to wander up and down,
Starving his Subjects, hazarding his Crown.

Nor are his high desires above his strength,
His Scepter and his P—— are of a length,
And she that plays with one may sway the other,   10
And make him little wiser than his Brother.
I hate all Monarchs and the Thrones they sit on,
From the Hector of *France* to the Cully of *Britain*.
Poor Prince, thy P—— like the Buffoons at Court,
It governs thee, because it makes thee sport;   15
Tho' Safety, Law, Religion, Life lay on't,
'Twill break through all to it's way to C——.
Restless he rolls about from Whore to Whore,
A merry Monarch, scandalous and poor.
To *Carewell* the most Dear of all thy Dears,   20
The sure relief of thy declining Years;
Oft he bewails his fortune and her fate,
To love so well, and to be lov'd so late;
For when in her he settles well his T——,
Yet his dull graceless Buttocks hang an Arse.   25
This you'd believe, had I but time to tell you,
The pain it costs to poor laborious *Nelly*,
While she employs Hands, Fingers, Lips and thighs,
E'er she can raise the Member she enjoys.

LXXIII

In Defence of Satyr

WHEN *Shakes. Johns. Fletcher*, rul'd the Stage,
They took so bold a freedom with the Age,
That there was scarce a *Knave*, or *Fool*, in *Town*,
Of any note, but had his *Picture* shown;
And (without doubt) though some it may offend,   5
Nothing helps more than *Satyr*, to amend
Ill Manners, or is trulier *Virtues Friend*.
Princes, may *Laws* ordain, *Priests* gravely Preach,
But *Poets*, most successfully will teach.

For as a passing *Bell*, frights from his *Meat*,   10
The greedy *Sick man* that too much wou'd Eat;
So, when a *Vice*, ridiculous is made,
Our *Neighbors* shame, keeps us from growing Bad,
But wholsome Remedies, few *Palates* please,
Men rather love, what flatters their Disease,   15
Pimps, *Parasites*, *Buffoones*, and all the *Crew*,
That under *Friendships* name, weak Man undoe,
Find their false service, kindlier understood,
Than such as tell bold *Truths* to do us good.
Look where you will, and you shall hardly find,   20
A *Man*, without some Sickness of the *Mind*.
In vain we Wise wou'd seem, while ev'ry *Lust*,
Whisks us about, as *Whirlwinds* do the *Dust*

    Here for some needless Gain, ⟨the⟩ Wretch is hurl'd
From *Pole*, to *Pole*, and *Slav'd* about the *World*;   25
While the reward of all his pains, and Care,
Ends in that despicable Thing, his *Heir*.

    There a vain Fop, *Mortgages* all his *Land*,
To buy that gawdy *Play-thing*, a *Command*,
To ride a *Cock-Horse*, wears a Scarfe, at's *Arse*,   30
And play the *Pudding*, in a *May-day-Farce*.
Here one whom *God* to make a *Fool*, thought fit
In spight of *Providence*, will be a *Wit*.
But wanting Strength, t'uphold his ill made choice,
Sets up with Lewdness, Blasphemy, and Noise,   35
There at his *Mrs*. Feet a *Lover* lyes
And for a tawdrey, painted *Baby* dyes
Falls on his Knees, adores, and is afraid
Of that vain *Idol*, he himself has made.
These and a Thousand *Fools* unmention'd here,   40
Hate *Poets* all, because they *Poets* fear
Take heed (they cry) yonder *Mad Dog* will bite,
He cares not whom he falls on in his fit;
Come but in's way, and strait a new *Lampoone*
Shall spread your mangled *Fame* about the *Town*.   45

But why am I this *Bug bear* to ye all?
My *Pen* is dipt in no such bitter Gall.
He that can rail at one he calls his *Friend*,
Or hear him absent wrong'd, and not defend;
Who for the sake of some ill natur'd Jeast,   50
Tells what he shou'd conceal, Invents the rest;
To fatal *Mid-night* quarrels, can betray
His brave *Companion*, and then run away;
Leaving him to be murder'd in the *Street*,
Then put it off with some *Buffoone* Conceit;   55
This, this is he, you shou'd beware of all,
Yet him a pleasant, witty *Man*, you call
To whet your dull Debauches up, and down,
You seek him as top *Fidler* of the *Town*.

But if I laugh when the *Court Coxcombs* Show,   60
To see that *Booby Sotus* dance *Provoe.*
Or chatt'ring *Porus*, from the Side *Box* grin,
Trickt like a *Ladys Monkey* new made clean.
To me the name of *Railer*, shalt you give,
Call me a *Man* that knows not how to live.   65

But *Wenches* to their *Keepers*, true shall turn,
Stale *Maids* of Honor, proffer'd *Husbands* scorn,
Great *Statesmen*, flatt'ry, and Clinches hate,
And long in Office dye without *Estate.*
Against a *Bribe, Court Judges*, shall decide,   70
The *City Knav'ry* want, the *Clergy* Pride.
E're that black *Malice*, in my Rhymes you find,
That wrong a Worthy *Man*, or hurts a *Friend.*
But then perhaps you say, why do you write?
What you think harmless *Mirth*, the *World* thinks
　　　Spight.   75
Why shou'd your *Fingers* itch to have a lash
At *Simius*, the *Buffoon*, or *Cully Bash*?
What is't to you, if *Alidores* fine *Whore*,
F**ks with some *Fop*, whilst he's shut out of *Door*?
Consider pray, that dang'rous *Weapon Wit*,   80
Frightens a *Million*, when a few you *hit*.

J.W.   139   O

Whip but a *Curr* as you ride through a *Town*,
And shall his *Fellow Currs* the Quarrel own.
Each *Knave*, or *Fool*, that's conscious of a Crime,
Tho he scapes now, looks for't another time.   85
   Sir, I confess all you have said is true
But who has not some *Folly* to pursue?
Milo turn'd *Quixot*, fancy'd *Battails*, *Fights*,
When the *Fifth Bottle*, had encreased the *Lights*.
War-like Dirt Pyes, our *Heroe Paris* forms,   90
Which desp'rate *Bessus*, without *Armour* storms.
Cornus, the kindest *Husband*, e're was born,
Still Courts the *Spark*, that does his *Brows* adorn.
Invites him home to dine, and fills his *Veins*,
With the hot Blood, which his dear *Doxy* drains.   95
   Grandio thinks himself a *Beau-Garcon*,
Goggles his *Eyes*, writes *Letters* up and down;
And with his sawcy *Love*, plagues all the *Town*.
While pleas'd to have his Vanity thus fed,
He caught with *G[osnall]*, that Old *Hag* a Bed. 100
But shou'd I all the crying *Follies* tell,
That rouse the sleeping *Satyr* from his *Cell*.
I to my Reader, shou'd as tedious prove,
As that Old *Spark*, *Albanus* making love.
Or florid *Roscius*, when with some smooth flam, 105
He gravely on the publick, tries to sham.
   Hold then my Muse, 'tis time to make an end,
Least taxing others, thou thy self offend.
The *World's a Wood*, in which all loose their way
Though by a diff'rent *Path* each goes *Astray*. 110

LXXIIIA

On the suppos'd Authour of a late Poem *in defence of* Satyr

To rack and torture thy unmeaning *Brain*,
In *Satyrs* praise to a low untun'd strain,
In thee was most impertinent and vain.
When in thy *Person* we more clearly see,
That *Satyr's* of Divine Authority, 5
For *God* made one on *Man*, when he made thee.
To shew there were some *Men*, as there are *Apes*.
Fram'd for meer sport, who differ, but in shapes:
In thee are all these contradictions joyn'd,
That make an *Asse* prodigious and refin'd. 10
A lump deform'd and shapeless wert thou born.
Begot in *Loves* despight and *Natures* scorn;
And art grown up the most ungraceful *Wight*,
Harsh to the *Ear*, and hideous to the sight,
Yet *Love's* thy bus'ness, *Beauty* thy delight. 15
Curse on that silly hour, that first inspir'd,
Thy madness, to pretend to be admir'd;
To paint thy grizly *Face*, to dance, to dress,
And all those Awkward Follies that express,
Thy loathsome Love, and filthy daintiness. 20
Who needs will be a Ugly *Beau-Garcon*,
Spit at, and shun'd by ev'ry *Girl* in *Town*;
Where dreadfully *Loves Scare-Crow*, thou art
      plac'd
To fright the tender *Flock*, that long to taste:
While ev'ry coming *Maid*, when you appear, 25
Starts back for shame, and strait turns chaste for
      fear.
For none so poor, or *Prostitute* have prov'd,
Where you made love t'endure to be belov'd.
'Twere labour lost, or else I shou'd advise.
But thy half *Wit* will ne're let thee be wise. 30

Half-witty, and half-mad, and scarce half-brave,
Half-honest (which is very much a *Knave*.)
Made up of all these Halfs, thou can'st not pass,
For any thing intirely, but an *Ass*.

LXXIIIb

The Answer

RAIL on poor feeble *Scribler*, speak of me,
In as bad Terms, as the *World* speaks of thee.
Sit swelling in thy Hole, like a vext *Toad*.
And full of *Pox*, and *Malice*, spit abroad.
Thou can'st hurt no *Mans Fame* with thy ill word, 5
Thy Pen, is full as harmless as thy Sword.

LXXIV

The Platonick Lady

I COULD Love thee till I dye,
    Wouldst thou Love mee modestly;
And ne're presse, while I live,
    For more than willingly I would give;
Which should sufficient be to prove   5
    I'de understand the Arte of Love.
I hate the thing is call'd Injoyment,
    Besydes it is a dull imployment,
It cutts of al that's Life and fier,
    From that which may be term'd Desire.   10
Just (like the Be) whose sting is gon,
    Converts the owner to a Droane.
I Love a youth sho'd give me leave
    His Body in my Arms to wreath;

To presse him Gently and to kisse,   15
    To sigh and looke with Eyes that wish.
For what if I could once Obtaine,
    I would neglect with flatt disdaine
I'de give him Libertye to toye,
    And play with mee and count it Joye.   20
Our freedome should be full compleate,
    And nothing wanting but the feate:
Let's practice then, and we shall prove
    These are the only sweets of Love.

LXXV

Song

1

PHILLIS misfortunes that can be exprest
Admit some gentle hours of peace and rest
But from Loves Empire I hope noe release
For though dispairing still my flames increase
And dull complaint can never ease a care   5
Thats caused by Absence norished by despair

2

Such conquering charms contribute to my chain
And ade fresh torments to my lingerin pain
That could blind Love judge of my faithfull flame
He would return the fugitive with shame   10
For haveing bin insenceble to Love
That does by constancy its merrit prove

3

But I that can thus slavishly complain
Of tedious absence and unjust disdain

Merit the scorn with which I am repay⟨d⟩   15
For she that calls not reas⟨on⟩ to her aid
deserves the punishment of Thersis hate
The utmost rigor of relentless fate

LXXVI

⟨Song⟩

YOUR glory Phillis is in being lov'd
but all your charmes consist in loving
A cruel beauty never conquering prov'd
kind kindl'd flames are the most moving
tis A mean harte that to your frown can yeald   5
soften my chaine and keep me still your slave
tyrants may force but neer can win the feild
while there remains one sensible or brave

LXXVII

Song

CLORIS to love without return
Is the efect of a mean soul
In hopeless flames ever to burn
Is past Tyranick loves controul
I by your charms and flattering Wit betrayed   5
Of my fond humble hart an offering Made
But your disdain has curd loves cruell paine
Prid and dispaire has brock his rigorous chaine.

2

though reason could not passhon cure
See what the sence of honour can   10

He that could your vain prid indure
Merits the scorn of every man
My long lost fredome fircely Ile persue
And flye the world rather than love renew
Soe though my hart neglected liberty   15
your own ungrateful hate has sett it free.

Continue still ingrate
My seeming hate youl gain
But my most wretched fate
Makes me still love me pain   20
Therefore in vaine your art
My wortheless love to loose
youl allways have the hart
Which you soe hardly use

Finish

LXXVIII

⟨Song⟩

CORRINA vainly I pretend
Your charming scorn still to outbrave
My fond resistance now must end
Soe glorious tis to be your Slave
That my ambition has noe higher Aime   5
Then humbly to adore (and) Serve
(with such a pure) and perfitt flame
Since mines soe inocent a flame
I doe your pitty though not love deserve
now humblely to adore and serve   10
is my ambitions highest aim

Corinna humblely I confess
My rude resistance now must end

Whilst you thouse thousand charmes posses
How vain to fredome I pretend   15

(*On verso*)

Vertues my lawfull prince my tyrant love
His fauls dominion (? cruelty) does prove

LXXIX

⟨*Draft of a Dialogue*⟩

DEAREST Armilla (did) could you once but (know)
                                                 guesse
How pleasantly and gentle Love does rain
your dull aversion to his power would cease
(and you would   fredome again)
And move you then some fredome   5
Such charming pleasurs mixt with that deare pain
that you would
youd then repine against the rigid fate
(which) and curse your selfe conceited ignorance
that first inclined you to delight in hate   10
that enymy to love and (innocence) common sence
it hinders mankind being fortunat
and robs the world of peace and innocence

Armilla Allexis cease all your attempts are vain
    My ferme resolves of hate ile still persue   15
If you such pleasure find in servil pain
you are recompenced by being pleased and true

Why did the gods bestow soe blest a forme divine
(to ruin and destroy all that behold)
And not forsee the danger of a storme   20
Thats raised by beauty (and) joynd with tyranny

none can presume to love but must resolve to dye
your endless rigor noe relefe affords

And joyn such beauty with such tyranny
why do you glory in your tyranny   25
And cant (p)revent the danger of a storme
(And) I must [love] with a
for thoug I di
Since (when) your bright eyes kindled faithfull flame
Its much more glorious to love on and dye   30
(for) nothing can be half soe great a shame
I chuse as a much more glorious fate
to dye your vasall then to have shame

LXXX

Some Impromptus ascribed to Rochester

1

Earle of Rochester's Conference with a Post Boy

SON of a Whore G—d damn thee, canst thou Tell
A Peerless Peer the readiest Way to Hell?
I've Outswill'd Bacchus, Sworn of my own Make
Oaths, Frighted Furyes, and made Pluto quake:
Sw—d Whore more ways than ever Sodoms Walls   5
Knew, or the Colledge of the Cardinals,
Witness Heroic Scars and Wounds: Ne're go!
Sear Cloths and Ulcers from the Top to th' Toe.
Frighted at my own Mischeif's I am fled,
And basely left my Life's Defender Dead.   10
But hang't why do I mention these poor Things?
I have blasphem'd G—d, and libell'd Kings;
The readiest way to Hell, Boy; Quick (Boy) Ne're stir
The readiest way, my Lord's by Rochester.

2

My Lord Rochester *attempting to Kiss the Duchess of* Cleveland, *as she was stepping out of her Chariot* at White-Hall-Gate, *she threw him on his Back, and before he Rose, he spoke the following Lines.*

> By Heavens! 'twas bravely done,
> First to Attempt the Chariot of the Sun,
> And then to fall like *Phaeton*.

3

Spoken Extempore *to a Country Clerk, after hearing him sing Psalms.*

> STERNHOLD and *Hopkins* had great Qualms,
> When they Translated *David's* Psalms,
>   To make the Heart full glad:
> But had it been poor *David's* Fate,
> To hear thee Sing, and them Translate,
>   By G—— 'twould have made him Mad.

4

Extempore to his Lady, who sent a servant on purpose desiring to hear from him, being very uneasy at his long silence

> *To his more than meritorious Wife*

> I AM by fate, slave to your will,
> And I will be obedient still.
> To shew my love, I will compose ye,
> For your fair fingers ring a posey,
> In which shall be express'd my duty,   5
> And how I'll be for ever true t'ye;
> With low made legs and sugar'd speeches,
> Yielding to your fair bum the breeches,
> To prove myself in all I can
>   Your faithful humble servant,   10
>   John.

5

TRUST not that thing call'd woman, she is worse
Than all ingredients cram'd in a Curse,
Were she but ugly, peevish, proud, a whore
Poxt, painted, perjurd so she were no more
I could forgive her, and connive at this,
Alledging still that she a woman is,
But she is far worse, in time she will forestall
The devil, and be the damning of us all.

LXXXI

Rochester's *Farewel*

TIR'D with the noysom Follies of the Age,
And weary of my Part, I quit the Stage;
For who in Life's dull Farce a Part would bear,
Where Rogues, Whores, Bawds, all the head Actors
    are?
Long I with Charitable Malice strove,   5
Lashing the Court, those Vermin to remove,
But thriving Vice under the rod still grew,
As aged Letchers whipp'd, their Lust renew;
What though my Life hath unsuccessful been,
(For who can this *Augean* Stable clean)   10
My gen'rous end I will pursue in Death,
And at Mankind rail with my parting breath.
First, ⟨then⟩ the *Tangier* Bullies must appear,
With open Brav'ry, and dissembled Fear:
M[*ulgrav*]e their Head, but Gen'ral have a care, 15
Though skill'd in all those Arts that cheat the fair,
The Undiscerning and Impartial *Moor*,
Spares not the Lover on the Ladies score.
Think how many perish by one fatal shot,
The Conquests all thy Goggling ever got.   20

Think then (as I presume you do) how all
The *English* Ladies will lament your fall;
Scarce will there greater Grief pierce every heart,
Should Sir George H[ewitt], or Sir C[ar] depart.
Had it not better been than thus to roam,   25
To stay and play the Cravat-string at home?
To strut, look big, shake Pantaloon, and swear
With H[ewitt], D[amme], there's no action there.
Had'st thou no friend that wou'd to R[owley] write,
To hinder this thy eagerness to fight?   30
That without danger thou a Brave might'st be,
As sure to be deny'd as S[alisbur]y.
This sure the Ladies had not fail'd to do,
But who such Courage would suspect in you?
For say, what Reason could with you prevail   35
To change Embroider'd Coat for Coat of Mail?
Let P[limout]h, or let M[ordan]t go, whom Fate
Hath not made Valiant, but desperate.
For who could not be weary of his Life,
Who's lost his Money, or has got a Wife?   40
To the more tolerable Alcaid of *Alcazzer*,
One flies from Creditors, the other from ⟨*Frazier*⟩;
'Twere Cruelty to make such sharp Remarks,
On all the little, forward, fighting Sparks;
Only Poor C[harls] I can't but pitty thee,   45
When all the pert young Voluntiers I see.
Those Chits of War, who as much mirth create
As the Pair Royal of the Chits of State,
Their names shall equal all succeeding Glory,
Chit S[underlan]d Chit G[odolphi]n, and Chit L[or]y
When thou let'st P[limout]h ⟨go⟩ twas such a Jest, 51
As when the Brother made the same request;
Had R[ichmon]d but got leave as well as he,
The Jest had been compleat and worthy thee.
Well, since he must, he'll to *Tangier* advance   55
It is resolv'd, but first let's have a Dance.
First, at her Highness Ball he must appear,

And in a parting Country Dance, learn there
With Drum and Fife to make a Jigg of War;
What is of Soldier seen in all the heap,   60
Besides the flutt'ring Feather in the Cap.
The Scarf, and Yard or two of Scarlet Cloath,
From Gen'ral *M[ulgrav]e* down to little *W[rot]h*?
There leave we them, and back to *England* come
Whereby the Wiser Sparks that stay at home,   65
In safe ideas by their fancy form'd,
Tangier (like *Mastrich*) is at *Windsor* Storm'd.
For now we talk of *Mastrich*, where he is he,
Fam'd for that brutal piece of Bravery?
He with the thick Impenetrable Skull,   70
The solid, hard'ned Armour of a Fool?
Well might himself to all Wars ills expose,
Who (come what will yet) had no Brains to lose.
Yet this is he, the dull, unthinking he,
Who must (forsooth) our future Monarch be.   75
This Fool by Fools (*A[rmstron]g* and *V[erno]n*) led,
Dreams that a Crown will drop upon his Head,
By great example he this Path doth tread,
Following such sensless Asses up and down,
(For *Saul* sought Asses when he found a Crown) 80
But *R[oss]* is risen as *Samuel* at his call,
To tell that God hath left the ambitious *Saul*.
Never (says Heaven), shall the blushing Sun,
See *P[roger]s* Bastard fill the Regal Throne.
So Heaven says, but *B[uckingha]m* says he shall, 85
But who e're he protects is sure to fall.
Who can more certain of Destruction be
Than he who trusts to such a Rogue as he?
What good can come from him who *Y[or]k*
        forsook,
T'espouse the Interest of this Booby Duke?   90
But who the best of Masters cou'd desert
Is the most fit to take the Traytors part.
Ungrateful! This thy Master-piece of sin,

Exceeds ev'n that with which thou did'st begin
Thou great Proficient in the Trade of Hell,   95
Whose latter Crimes still do thy first excel:
The very top of Villany we seize,
By steps in Order, and by just degrees
None e're was perfect Villain in one day,
The murder'd Boy to Treason led the way;   100
But when degrees of Villany we Name,
How can we choose but think of B[uckingha]m?
He who through all of them has boldly ran,
Left ne're a Law unbroke by God or Man.
His treasur'd sins of Supererrogation,   105
Swell to a summ enough to damn a Nation:
But he must here, *per* force, be left alone,
His acts require a Volumn of their own:
Where rank'd in dreadful order shall appear,
All his Exploits from *S[hrewsbur]y* to *Le M[arr]*.
But stay, methinks! I on a sudden find,   111
My Pen to treat of th'other Sex inclin'd;
But where in all this choice shall I begin?
Where, but with the renowned *M[azarin]e*?   114
For all the Bawds the Courts rank Soil doth bear
And Bawds and States-men grow in plenty there
To thee submit and yield, should we be Just,
To thy experienc'd and well travell'd Lust:
Thy well known Merits claim that thou should'st
   be,
First in the Glorious Roll of Infamy.   120
To thee they all give place, and Homage pay,
Do all thy Letcherous Decrees obey;
Thou Queen of Lust, thy Bawdy Subjects they.
While *S[usse]x*, *B[roghi]ll*, *Betty F[elto]n* come,
Thy Whores of Honour, to attend thy Throne;   125
For what proud Strumpet e're could merit more
Than be Anointed the Imperial Whore?
For tell me in all *Europe*, where's the part,
That is not conscious of thy Lewd desert.

The great *Pedalian* Youth, whose Conquests run 130
O're all the World, and Travall'd with the Sun,
Made not his Valour in more Nations known.
Than thou thy Lust, thy matchless Lust have
   shown,
All Climes, all Countries, do with Tribute come,
(Thou World of Lewdness) to thy boundless Womb:
Thou Sea of Lust, that never ebb doth know,
Whither the Ruines of all Nations flow,
Lewd *Messaline* was but a Type of thee
Thou highest, last degree of Letchery:
For in all Ages, except her and you,   140
Who ever sinn'd so high, and stoop'd so low.
She to th'imperial Bed, each Night did use,
To bring the stink of the Exhausted Stews;
Tir'd (but not satisfy'd) with man did come,
Drunk with abundant Lust, and reeling home.   145
But thou, to our admiring Age, doth show
More sin than Inn'cent Rome did ever know;
And having all her Lewdnesses out-ran,
Takes up with Devil, having tir'd Man:
For what is else that loathsom uggly Black,   150
Which you and *S[usse]x* in your Arms do take?
Nor does Cold Age, which now rides on so fast,
Make thee come short of all thy Lewdness past:
Though on thy Head, Grey-hairs like *Etna's* Snow
Are shed, thou'rt Fire and Brimstone all below.
Thou monstrous thing, in whom at once doth rage
The Flames of Youth, and impotence of Age.
My Lady *D——s* takes the second place,
Proud with thy favour and peculiar grace;
E'n she with all her Piety and Zeal,   160
The hotter flames that burn in thee does feel.
Thou dost into her kindling breast inspire,
The Lustful seeds of thy Contagious fire;
So well the Spirit and the Flesh agree,
Lust and Devotion, Zeal and Letchery.   165

Important use Religion's made,
By those who wisely drive the Cheating Trade;
As Wines Prohibited securely pass.
Changing the Name of their own Native place.
So Vice grows safe, drest in Devotions Name,   170
Unquestion'd by the Custom-house of Fame:
Where e're so much of Sanctity you see,
Be more Suspicious of hid Villany;
Whosoever Zeal is than his Neighbours more
If Man, think he's a Rogue, if Woman Whore: 175
And such a thing art thou Religious Pride,
So very Lewd, and yet so Sanctify'd.
Let now the D[utches]s take no further care
Of humorous Stallions, let her not dispair,
Since her Indulgent Stars so kind have been   180
To send her B——y and M[azarin]e
This last doth banist M[onmouth]s Place supply,
And Wit supplanted is by Letchery.
For M[onmout]h ⟨s⟩he had Parts, and Wit, and
     Sense,
To all which M[azarin]e had no pretence;   185
A proof that since such things as ⟨s⟩he prevail
Her H[ighness's] Head is lighter than her Tail
But stay I P[ortsmout]h almost had forgot,
The common Theam of every Rhiming Sot;
She'll after railing make us laugh a while,   190
For at her Folly who can choose but smile?
While them who always slight her great she makes,
And so much pains to be despis'd she takes.
Goes sauntring with her Highness up to Town,
To an Old Play, and in the Dark come down;   195
Still makes her Court to her as to the Queen,
But still is Justl'd out by M[azarin]e
So much more Worthy a kind Bawd is thought,
Than ever she who her from Exile brought.
O P[ortsmout]h, foolish P[ortsmout]h! Not to take
The offer the great S[underlan]d did make,   201

When Cringing at thy Feet; e're *M[onmout]h*
    bow'd,
The Golden Calf, that's Worshipp'd by the Crowd.
But thou for *Y[or]k,* who now despises thee,
To leave both him and Pow'rful *S[haftsbur]y:*
If this is all the Policy you know,
This all the skill in States you boast of so,
How wisely did thy Country's Laws ordain,
Never to let the foolish Women Reign.
But what must we expect, who daily see   210
Unthinking *C[harle]s,* Rul'd by Unthinking thee.

NOTES

NOTES

LIST of printed books and manuscripts referred to in the notes with symbols by which they are represented. Short titles only of printed books are given.

N.B.—Every note begins with an indication of the exact source of the text, and this is followed by a list (which does not pretend to be exhaustive) of some of the other chief editions and manuscripts where versions of the poem are to be found. 'Etc.' signifies 'and other later editions'.

PRINTED BOOKS

1680—Poems on Several Occasions. By the Right Honourable, the E of R——. Printed at Antwerp, 1680. Small 8vo. (Copy in the Folger Library, Washington, D.C.)

1685—Poems on Several Occasions. Written by a Late Person of Honour. London, Printed for A. Thorncome, 1685. Small 8vo. (British Museum 11623, a, 37.)

Val.—Valentinian: A Tragedy As 'tis Alter'd by the Late Earl of Rochester, And Acted at the Theatre Royal. London: Printed for Timothy Goodwin, 1685. 4to. (Nottingham University Library.)

1691—Poems, &c. on Several Occasions: With Valentinian, A Tragedy. Written by the Right Honourable John Late Earl of Rochester. London, Printed for Jacob Tonson, 1691. 8vo. (Bodl. Don. e. 74.) (This book was reprinted with no substantial alterations in 1696 and 1701. The 1696 edition is referred to as '1696'.)

1701—Poems on Several Occasions. By the R.H. the E. of R. London, Printed for A.T. 1701. Small 8vo. (Bodl. ϕ. f. 119*.)

1707—The Miscellaneous Works of the Right Honourable The Late Earls of Rochester and Roscommon. London Printed: And sold by B. Bragge, 1707. 8vo. (Re-issued by Edmund Curll with cancel title-page as 'The Second Edition' in the same year. See Introduction, p. xliii.) (Dyce Collection, South Kensington, 8284.)

1709—The Works of the Right Honourable the Earls of Rochester and Roscommon. The Third Edition. London. Printed for E. Curll, 1709. 8vo. (Bodl. Vet. A. 4.)

UNC—Upon Nothing A Poem by the Right Honourable John late Earl of Rochester Now first Correctly Printed London Printed for E. Curll, 1711. (Brit. Mus. 161, m. 20.)

1714—The Works of John Earl of Rochester. Containing Poems On Several Occasions: His Lordship's Letters to Mr. *Savil* and Mrs. —— with Valentinian, A Tragedy. London: Printed for Jacob Tonson, MDCCXIV. 12mo. (Collection of the Editor.)

E—Epicedia Academiae Oxoniensis, In Obitum Serenissimae, Mariae Principis Arausionensis. Oxoniae, Excudebat A. & L. Lichfield, Acad. Typogr. Impensis Ric. Davis. 1661. 4to. (Bodl. J. 21, Art.)

Kemp—A Collection of Poems, Written upon several Occasions, By Several Persons. Never Before in Print. London, Printed for Hobart Kemp, 1672. Small 8vo. (Brit. Mus. C. 57, K. 20.)

Collins—A Collection of Poems Written upon Several Occasions By several Persons. With many Additions, Never before in Print. London, Printed for *Tho. Collins*, 1673. Small 8vo. (Brit. Mus. 11631, aa. 9.)

Female Poems—Female Poems on Several Occasions. Written By Ephelia. The Second Edition, with large Additions. London. Printed for James Courtney, 1682. Small 8vo. (Brit. Mus. 11631, C. 20).

RRR—Rome Rhym'd to Death. Being a collection of Choice Poems: In two parts Written by the E. of R. Dr. Wild, and others of the best Modern Wits. London Printed for John How, 1683. 8vo. (Bodl. Firth, f. 96.)

DMP—Miscellany Poems. Containing a New Translation of Virgills Eclogues, Ovid's Love Elegies, Odes of Horace, and Other Authors; With Several Original Poems. By the Most Eminent Hands. London, Printed for Jacob Tonson, 1684. 8vo. (The first part of 'Dryden's Miscellany'.) (Bodl. 280, m. 304.)

Tate—Poems By Several Hands, and on Several Occasions Collected by N. Tate. London: Printed for J. Hindmarsh, 1685. 8vo. (Brit. Mus. 11626, d. 60).

ABM—Miscellany, Being a Collection of Poems By Several Hands. Together with Reflections on Morality, Or Seneca Unmasqued. London: Printed for J. Hindmarsh, 1685. 8vo. (Aphra Behn's Miscellany.) (Brit. Mus. 1078, l. 9.)

SCNIP—A Second Collection of the Newest and Most Ingenious Poems, Satyrs, Songs &c Against Popery and Tyranny, Relating to the Times. Most of which never before Printed. London. MDCLXXXIX. 4to. (Brit. Mus. 1077, h. 32.)

TPCP—The Third Part of the Collection of Poems on Affairs of State Containing Esquire Marvel's further Instructions to a Painter. And the late Lord Rochester's Farewell. London MDCLXXXIX. 4to. (Brit. Mus. 1077, h. 32.)

POAS—Poems on Affairs of State: From the Time of Oliver Cromwell, to the Abdication of K. James the Second. Written by the greatest Wits of the Age. Printed in the Year 1697. 8vo. (Collection of the Editor.)

SPC—State Poems; Continued from the time of O. Cromwel, to this Present Year 1697. Written By the

Greatest Wits of the Age, Printed in the Year MDCXCVII. 8vo. (Brit. Mus. 1077, e. 26.)

Examen Poeticum—Examen Poeticum: Being The Third Part of Miscellaneous Poems. Containing Variety of New Translations Of the Ancient Poets. Together with many Original Copies, By the Most Emenent Hands, London: Printed by R.E. for Jacob Tonson, MDCXCIII. 8vo. (The third part of 'Dryden's Miscellany'.) (Brit. Mus. 1076, k. 27.)

EM—The Empress of Morocco. A Tragedy. With Sculptures. As it is Acted at the Duke's Theatre. Written by Elkanah Settle, Servant to his Majesty. London, Printed for William Cademan, 1673, 4to. (Brit. Mus. 841, c. 21.)

Love in the Dark—Love in the Dark, Or the Man of Bus'ness. A Comedy: Acted at the Theatre Royal. Written By Sir Francis Fane, Junior; Printed by T. N. for Henry Herringham, 1675. 4to. (Brit. Mus. 644, d. 82.)

Circe—Circe, A Tragedy. As it is Acted At His Royal Highness the Duke of York's Theatre. By Charles D'Avenant, L.L.D. London, Printed for Richard Tonson, MDCLXXVII. 4to. (Brit. Mus. 644, g. 55.)

Hayward—The Collected Works of John Wilmot Earl of Rochester Edited by John Hayward the Nonesuch Press 16 Great James Street, W.C. MCMXXVI. 4to. (Limited edition.)

Welbeck Miscellany—Welbeck Miscellany No. 2 A Collection of Poems by Several Hands Never before published 1934 (ed. Francis Needham at Welbeck Abbey, Notts.). Small 8vo. pamphlet.

Thorpe—Rochester's Poems on Several Occasions Edited by James Thorpe Princeton New Jersey, 1950. Small 8vo. (A facsimile reprint of the Huntington Library copy of 1680 with introduction, notes, etc.)

MANUSCRIPTS

Portland MS.—Folio album bound in full black morocco with lettering in gold on spine 'Earl of Rochester Autograph Poems' containing 24 leaves in which are inserted poems in three hands, one of which is Rochester's, and one Lady Rochester's. Bookplate of 6th Duke of Portland. This Album is part of the Portland Collection deposited in the Library of the Univeristy of Nottingham.

Portland Miscellany—Folio volume in old leather binding with bookplate of the Sixth Duke of Portland. There are two seals on binding with arms of the First Earl of Pomfret and his wife. The volume contains a miscellany of poems mostly written in a neat scribal hand. These include the obscene play called 'The Destruction of Sodom' and poems by Rochester, Dryden, Marvell, Oldham and others. This volume is part of the Duke of Portland's collection at Welbeck Abbey.

MS. 636F—MS. Eng. 636F in the Houghton Library, University of Harvard, a small folio volume containing a miscellany of poems transcribed in a neat late seventeenth-century hand, probably c. 1680. It contains 79 poems by Rochester, Dryden, Etherege, Butler, Lee and others.

MS. 624F—MS Eng. 624F in the Houghton Library, University of Harvard. Small quarto volume formerly belonging to Edward Dowden, contains transcripts of poems in a late seventeenth-century hand.

MS. 623F—MS. Eng. 623F in the Houghton Library, University of Harvard. A collection of poems on loose sheets 'Written by Various Hands chiefly of the Seventeenth Century' formerly belonging to 'the noble family of Huntingdon'. It includes 66 folio sheets apparently torn out of a manuscript miscellany containing transcripts in a late seventeenth-century hand of poems by Rochester and others.

Osborn MSS.—Manuscripts in the collection of Professor James M. Osborn, 77 Edge Hill Road, New Haven, Conn., U.S.A.

Harl. MS. 6207
Harl. MS. 7003 }—British Museum Harleian MSS. with these numbers.

Add. MS. 27408
Add. MS. 28692
Add. MS. 21094 }—British Museum Additional MSS. with these numbers.
Add. MS. 6207

Sloane MS. 655
Sloane MS. 1731A }—British Museum Sloane MS. with these numbers.

Rawl. Poet. 90
Rawl. Poet. 123 }—Bodleian Library Rawlinson Eng. Poet. MSS. with these numbers.
Rawl. Poet. 173

Tanner 89—Bodleian Library Tanner MS. with this number.

Douce 357—Bodleian Library Douce MS. with this number.

Sancroft 53—Bodleian Library Sancroft MS. with this number.

Bodl. Add. MS. 301—Bodleian Library Additional MS. with this number.

The following abbreviations are used for the titles of periodicals:

T.L.S.—Times Literary Supplement.
R.E.S.—Review of English Studies.
M.L.N.—Modern Language Notes.
N. and Q.—Notes and Queries.

I. *To His Sacred Majesty* etc.: 1691, pp. 121, 122; first printed in *Britannia Rediviva, Oxoniae* MDCLX, a volume of Latin and English verses published at Oxford in honour of the Restoration. This poem occurs on sig. Aa, and is signed 'Rochester, Wadh. Col.' The Wilmot mentioned in *l.* 18 is Henry Wilmot, first Earl of Rochester, the poet's father. See Introduction, p. xv. This poem and the two that follow are said by Anthony à Wood in *Athenae Oxonienses* (ed. Bliss, III, 1231) to be the work of Robert Whitehall (see Introduction, p. xvii). There is a copy of verses signed by Whitehall in *Britannia Rediviva*; it is distinctly inferior to the verses ascribed Rochester.

II. *In obit. Seren Mariae*, etc.: 1691, p. 123; E. This and the following poem were first printed on sigg. A2v. and G1 and G1v. respectively of E, a collection of verses in Latin, Greek, Hebrew and English on the death of Mary, Princess Royal of England and Princess of Orange, who died of smallpox at Whitehall on 24th December 1660.

1 concilia] E convitia. *2* nequat for 'nequeat'] E nequit. *9* par] certainly the correct reading. 1696 and later edd. read 'per'.

III. *To her Sacred Majesty*, etc.: 1691, pp. 124–7; E. The poem is addressed to the Queen Mother Henrietta Maria, widow of Charles I.

15 young daughter] Elizabeth (1636–50), second daughter of Charles I. *18 Glocester*] Henry, Duke of Gloucester (1639–60), third son of Charles I). *24* to the firm shore] E unto the shore. *31* Curses] E cures. *46 Princess*] Henrietta Anne, afterwards Duchess of Orleans, younger sister of the Princess of Orange who left England and returned to France with her mother on 25th January 1660.

IV. *A Dialogue between Stephon and Daphne*: 1691, pp. 3–9. Rochester is called Strephon in several of

the elegies published on his death and also by
Charles Blount in his *Miscellaneous Works*, 1695,
p. 117.

V. *A Pastoral Dialogue between Alexis and Strephon*:
1691, pp. 10–15; Portland Miscellany. This poem
was printed as a broadside 'by Benj Billinley at
the Printing House in Cornhil, 1682' (copy in B.M.
1875, d. 6 (74)).

VI. *Womans Honour*: 1691, pp. 22, 23; 1680; 1685;
Female Poems; MS. 636F; Portland Miscellany.
1 bid] 1680 bad. *10* where he alone] 1680 alone
where he.

VII. *Grecian Kindness*: 1691, p. 24; 1701. Neither this
nor the two following poems appear in 1680, 1685
or MS. 636F.

VIII. *The Mistress*: 1691, pp. 25–7.

IX. *A Song*: 1691, pp. 28, 29.

X. *To Corinna*: 1691, pp. 30, 31; 1680; 1685; Portland
Miscellany. This poem also appears, attributed to
Rochester, in *The Theater of Music*, 1685, and *The
New Treasury of Music*, 1695. The version in the
Portland Miscellany (p. 56) omits stanza 3.

XI. *A Song of a Young Lady to her Ancient Lover*:
1691, pp. 32, 33. Not in 1680, 1685 or MS. 636F.

XII. *A Song*: 1691, pp. 34, 35; 1680; 1685; Female
Poems; Portland Miscellany.

XIII. *To a Lady in a Letter*: 1691, pp. 36–8; 1680; 1685;
MS. 636F; Portland MS. The version in Portland
MS. (f. 4) is in Rochester's autograph written on
both sides of a folded sheet of paper. It differs considerably from that printed in 1691. The versions
found in 1680, 1685 and MS. 636 resemble the text

in the Portland MS. but are not so full. The following is the version in the Portland MS. There are two corrections both in Rochester's hand. In *l.* 1 'perfect' has been substituted for 'happy', and in *l.* 23 'lusty juice of' for 'juice of lusty'.

How perfect Cloris, & how free
Would these enjoyments prouve,
But you wth formall jealousy
Are still tormenting Love

Let us (since witt instructs us how)   5
Raise pleasure to the topp,
If Rivall bottle you'l allow
I'le suffer rivall fopp,

Ther's not a brisk insipid sparke
That flutter in the Towne   10
But wth y^{r} wanton eyes you marke
Him out to be y^{r} owne.

Nor ever thinke it worth y^{r} care
How empty nor how dull
The heads of y^{r} admirers are   15
Soe that their ^{backs}_{purse} bee full.

All this you freely may confess
Yett wee'l not disagree
For did you love you pleasures less
You were not fitt for mee.   20

Whilst I my passion to persue
Am whole nights taking in
The Lusty juice of Grapes, take you
The juice of Lusty Men—

Upraide mee not that I designe   25
Tricks to delude y^{r} charmes
When running after mirth & wine
I leave y^{r} Longing Armes

For wine (whose power alone can raise
  Our thoughts soe farr above)   30
Affords Idea's fitt to praise
What wee think fitt to Love.

XIV. *The Fall*: 1691, pp. 39, 40; 1680; 1685; Female
Poems; Add. MS. 27408; Portland Miscellany.

XV. *Love and Life*: 1691, pp. 41, 42; 1680; 1685;
Female Poems; Tate; MS. 636F; Add. MS. 27408;
Portland Miscellany; Rawl. Poet. 90. This was one
of Rochester's best known lyrics. Besides the collections listed above, it occurs in a number of song-
books of the period recorded by Thorpe, pp. 179,
180.
The version in MS. 636F (p. 246) reads as follows:

Song

See my past life is now no more
  The flying howers are gone
Like Transitory dreames slept o're
Those Images are kept in store
  By Memory alone

(2)

The time that is to come is not
  How can it then be mine
This present moment is my Lott
And that as soon as it is gott
  Phillis is onely thine

(3)

Then talke no more of Constancy
  False hearts and broaken vows
If I by Miracle can be
This long lived Minute true to thee
  Tis all that Fate allowes

The first line of the version found in Rawl. Poet. 90, f. 132v. reads: 'All my past Joyes are mine no more'.

XVI. *A Song*: 1691, pp. 43, 44; 1680; 1683; Portland Miscellany; MS. 636F; Add. MS. 27408. Pencil note in Bodleian copy of 1691 'Before 1677'. Thorpe (p. 180) lists a number of song-books where it appears without attribution to Rochester.

XVII. *A Song*: 1691, pp. 44, 45; 1680; 1685; Portland Miscellany. 1680 and the Portland Miscellany have the following additional stanza:

> Then give me *Health*, *Wealth*, *Mirth* and Wine,
> And if busie *Love* intrenches,
> There's a sweet soft Page of mine,
> Do's the trick worth *Forty Wenches*.

XVIII. *A Song*: 1691, pp. 46–8; 1680; 1685; Portland Miscellany. Title in Portland Miscellany (pp. 57, 58), 'The Submission'.

XIX. *Upon his leaving his Mistress*: 1691, pp. 49, 50; 1680; 1685; Female Poems; Tate; MS. 636F.

XX. *Upon Drinking in a Bowl*: 1691, pp. 51, 52, 1680; 1685; Female Poems; MS. 636F; Portland Miscellany. It also appears in *The Works of Anacreon and Sappho. Done from Greek*, London, 1713 and some other collections listed by Thorpe. The title in the Portland Miscellany is 'Nestor'. This poem is a free adaptation or 'imitation' of the eighteenth ode of Anacreon, beginning

> Τον ἄργυρον τορεύων
> Ἥφαιστε μοι ποίησον

Rochester's lyric is an interesting example of the principle of 'imitation', which he used so successfully in satire, applied to lyric poetry. Oldham made a free translation of the same ode of Anacreon which appears under the title of *The Cup* in his *Poems and Translations* (London, 1683), and the various editions of his *Works*.

12 Mastrick] Maastricht, capital of the province of Limburg in Holland and an important fortress in the seventeenth century. Rochester is referring to the taking of the city by the French after a siege that lasted from 6th June till 1st July 1673. Charles II was allied with Louis XIV at this time, and an English contingent under the Duke of Monmouth was with the French besieging army. The poet is also probably making a sly allusion to a mimic siege of Maastricht, which was staged at Windsor for the amusement of the Count in the Summer of 1674. (See Arthur Bryant, *Charles II*, p. 248.)

13 Yarmouth Leaguer: Here again Rochester is referring to the operations against the Dutch in 1673. 'Leaguer' in seventeenth-century English means 'a military camp, esp. one engaged in a siege' (O.E.D.). In July 1673 Prince Rupert's fleet was off the coast of Norfolk with an English force on board, which it was intended to land on the Dutch coast. It was decided to disembark them at Yarmouth, while Rupert dealt with the Dutch fleet under De Ruyter. De Ruyter, however, offered a stout opposition, and, after an indecisive naval action off Kykduin on August 11th, the plan for an invasion of Holland was abandoned. Rochester seems to be applying the term 'leaguer' to the camp formed at Yarmouth when the troops were waiting for Rupert to re-embark them in the summer of 1673. If 'Mastrick' in *l.* 12 refers to the mimic battle at Windsor in the summer of 1674, it would appear that Rochester is laughing at the fire-breathing heroes who failed to invade Holland in 1673 and had to be content with a mock-fight at Windsor in 1674.

15 Sir Sindrophel: 1680, 1685 read Sydrophel(l).
The reference is to Sidrophel, the comic astrologer
in Butler's *Hudibras*, II, 3. *24* love] 1680 c**t.

XXI. *A Song*: 1691, pp. 53, 54, 1680; 1685; Female
Poems; Rawl. Poet, 173. Pencil note in Bodleian
copy of 1691 'Before 1677'. This poem also appeared
anonymously in an undated broadside, 'London
Printed for W. Thackeray, T. Passinger and W.
Whitwood.' The text of the broadside is reprinted in
The Roxburghe Ballads, ed. Ebsworth, IV, 134, 135.
Ebsworth dates the poem 'about 1677'.

XXII. *A Song*: 1691, pp. 55, 56; 1685; Female Poems;
Portland Miscellany. The second stanza of this poem
appears in the following version in Val., Act V,
sc. v, p. 75:

A Song

Kindness hath resistless Charms,
   All beside can weakly move:
Fiercest Anger it disarms,
   And clips the wings of flying Love.

2

Beauty doth the heart invade,
Kindness only can perswade;
It guilds the Lovers servile-chain
And makes the Slave grow pleas'd and vain

Title in Portland Miscellany, p. 58, is 'To Thirsis'.

XXIII. *The Answer*: 1691, pp. 56, 57; 1680; 1683;
Female Poems; Portland MS.; Portland Miscellany.
5–8 The reading adopted in the text is that of a contemporary erratum slip pasted in the copy of 1691 in
the Houghton Library at Harvard (1543. 42. 260*).

This slip corrects the following obviously faulty reading of 1691:

> You insisted on your Slave
> > Humble Love you soon refus'd:
> > Which ingloriously you us'd.
> Hope not then a Pow'r to have.

It is curious that the faulty reading of *l.* 5 ('You insisted', etc.) reappears in all Tonsons subsequent editions (1696, 1701 and 1713), though the correct line order is restored. 1680, 1685 and the Portland Miscellany have the correct reading ('You insulted', etc.). The following version of the first sixteen lines of the poem is found in Lady Rochester's handwriting in Portland MS., f. 13, on a small sheet of paper with writing on one side:

> Nothing ades to Loves fond fire
> More then scorn and cold disdain
> I to cherish your desire
> Kindness used but twas in vain
> You insulted on your Slave   5
> To be mine you soon refused
> Hope not then the power to have
> Which ingloriously you used
>
> Thinke not Thersis I will ere
> By my love my Empire loose   10
> You growe constant through dispare
> Kindness you would soon abuse
> Though you still possess my hart
> Scorn and vigor I must fain
> There remains noe other art   15
> Your love fond fugitive to gain

There are several corrections in the MS. in Lady Rochester's hand. In *l.* 3 'cherish' has been substituted for 'lighten', and in *l.* 11 'growe' for an illegible word; 'My' is deleted before 'kindness' in *l.* 12

and in *l.* 15 'there' is substituted for 'since'. It is quite possible that Lady Rochester is the author of this poem and that she wrote it as an answer to no. XXII. See *Rochester, Portrait of a Restoration Poet* by V. de S. Pinto, p. 64. The following variants occur in 1680:

5 o're] 1680 on.   *23* the] 1680 your.   *24* kill] 1680 sell.

XXIV. *A Song to Chloris*: 1691, pp. 59–61; 1680; 1685; MS. 636F; Portland Miscellany. 1680, 1685 and the Portland Miscellany have the following additional stanza:

> Frighted she wakes, and waking Friggs.
> > Nature thus kindly eas'd,
> In Dreams rais'd by her murm'ring *Piggs*,
> And her own Thumb between her Leggs,
> > She innocent and pleas'd.

MS. 636F has the following version of stanza 5:

> Frighted all this away she flyes
> > Not blushes to her face
> Nor the bright Lightning from the Skies
> Nor Love shott by her brighter eyes
> > Flew halfe so swift a pace.

XXV. *Constancy*: 1691, pp. 62, 63; 1680; Portland Miscellany. A version of this poem also appears on f. 11 of Add. MS. 27408 on the same sheet and in the same hand as several authentic poems of Rochester. This version is headed 'To Madam P ff G'. The version in the Portland Miscellany, pp. 38, 39, is headed 'Lett^r' and begins with the word 'Madam'. It is followed by an obscene 'Answer' in the same metre. Mr D. Vieth states that he has evidence that this poem is not by Rochester, but until his evidence is forthcoming, it must remain in the Rochester canon as it is attributed to him in 1680, 1685 and 1691.

XXVI. *A Song*: 1691, p. 64; ABM. Not in 1680, 1685 or MS. 636F. Title in ABM, p. 43, is 'Song by the Earl of *Rochester*'.

XXVII. *A Song:* Examen Poeticum, pp. 381, 382. This poem does not appear in 1680, 1685, 1691 or MS. 636F. It appears to have been printed for the first time in Examen Poeticum, and it was reprinted in some of the eighteenth-century editions of Rochester's works. In Examen Poeticum the poem is headed 'A Song by the Earl of *Rochester*' and I have no doubt that this attribution is correct. The same collection includes several poems of markedly inferior quality ascribed to '*My Ld. R.*', which have been reprinted in various editions of Rochester's works. I do not believe that any of them are by Rochester. On p. 424 there appears another poem attributed to Rochester, see below, no. XXX and note.

XXVIII. *A Song ⟨from Valentinian⟩*: Val., p. 42. This song occurs in Act IV, sc. ii, of the play, where it is sung by the servants of the lustful Emperor Valentinian as part of his plan to seduce the virtuous Lucina, whom he has lured to his palace by a trick. In the text of the quarto edition, the poem is printed in italic type with the headings 'Nymph', 'Shepherd' and 'Chor.' in roman. This arrangement of founts is reversed in the text of the present edition.

A different version of this poem appears on pp. 125, 126 of Female Poems. This collection contains a dozen other poems ascribed to Rochester elsewhere on good authority. The following is the version in Female Poems:

> Insulting charmer of my languish'd Heart.
>> Canst thou feel Love, and yet not let me go?
> Since of my self from thee I cannot part;
>> Devise some gentle way to let me go.

For what with ease thou didst obtain,
    And I with more did give;
In time will make thee false and vain,
    And me unfit to live

Then let our flaming Hearts be joyn'd
    Whole in the smoking Fire,
Ere you prove false or I prove kind,
    Together both expire.

XXIX. ⟨*Song*⟩: Portland MS., f. 1, in Rochester's autograph on both sides of a small sheet of paper. It was first printed by Mr. F. Needham in *The Welbech Miscellany*, p. 51, and it is quoted in full in Rochester, *Portrait of a Restoration Poet*, by V. de S. Pinto (1935), p. 64. The punctuation in the text is partly mine; there is no punctuation in the MS. except a comma after 'Worth' (*l.* 5), another after 'brest' (*l.* 12) and a full stop after 'by' (*l.* 12).
13. The word 'powerfull' is crossed out before 'God' in the MS. and 'Els' added before 'the'. An illegible word is crossed out before 'heavnly' and 'his' seems to be substituted, though this is not quite clear.
16 'Had soe' is written above two words that have been crossed out. They are possibly 'Must have'.

XXX. *Song*: Portland MS., f. 2, in Rochester's autograph on one side of a small sheet of paper. I have preserved the punctuation of the original, but have added a colon after 'vanquish' in *l.* 2 and a comma after 'posses' in *l.* 3.
The following slightly different version of the poem appears on p. 424 of Examen Poeticum (see above, note to no. XXVII, p. 174):

Too late, alas! I must confess
    You need no Arts to move me
Such charms by Nature you possess
    'Twere madness not to love you [*sic*].

> Then spare a Heart you may surprise
> And give my tongue the glory
> To boast, tho my unfaithful Eyes
> Betray a tender story.

This poem is headed in Examen Poeticum 'A Song in Imitation of Sir John Eaton's Songs by the late Earl of Rochester:' It follows 'A Song by Sir John Eaton' beginning

> Tell me not I my time misspend,
> Tis time lost to reprove me,
> Persue thou thine, I have my end
> So *Cloris* only love me.

XXXI. ⟨*Song*⟩: Portland MS., f. 3, in Rochester's autograph on one side of a small sheet of paper. First printed on p. 120 of my *Rochester, Portrait of a Restoration Poet* (1935). The punctuation is mine. There is no punctuation in the MS.

XXXII. *Impromptus*: A number of impromptu verses have been ascribed to Rochester. These two specimens are probably the best authenticated. They are quoted by Thomas Hearne, the Oxford antiquary, in his diary under the date of 17th November 1706. Hearne was well acquainted with Francis Giffard, Rochester's former tutor (see Introduction, p. xvi), and his information may be regarded as reliable. The text used is that of *Reliquiae Hearnianae*, edited by Philip Bliss, 2nd edition, London, 1869, i, 119, 120.

(1) Hearne introduces these lines in his diary with the following words:

'King Charles II, duke of York, duke of Monmouth, Laurendine and Frazier (the King's physitian,) being in company, my lord Rochester, upon the king's request, made the following verses.' In his notes Hearne describes Monmouth as 'a half witted man,'

Laurendine as 'a deformed person', Frazier as 'a mean empty physitian' and York as one who 'would not take a jest'. His note on the last line is 'This well said of the king, who was negligent and careless, though otherwise a man of very strong parts.'

(2) Hearne's note on this famous epigram is as follows:

'The lord Rochester's verses upon the king on occasion of his majesties saying, he would leave every one his liberty in talking, when he himself was in company, and would not take what was said at all amiss.'

1707 (p. 135) gives the lines in the form of an inscription 'Posted on White-Hall-Gate':

> Here lives a great and Mighty Monarch
>> Whose promise none relies on;
> He never said a Foolish Thing,
>> Nor ever did a Wise One.

In 1709 (p. 75) they appear in their best known form as 'The King's Epitaph':

> Here lies a Great and Mighty King,
>> Whose Promise none rely'd on:
> He never said a Foolish Thing,
>> Nor ever did a Wise One.

Other impromptus ascribed to Rochester will be found in the Appendix, no. LXXX.

XXXIII. *The Advice*: 1691, pp. 16–18; Kemp; Collins. Neither this nor the next poem appears in 1680 or 1685. The versions of the two poems printed in Kemp and Collins differ slightly from that which appears in 1691. No author's name is attached to them in either of the miscellanies.

24 1691 has a full stop at the end of this line, but it is crossed out in ink in the Bodleian copy.

XXXIV. *The Discovery*: 1691, pp. 19–21; Kemp; Collins.

XXXV. *Could I but make my wishes*, etc.: Portland MS., f. 7. In Rochester's autograph on a small folded sheet with writing on both sides. This poem was first printed by Mr. F. Needham in *The Welbeck Miscellany* (1934), p. 52. I have retained the punctuation of the MS. but have added a semi-colon at the end *l.* 4, full stops at the end of *ll.* 6, 8, 14, 16 and a question mark at the end of *l.* 10.
19 This line was originally 'That not the humble Love of many yeares'. The words 'That not the humble' and 'of' have been crossed out in the MS. and 'Regardless of A' and 'soe' substituted. *21* in] this word is substituted for 'from' crossed out in the MS.

XXXVI. *A very Heroical Epistle In answer to Ephelia*: 1680, pp. 140–2; 1685; 1707; Female Poems; Portland Miscellany. This poem also appeared anonymously in a broadside ('Printed in the Year 1679') with 'My Lord All Pride' (see below, no. LXI) under the title 'A Very Heroical Epistle from my Lord All-Pride to *Doll-Common*'. This is followed by 'The Argument': 'Doll-Common being forsaken by my *Lord-All Pride* and having written him a most lamentable Letter, his Lordship sends her the following answer.' The broadside is reprinted in *The Roxburghe Ballads*, ed. Ebsworth, IV, 3, 575. The poem seems to be a reply to some lines called *Ephelia to Bajazet* which immediately precede it in 1680, Female Poems and the Portland Miscellany. *Ephelia to Bajazet* is almost certainly the work of Sir George Etherege. It is referred to as his in the following lines from *A Familiar Epistle to M*ʳ *Julian, Secretary to the Muses*, attributed to Buckingham and printed as his in his *Miscellaneous Works* (1705) and Works (1715) as well as in several miscellanies.

Poor *George* grows old, his Muse worn out of
   fashion,
Hoarsly she sings Ephelias *Lamentation*.

Bajazet and My lord All-Pride were nicknames for Rochester's enemy John Sheffield, Earl of Mulgrave (afterwards Marquis of Normanby and Duke of Buckinghamshire). Ephelia (possibly a variant of Ophelia) is probably the person whose name appears on the title-page of Female Poems. p. 55
55 Damocles: 1680 Democles, an obvious misprint.

XXXVII. *The Imperfect Enjoyment*: 1680, pp. 28–30; 1685; 1707, etc.; MS. 636F; Portland Miscellany.

XXXVIII. *The Ninth Elegy In the Second Book of Ovid's Amours, Translated*: 1691, pp. 11–117; 1680; 1695; DMP; MS. 636F; Portland Miscellany. In 1691 and DMP the Latin text is printed opposite the English version. The title in DMP (p. 19) is 'Elegy the Ninth. *Englished by the late* Earl of Rochester'. In the Portland Miscellany it is simply headed 'Ovid'.

XXXIX. *The latter End of the Chorus of the Second Act of Seneca's Troas, translated*: 1691, pp. 119, 120; 1680; MS. 636F; Portland Miscellany. 1691 prints the Latin text opposite the English version. The poem is a free rendering of the *Troades* of Seneca, *ll.* 397–408. Title in Portland Miscellany is Seneca's Troas, Act 2, Chorus. Charles Blount wrote to Rochester to thank him for a copy of this poem on 7th February 1679/80. His letter is printed in *The Miscellaneous Works of Charles Blount Esq.*, 1695, p. 117. It is addressed 'To the Right Honourable the Most Ingenious Strephon' and begins as follows:

'My Lord

I had the Honour yesterday to receive from the Hands of an Humble Servant of your Lordship's your most incomperable Version of that Passage of *Seneca's*, where he begins with,—*Post mortem nihil est, ipsaque mors nihil*, &c—and must confess, with your Lordship's Pardon, that I cannot but esteem the Translation to be, in some measure, a confutation of the Original, since what less than a divine and immortal Mind could have produced what you have written? Indeed the Hand that wrote it may become *Lumber*, but sure, the Spirit that dictated it, can never be so: No, my Lord, your mighty Genius is a most sufficient Argument of its own Immortality . . .'

6 or] 1680, *nor*. *14* the everlasting] 1680 MS. 636F, Portland Miscellany. God's everlasting. *14* G⟨ao⟩ls] All the early editions read 'Goals', a spelling that was fairly common in the seventeenth century.

XL. *Lucretius, in his First Book*: 1691, pp. 109, 110, A free version of *ll.* 44–8 of the *De Rerum Natura*, Book I.

XLI. ⟨*Draft of Translation from Lucretius*⟩: Portland MS., f. 5. In Rochester's autograph on one side of a folio sheet. A free version of Lucretius, *De Rerum Natura*, I. 1–6. Punctuation is that of the MS. except for a full stop inserted at the end of *l.* 8.
5 vast regions] These words are written above an illegible word which has been crossed out. *6* the word 'borrow'd' has been crossed out before 'groves' and the words 'of ships' inserted above 'groves on'.

XLII. *Prologue* ⟨*to the Empress of Morocco*⟩: EM. sig. A3, A3v.; Collins; 1691. Text used is that of the quarto of 1673, title that of the version printed in

1691, p. 134, with addition of the words 'to *The Empress of Morocco*'. The text in the quarto is preceded by '*The first* Prologue *at Court*' stated to be 'Written by the Earl of Mulgrave'. Rochester's prologue seems to have been spoken at the second Court performance. It is followed in the quarto by the words 'Written by the Earl of Rochester'. The Court performances of *The Empress of Morocco* probably took place in the spring of 1671/2 (see *Rochester, Portrait of a Restoration Poet*, by V. de S. Pinto, pp. 114, 115).

The words 'To the King' printed after *l.* 22 are from the text of 1691; they do not appear in EM. The Lady Elizabeth Howard who spoke this prologue is not Sir Robert Howard's sister whom Dryden married in 1663, but Lady Betty Howard, daughter of the Earl of Suffolk, who married Thomas Felton in July 1673 (*Savile Correspondence* ed. Camden Society, p. 39) and died in December 1683 (Luttrell's Diary, i, 153).

XLIII. Prologue: SPC, pp. 214, 215; 1707. Title in SPC is 'Prologue by the E. of R——r.' It is reprinted in *A New Collection of Poems Relating to State Affairs*, 1705. There are two MS. versions in the British Museum. One on f. 1 of Add. MS. 21094 (no author's name) is almost identical with the text in SPC. The other on f. 3 of Sloane MS. 655 is headed 'Prologue E. of R.', and is identical with the version in SPC up to *l.* 17, but after that 24 lines follow from a poem called *Tunbridgalia: or the Pleasures of Tunbridge*, which appear on p. 211 of SPC, where the poem is attributed to 'Mr Peter Causton, Merchant'.

XLIV. *Epilogue* ⟨*to Circe*⟩: Circe, p. 59; 1691; Portland Miscellany. Title in quarto edition is *The Epilogue by the Earl of Rochester*. Title in Portland Miscellany, p. 225, is 'The Epilogue to Circe. by: ye E

R——'. The use of italic and roman types in the quarto ed. is reversed in the present text.

14–16: cf. no. L, *ll.* 41–4.

XLV. *Epilogue ⟨To Love in the Dark⟩*: Love in the Dark, sig. N4, N4v; 1691. No author's name is attached to this epilogue in the quarto edition, where it is simply headed 'Epilogue, As it was spoken by Mᵣ *Haines*'. As *Love in the Dark* was dedicated by Fane to Rochester, it is highly probable that the attribution of it to him in 1691 is correct. In the present text the use of italic and roman types in the quarto version has been reversed.

Love in the Dark was produced at Drury Lane in May 1675. Rochester's epilogue is full of satiric allusions to the rival company at Dorset Garden.

4 Smiths in Sattin] This and other passages in the epilogue refer to the recent staging of Shadwell's opera *Psyche* at Dorset Garden in February 1674/5. This was apparently a gorgeous production with elaborate scenic effects. The '*Smiths* in Sattin' are presumably the Cyclops, who, according to the stage direction at the head of Act III, sc. i, were shown at the Court of Cupid 'forging great vases of silver'. The scene opens with a dance of the Cyclops 'hammering the Vases upon Anvils'. *10, 11* Probably these lines refer to Act V, sc. i, of *Psyche*, where the scene 'represents Hell'. 'In the Middle arises the Throne of *Pluto* . . . With the Throne of *Pluto* arise a great Number of Devils and Furies.' *13* losing *Loadum*] Loadum or Lodam was an old English card game and 'losing Loadum' a form of the game in which the loser won. See quotations under 'Loadum' in O.E.D. *31* Opposite this line 1691 prints '(Major Mohun)' in the margin. The reference is to Michael Mohun (? 1620–84), one of the best known actors of the King's company. He began his career as an actor under Beeston in the reign of Charles I, served in the royalist army where he attained the rank of Major, and joined the Drury lane company at the Restoration. *36 the Traytor*] *The Traitor*, a tragedy by James Shirley first acted in 1631 and published in 1635. It was revived several times after the Restoration and was a favourite play of Pepys who saw 'Mr Moon' (i.e. Mohun) act 'very well' in it on 22nd November 1660. *38 Cethegus*] In Ben Jonson's *Catilines' Conspiracy*. Mohun took the part of Cethegus in this play when it was revived by the King's company in December 1668 (see Pepys's *Diary*, ed. Wheatley, VIII, 171).

XLVI. *Sab: Lost*: Portland MS. f. 6. In Rochester's autograph on one side of a quarto sheet. There is no clue to the meaning of this strange dramatic fragment. It is tempting to connect it with Rochester's attempted abduction of Elizabeth Malet on 26th May 1665 (see *Rochester, Portrait of a Restoration Poet*, by V. de S. Pinto, pp. 47–50).

XLVII. *A Scaen of Sir Robert Howard's Play*: Add MS. 28692, ff. 70–5. This MS. is in a small folio which also contains a version of Rochester's *Valentinian* entitled 'Lucina's Rape or the Tragedy of Valentinian'. The contents of the volume are written in a very neat scribal hand. In the Folger Library, Washington, D.C., there is another small folio volume with exactly the same contents. It appears to be a rough copy from which Add. MS. 28692 was made. This Scene was apparently written by Rochester to be inserted in a heroic play called *The Conquest of China* planned by Sir Robert Howard in 1672. In a letter written by him to Rochester on 7th July (? 1672) he speaks of the 'sceen you are pleas'd to write', and declares that he will not 'repine to see how far you [Rochester] exceed mee' (Harl. MS. 7003, f. 56, Prinz, *John Wilmot Earl of Rochester*, pp. 286, 287). Howard seems to have abandoned his project when he heard that Elkanah Settle was writing a play with the same title. Settle's *The Conquest of China, By the Tartars* was produced in 1673/4 and published in 1675. Many years later, in 1697, Howard thought about the sketch again and asked Dryden to help him to complete it, but the work was never carried out (see *Rochester, Portrait of a Restoration Poet*, by V. de S. Pinto, pp. 121–4).

XLVIII. *From Valentinian*: Val., pp. 31, 32; Add. MS. 28692. The scene is a 'Grove and Forest'. In the preceding scene (III, 2), Lucina, the chaste wife of Maximus, is walking there with her ladies when she receives news that her husband has been suddenly called back to court by the Emperor, who has already solicited her love. She asks Marcellina to play on her lute to her and she sleeps. Scene 3 opens with a 'Dance of Satyrs' and here apparently an elaborate masque by Sir Francis Fane (printed in Tate) was presented. It consists of a dialogue in verse in which Venus, Mercury and other deities take part and was intended to represent Lucina's dream. At the point at which the extract begins Lucina awakes and addresses the two ladies, Claudia and Marcellina.

XLIX. *The Soliloquy of Maximus*: Val., pp. 56, 57; Add MS. 28692. In Val. this fine dramatic lyric is printed continuously. I have preferred to follow the arrangement of Add. MS. 28692, where it is divided into stanzas.

L. *The Maim'd Debauchee*: 1691, pp. 100–3; 1680; 1685; Female Poems; MS. 636F; Portland Miscellany. Rymer in his Preface to 1691 calls this poem

Rochester's 'Gondibert'. The metre is that of Davenant's *Gondibert*, which Rochester may have intended to parody. Title in MS. 636F is 'The Disabled Debauchee' and in Portland Miscellany 'The Disabled Debauch'.

3 Rivall] MS. 636F Royall. *14* Love] 1680, 1685, MS. 636F, Portland Miscellany Pox.

Between stanzas 9 and 10, 1680, 1685, MS. 636F and Portland Miscellany insert the following stanza, which is omitted in all Tonson's editions:

Nor shall our *Love-fits Cloris* be forgot,
When each the well-look'd *Link-Boy* strove t'enjoy
And the best Kiss, was the deciding *Lot*,
Whether the *Boy* us'd you, or I the *Boy*.

(Text of 1680.)

43, 44 Cf. La Rochefoucauld, *Les Maximes*, XCIII: 'Les vieillards aiment à donner de bons préceptes, pour se consoler de n'être en état de donner de mavvais exemples'. Rochester probably read La Rochefoucauld's *Maximes* (*Réflexions Morales*) in one of the five editions that appeared between 1665 and 1678. Cf. note to no. LXIV, *ll.* 140–56).

LI. *Upon Nothing*: 1691, pp. 104–8; 1680; 1685; RRR; Tate; UNC; Portland Miscellany. This is one of Rochester's best known poems. It was printed in two undated broadsides without the author's name about 1679. Both of them attribute it to 'A Person of Honour'. They were reprinted together from copies in Texas University Library as a Christmas card by Professor R. H. Griffith in 1946. Both misprint the word 'ev'n' in *l.* 1 as 'Eve' and one has 'Light' for 'Life' in *l.* 15. UNC is a separate edition of the poem published by E. Curll in 1711 (26th April according to a MS. note in the Brit. Mus. copy). It is a pamphlet of eight octavo pages claiming to be the 'First Correctly Printed' (see Introduction, p. xliii). Actually, it is merely a reprint of the 'Light' broadside. Professor Griffith appended the following illuminating note to his Christmas card edition, which he has kindly allowed me to reprint. 'The background of the poem is philosophy from Genesis and Plato through Aristotle and St. Augustine to Aquinas. Did God create Nothing or is it coeval with Him? Did God create Matter, is it coeval with Him, is it the offspring of Nothing? Did Matter ever exist without Form? *Form* in stanza 5 is Aristotelian, as "Idea" is Platonic, and each (Idea, Form) has power to attract Matter towards itself. Are Nothing and Matter God's Adversary gods?'

LII. *A Letter from Artemisa in the Town*, etc.: 1691, pp. 65–81; 1680; 1685; MS. 636F.; MS. 623F; Rawl. Poet. 123; Portland Miscellany. There are two broadside editions of this poem. One is a folio of four leaves with a title-page 'Printed for William Leach at the Sign of the Crown in Cornhil MDCLXXIX' (Bodl. Ashm. 1094), and the other consists of two leaves with no title-page or imprint. Both ascribe the poem to 'A Person of Quality'. Rawl. Poet. 123 is a manuscript book of poems which once belonged to John Oldham and contains transcripts of a number of poems in his autograph, including this poem and also Rochester's *Satyr Against Mankind*. There are a few corrections in the margin in another hand which closely resembles Rochester's.

28 Rawl. Poet. 123 has 'As Men that marry, or as Maids', the second 'as' corrected in the margin to 'like'. 29 Rawl. Poet. 123 reads 'Because 'tis ye worst thing y^t they can do', corrected in margin to the reading of the text. 34 Change] Corrected in

margin of Rawl. Poet. 123 to 'chance'. *59* whatever
is] Marginal correction in MS. 636F 'All yᵗ which'.
60 or] Corrected in margin of Rawl. Poet. 123 to
'and'. *63* is] Rawl. Poet. 123 have, corrected in
margin to 'is'. *64* they] Corrected in margin of
Rawl. Poet. 123 to 'they'll'. *68, 69* Marginal note in
Rawl. Poet. 123 'dele'. *70 Bovy's*] Rawl. Poet. 123
B——, expanded in marginal note to 'Boveys'.

James Bovey was an eccentric of Restoration London whose ugliness was a by-word. According to
Aubrey (Brief Lives, ed. Clark, I. 112–15), he was
born in 1622, and was the son of a merchant. He
was in business till he was thirty-two, when he re-
tired and was admitted to the Inner Temple as a
student of 'Lawe Merchant'. Aubrey describes his
appearance as follows: 'he is about 5 foot high,
slender, strait, haire exceeding black and curling at
the end, a dark hazell eie, of a midling size, but the
most sprightly that I ever beheld. Browes and beard
of the colour of his hair.' Pepys met him on 20th
May 1668 and describes him as 'a solicitor, and
lawyer and merchant all together, who hath travelled
very much, did talk some things well; but only he is
a Sir Positive'. Oldham alludes to Bovey's ugliness
in *The Eighth Satyr of Monsieur Boileau, Imitated*:

> Gold to the loathsom'st object gives a grace,
> And sets it off, and makes ev'n *Bovey* please.

75 through] Marginal correction in Rawl. Poet. 123
'by'. *84* Fool] Marginal correction in Rawl. Poet.
123 'Fop'. *86* Your beastly] marginal correction in
Rawl. poet. 123, 'That needful'. *101* is] Marginal
correction in Rawl. poet. 123 'dos'. *104* held then]
MS. 636F still thought ('still' correction in a different hand). *105* in] Rawl. Poet. 123 has 'of', corrected in margin to 'in'. *125* trust us, his Follies]
Marginal correction in Rawl. Poet. 123 'trust in his

Follies w^ch'. *130* happy] Rawl. Poet. 123 joyful, corrected to 'happy'. *136* not] Rawl. Poet. 123 &, corrected in margin to 'not'. *143* Miniature] Rawl. Poet. 123 Miniature, corrected in margin to 'Mimicker'. *153* rose] Rawl. Poet. 123 corrects in margin to 'reacht'. *161* Fool of parts] Fool, corrected in margin of Rawl. Poet. 123 to 'Man'. *175* so] Marginal correction in Rawl. Poet. 123 'too'. *183* Foster] Rawl. Poet. 123 Fauster, corrected in margin to 'Foster'. This is probably the Mrs. Foster, a friend of the actress Mrs. Knipp, with whom Pepys dined (and was 'mighty merry' on 23rd April 1668, and whom he met again with Mrs. Knipp on 6th May of the same year. I cannot identify her 'Irish Lord'. *183* Nokes] An obsolete word for 'a ninny or fool'. O.E.D. quotes B.E.'s *Dictionary of the Canting Crew*, 1700, which gives this meaning. *184* Morris] Rawl. Poet. 123 Maurice, corrected in margin to 'Morris'. Nothing seems to be known about Betty Morris. John Hayward in his note on the passage states that she was 'a well known bawd' but quotes no authority. Cokes] An obsolete word (possibly related to 'Cockney') for 'a silly fellow, fool, ninny' (O.E.D.). Rochester may have been thinking of Ben Jonson's gull Master Bartholomew Cokes in *Bartholomew Fair*. *196* Bed] Rawl. Poet. 123 Head, corrected in margin to 'Bed'. *222* Pease] Rawl. Poet. 123 Peace, corrected in margin to 'Pease'. *236* Town] Rawl. Poet. 123 Times, corrected in margin to 'Town'. *239* a Blood] Rawl. Poet. 123 alone, corrected in margin to 'a Love'. *254* kind] Rawl. Poet. 123 such, corrected in margin to 'kind'. *257* Still] Marginal correction in Rawl. Poet. 123 'well'.

LIII. *Tunbridge Wells*: SPC, pp. 218–23; A New Collection of Poems Relating to State Affairs, 1705;

1707; Douce 357. The title of the poem in SPC is 'Tunbridge-Wells. *By the Earl of Rochester, June 30, 1675*'. The same collection includes several other poems attributed to 'the Lord R———' which have been reprinted as Rochester's, but I think it is unlikely that he had anything to do with them. The version in Douce 357 (ff. 136–8) is longer and more indecent than the printed text. It is endorsed 'Lord R. fecit Sep. 20. 81.' The date is probably that on which the copy was made. 1707 prints four additional lines at the end of the poem. In the present edition these lines appear in square brackets as *ll*. 177–80. They are in Rochester's best satiric manner and I have no doubt that they are authentic.

Tunbridge Wells became a fashionable watering-place in the reign of Charles II. See the amusing account of it in Chapter X of *The Memoirs of Count Grammont*.

14 Sir Nicholas Cully]. A ridiculous character in Etherege's *The Comical Revenge* (1664). *48 Canonical Elves*] Rochester may well have been thinking of the opening lines of Chaucer's *Tale of the Wyf of Bath*, where the poet slyly suggests that, while the fairies and elves have been driven out of Britain by the Churchmen, their place has actually been taken by the friars:

> For ther as wont to walken was an elf,
> Ther walketh now the limitour him self.

63 Cobb] the name of the garrulous water-bearer in Ben Jonson's *Every Man in his Humour*. *64 Bayes*] A marginal note in SPC glosses this word as 'Parker'. This is Samuel Parker (1640–88), afterwards Bishop of Oxford. The name Bayes was applied to him by Andrew Marvell in his pamphlet *The Rehearsal Transprosed* (1672/3). It was, of course, the name given by Buckingham to his caricature of Dryden in *The Rehearsal*. Marvell suggests that Mr. Bayes and Parker are alike 'in their understandings, in their humour, in their contempt and quarrelling of all others, though of their own profession'. *64* Importance comfortable] Marvell in *The Rehearsal Transprosed* twits Parker for his use of the phrase 'matters of a closer and more comfortable Importance' (see Works, ed. Grosart, III, 9, 10). *65* Arch-deaconry] Parker, who had formerly been Chaplain to Archbishop Shelldon, was appointed to the Archdeaconry of Canterbury in 1670. *69 Marvel*] Andrew Marvell (1621–78), the famous poet and politician, whose devastating satire in *The Rehearsal Transprosed* was directed against Parker. This is the only reference to Marvell in Rochester's works; Aubrey records that Marvell thought highly of Rochester as a satirist (see Critical Comments, I). *88* Mum] A kind of German beer very popular in England in the seventeenth and eighteenth centuries. The reading of this passage in SPC is

Mum, Bacon, Women and Sempstresses

Hayward reads 'Mum-bacon women' and tries to equate an imaginary word 'Mum-bacon' with 'chaw bacon'. Rochester's meaning, however, is obviously that the crowd included 'Chandlers' (i.e. candle-sellers), Mum-women (i.e. sellers of mum), Bacon-women and Sempstresses. *111* Cribbidge] This game seems to have been introduced into England in the seventeenth century. The first reference to it quoted by the O.E.D. is dated 1630. *118 Scotch Fiddle*] According to the O.E.D. 'Scotch (or Welsh) Fiddle' was a cant term for the itch. *167* Ape] Rochester may have had in mind Spenser's Ape in *Mother Hubberds Tale*, who goes to court 'cloathed like a gentleman' and is shown as the type of the degenerate cowriter who wastes his time with 'thriftles games' and with 'courtizans and costly riotise.' (*ll.* 655–810).

LIV. *An Epistolary Essay from M.A. to O.B.*, etc.: 1691, p. 82; 1680, 1685; MS. 636F; MS. 623F; Portland Miscellany. This poem is almost certainly an epistle from Rochester to John Sheffield, Earl of Mulgrave (afterwards Marquis of Normanby and Duke of Buckinghamshire), and it was probably written in 1669 just before the two men quarrelled. What the initials 'M.G.' and 'O.B.' stand for has never been explained. They may represent some fanciful nicknames like 'Mercurius Gallicus' and 'Ovidius Britannicus'. In MS. 636F the poem is headed 'To my Lord Mulgrave, from Rochester. An Epistolary Essay from M.G. to O.B. on their Mutuall Poems'. In MS. 623F it is headed 'To my Lord Mulgrave' and signed 'Rochester', and in the Portland Miscellany 'From E.R. to E.M.' In the list of contents of the projected edition of Rochester's poems for which Francis Saunders obtained a licence from the Stationers' Company on 19th November 1690 (*Stationers' Register*, ed. Roxburghe Society, III, 377), the first item is 'An Epistolari Essay from E.R. to E.M.' A pencil note in the Bodleian copy of 1691 rather absurdly alters the initials to 'M.C.' and 'D.B.' and expands them to 'Martin Clifford' and 'Duke of Buckingham'.

10 the *British Prince*] This allusion helps to date the poem. The work to which Rochester refers is *The British Princes: An Heroick Poem* by the Hon. Edward Howard. This poem was published on 19th May 1669 (*Term Catalogues*, ed. Arber, I, 10); it had a bad reception and became the laughing-stock of the Wits. Rochester and Mulgrave quarrelled in November, 1669. The *Epistolary Essay* was, therefore, probably written between May and November 1669.

LV. *An Allusion to Horace*: 1680, pp. 40–3; 1685; 1707; 1714; MS. 636F; Portland Miscellany. 1714 prints the Latin text of Horace's 10th satire of the First Book opposite Rochester's poem. This was one of Rochester's best known works. To judge from allusions in the poem to contemporary events, it was written in the spring of 1675. Where 1680 gives initials only for the proper names, they have been expanded with the help of 1714.

11 Crowns] John Crown (d. ? 1703), author of various plays and poems as well as of a prose romance. *18 S[ettle]*] Elkanah Settle (1648–1724). City poet and author of a number of plays, including *The Empress of Morocco* (1673), for which Rochester wrote an epilogue (see above, p. 53). He is the *Doeg* of Dryden's satire in *Absalom and Achitophel*, Part II. *19 O[tway]*] Thomas Otway (1652–85), the well-known Restoration dramatist. It must be remembered that this passage was written before the production of his best plays, *The Orphan* (1680) and *Venice Preserved* (1682). *32 E[therege]*] Sir George Etherege (1635–1688), the famous wit and dramatist, a close friend of Rochester, whose praise of his originality in this couplet is well deserved. *35 F[latman]*] Thomas Flatman (1637–88). His *Poems and Songs* appeared in 1674. *37 Lee*] Nathaniel Lee (? 1653–92), the well-known dramatist. Rochester is referring in *ll.* 37 and 38 to his second play *Sophonisba, or Hannibal's Overthrow*, produced at Drury Lane in April 1675 and printed in the same year. It is one of the most extravagant and bombastic of the 'heroic' rhyming plays and fully deserves Rochester's censure. A fair specimen

of Scipio's language in the play is the following
speech addressed to Sophonisba in Act IV, sc. i:

> When Ladies rail, a Soldier must be mute:
> Besides I have no leisure to dispute.
> As Helen did to Troy perdition bring,
> Where'er you come, your Eyes destruction fling.
> When will your thirsty Charms with Blood be
>   cloy'd?
> Two Kings you have like that fair Greek
>   destroy'd.

Hannibal speaks like 'a whining Amorous Slave' in
the following speech in Act III, sc. i:

> My heart to others rough, the Soldiers crime,
> As Rocks to Seas, or stubborn Oaks to Wind
> Shall bow to you, as those must yield to Time:
> Forgive my temper, Harden'd with the Steel,
> In which I stood, almost Immortal Man,
> Till Love let fall a Blow, that made me reel,
> And pointed Beauty through my Armour ran.

40 B[usby's]] Richard Busby (1606–95), the famous
headmaster of Westminster School, where Lee, like
Dryden, was educated. He was a fine classical
scholar and must have been astonished at the way
in which his former pupil treated Roman history in
Sophonisba if he ever read the play. Cf. with this
passage no. LXIV, which probably refers to Lee.
43 Shadwel] Thomas Shadwell (? 1642–92), the well-
known dramatist, a favourite of the Court Wits,
and an intimate friend of Rochester, Dorset and
Sedley. *ll*. 44–9 are an acute criticism of his powerful,
realistic comedies. *Wicherley*] William Wycherley
(? 1640–1712), the famous dramatist. This criticism
was probably written after the production of his
best play *The Country Wife* in January 1674/3. *54
Waller*] Edmund Waller (1606–87), the old courtly

poet whose works were much admired at the Restoration Court. Etherege makes his Dorimant quote some lines of Waller in *The Man of Mode*. Dorimant was generally supposed to be a portrait of Rochester, and John Dennis in his *Defence of Sir Fopling Flutter* gives a list of the qualities of Rochester which are found in Dorimant, the last of them being 'his repeating, on every occasion, the Verses of *Waller*, for whom that noble lord had a very particular esteem'. *59 Buckhurst*] Charles Sackville, Lord Buckhurst, afterwards Earl of Middlesex and Earl of Dorset (1643–1706), the famous courtier, poet and wit, one of Rochester's most intimate friends. The use of the title 'Buckhurst' seems to indicate that the poem was written before 4th April 1675, when Sackville was created Earl of Middlesex. See *Charles Sackville, Poet and Patron of Literature*, by Brice Harris (University of Illinois Press, 1940), p. 62. *63 warm*] the Folger and some other issues of 1680 misprint this word as 'worm'. All the 1680 edd. have a full stop at the end of this line, obviously a mistake for a comma. *64 Sidley*] Common spelling of the name of Sir Charles Sedley (1639–1701), another celebrated member of the circle of Court Wits. A number of Sedley's love poems, to which Rochester is referring here, had appeared in Kemp's collection of 1672 and Collins's of 1673. See *Sir Charles Sedley, A Study in the Life and Literature of the Restoration*, by V. de S. Pinto (Constable, 1927). *71 D[ryden]*] John Dryden (1631–1700) was a man of forty-four when this poem was written; he was Poet Laureate and author of a number of successful plays. In *ll.* 71, 72 Rochester is doubtless referring to the period in Dryden's career when he was intimate with the Court Wits. In 1673 he dedicated one comedy, *Marriage à-la-Mode*, to Rochester, and another, *The Assignation*, to Sedley. Both these dedications show that at that time he was on very friendly terms with two of the most prominent of the 'tearing blades'. *In Marriage à-la-Mode* he attempts with considerable success to emulate the 'nice way of wit' of the courtiers. *81–4* Rochester is certainly referring here to Dryden's strictures on the 'poets of the last age' in his Epilogue to *The Second Part of the Conquest of Granada* and his *Defence of the Dramatic Poetry of the Last Age* (both published in 1672). In the Epilogue he writes that

> *Johnson* did mechanic humour show,
> When men were dull, and conversation low.

In *The Defence of the Epilogue* he criticizes the language of Shakespeare and Fletcher severely: 'But, malice and partiality set apart, let any one who understands English, read diligently the works of Shakespeare and Fletcher, and I dare undertake, that he will find in every page either some solecism of speech or some notorious flaw in sense.' Other passages in Dryden's writings which Rochester may have had in mind are the famous 'character' of Shakespeare in *An Essay of Dramatic Poesy* (1668), where he declares that Shakespeare 'is many times flat, insipid; his comic wit degenerating into clenches, his serious swelling into bombast', and the passage in the preface to *An Evening's Love or the Mock Astrologer* (1671), where he comments on Ben Jonson's lack of 'wit'.

94 Mustapha] *The Tragedy of Mustapha, Son of Solyman the Magnificent*, a 'heroic' rhyming tragedy by Roger Boyle, Earl of Orrery, produced in April, 1665 and printed in 1668. *The English Princess*] If this reading is correct the reference must be to *The English Princess, Or the Death of Richard III*, by John Caryll, staged and published in 1667. *1714* reads *Island Princess*; if this is the correct reading Rochester would be referring to the altered version of this play of Beaumont and Fletcher staged at the King's House in January 1668/9. *109 Betty M[orice]]* See above, note to *l.* 184 of LI. *110 B[uckley's]*] The name is completed in this form in MS. 636F, Portland Miscellany and 1714. 1707, 1709, and later editions read 'Buckhurst's'. Buckley is the usual contemporary spelling of the name of Henry Bulkley, a well-known courtier and Master of the Household to Charles II. *112* Pur-blind *Knight*] probably Sir Car Scroope (1649–80), a minor court wit and versifier. See note to nos. LXXIII, LXXIIIA, LXXIIIB. *118, 119* The names in this list are given in this form in 1714 and most of the later editions. MS. 636F has the following version:

> Sedley, Shadwell, Buckhurst, Wicherley,
> Godolphin, Butler, Shephard, Buckingham.

Professor J. H. Wilson has suggested to me that Sheppard's name may have been substituted for that of Savile (Rochester's friend Henry Savile) when Sheppard became better known later on as a member of the circle of Wits. *119 S[heppard]*] Sir Fleetwood Sheppard (1634–98) was a protégé of the Earl of Dorset, a minor poet and steward to Nell Gwyn. G[odolphin]] Sidney Godolphin (1645–1712), the well-known statesman, in his youth one of the minor Wits at the court of Charles II. B[utler]] Samuel Butler (1612–80), 'the famous satirist,' author of *Hudibras*. B[uckingham]] George Villiers, Second Duke of Buckingham (1628–87), Dryden's Zimri, an intimate friend of Rochester.

LVI. *Satyr ⟨commonly called Timon, a Satyr⟩*: 1680, pp. 105–10; 1685; MS. 636F; Portland Miscellany.

This poem appears as Rochester's in 1680, 1685 and some of the eighteenth-century editions of his works as well as in MS. 636F. It is not ascribed to any author in the Portland Miscellany, where it is simply headed 'Satyr'. It is attributed to Buckingham in Buckingham's *Miscellaneous Works* (1704) and elsewhere. In Buckingham's *Works* (1715) it is attributed to 'the Duke of Buckingham, and the Earl of Rochester'. Both Giles Jacob in his *Poetical Register* (1723) and Horace Walpole in his *Catalogue of Royal and Noble Authors* (1758) state that the poem was written jointly by Buckingham and Rochester. Pope apparently believed it to be the work of Rochester (see p. lix above). It is quite probable that both this and the following poem (no. LVII) were written by Rochester in collaboration with one or more of his friends.

Harold F. Brooks in an article contributed to N. and Q., 28th May 1938, showed from a study of allusions to contemporary events in the poem that it must have been written in the spring of 1674.

The basis of the poem is probably the Third Satire of Boileau, and Timon's opening lines owe something to the opening of Horace's Ninth Satire of the First Book. In the 1739 and other eighteenth-century editions of Rochester's works it is called *The Rehearsal, a Satire* and in Buckingham's *Works* (1718), *Timon, a Satyr, in Imitation of Monsieur Boleau, upon several Passages in some new plays then Acted upon the Stage.* 15 *The praise of pious Queens*] I have been unable to find any work with this precise title. I think Rochester is probably alluding to one of the works of Thomas Heywood (1574–1650) in praise of famous women. He may well have had in mind such a popular work as Heywood's *The Exemplary Lives and Memorable Acts of Nine the Most Worthy Women of the World*

(London, 1640), which gives an account of nine celebrated women, three Jewish, three Gentile and three Christian, ending with Queen Elizabeth, who is described as 'a Vestall for virginitie, a Mirrour of Majestie, no lesse celebrated for religious pietie, than regall dignitie'. The work is illustrated by woodcuts; a copy may well have been in the possession of Rochester's pious mother and have amused him when he was a child. *16 S[hadwell's]* unassisted former *Scenes*] 1680 prints only the initial of the proper name here and elsewhere in the poem. The full names appear in Buckingham's *Works* and in the eighteenth-century editions of Rochester's *Works*. The fact that Shadwell received help from Sir Charles Sedley in the writing of his comedies is alluded to by Dryden in the well-known couplet in *Mac Flecknoe*:

> And let no alien Sedley interpose
> To lard with wit thy hungry Epsom prose.

In the dedication of *A True Widow* (1679), Shadwell acknowledges that this comedy 'had the benefit' of Sedley's 'correction and alteration'. If *Epsom Wells* 1672) was the first play of Shadwell's in which Sedley assisted him, the 'unassisted former scenes' would refer to his early comedies *The Sullen Lovers* (1668), *The Humorists* (1671) and *The Miser* (adapted from Molière) (1672), and the pastoral play *The Royal Shepherders* (1669). *32 Savill*] Henry Savile (1642–85), one of Rochester's closest friends. See *The Rochester-Savile Correspondence*, ed. J. H. Wilson (Columbus, Ohio, 1941). *46 ⟨to⟩*] this word is omitted in the Folger copy of 1680, but appears in some of the other 1680 editions. *55 French Kings success*] The successes of the armies of Louis XIV in Flanders and the Rhineland in the war which began in 1672. *57 two Women at one time*]

The reference is to Louis XIV's two mistresses, Louise de la Vallière and Madame de Montespan. *69 Terse*] The usual English seventeenth-century word for the wine which we call claret. *71 Champoon*] champagne. Although wine had been made in Champagne from very early times, the kind of sparkling wine which we call champagne is said to have been invented by a monk called Dom Perignon in the reign of Louis XIV; the same monk is said also to have invented corked wine-bottles. Champagne was a fashionable novelty at the court of Charles II. *75 M[ordaunt]*] Some of the eighteenth-century editions complete this name as '*Mordaunt*' and some as '*Mazarine*'. If '*Mordaunt*' is the correct reading, the reference is probably to Lady Mary Mordaunt, daughter of the Earl of Peterborough, who was afterwards divorced by her husband, the Duke of Norfolk. '*Mazarine*' would refer to Hortense Mancini, the famous Duchess of Mazarin. It is unlikely, however, that this is the correct reading, as the Duchess did not reach England till the winter of 1675/6. See below, note to no. LXXXI, *l.* 114. *91 Porter B[lunt]*] This may refer to Mountjoy Blount, Earl of Newport (1597–1666), an old Cavalier who was made a Gentleman of the Bedchamber of Charles II after the Restoration. *92 Harris*] This is probably the actor Henry Harris, an original member of Sir W. Davenant's company, who acted Romeo to Betterton's Mercutio. See note in Pepys's *Diary*, ed. Wheatley, III, 203. *Cullen*] This must be Elizabeth, wife of Brien Cokayne, Viscount Cullen. She was noted for her extravagance and beauty. Two portraits of her by Lely survive, one 'whole length as Venus perfectly nude'. See G.E.C. Peerage, III, 563 n. *105 Falkland*] The famous Lucius Cary, second Viscount Falkland (1610–43). The lady was probably thinking less of his verses than of his personality. See the celebrated description of him in Book IV of Clarendon's *History of the Rebellion*. *Sucklings, easie Pen*] The 'ease' of the poetry of Sir John Suckling (1609–42) was highly esteemed in the Restoration period. Dryden praised him in *An Essay of Dramatic Poetry* for expressing 'the conversation of a gentleman', and as late as 1700 Congreve's Millamant delights in 'natural easy Suckling'. *111. my Lord of O[rrery]*] Roger Boyle, first Earl of Orrery (1621–79), author of a number of rhyming 'heroic' tragedies and two comedies. Mustapha and Zanger are both characters in his very popular tragedy *Mustapha* first produced in August 1664 and greatly admired by Pepys, who saw it several times. It was published in 1668 in a folio with the same author's *History of Henry the Fifth*. *115, 116* These two very flat lines are from Orrery's tragedy *The Black Prince*. This play was produced in October 1667 and printed in a folio with the same author's *Tryphon* in 1669. The lines quoted in the text are *ll*. 273, 274 of Act II, sc. 1, of *The Black Prince*. They are spoken by the Prince to Delaware. In the folio of 1669 they appear in the following version:

And which is worse, if worse then this can be,
She for it ne're excus'd her self to me.

120–3 E[therege]] 'Airy Songs' and 'soft Lampoons' describe very aptly the extant lyrics and satires of Sir George Etherege. In the following lines Rochester is probably twitting him for his lack of a formal education. The 'Two talking *Plays* without one *Plot*' are *Love in a Tub* (1664) and *She Wou'd If she Cou'd* (1668). This poem was written before the appearance of Etherege's third play, *The Man of Mode*, staged in March 1675/6. *124 S[ettle]*,... *Morocco*] The reference is to Elkanah Settle's *The Empress of Morocco*, for which Rochester wrote a prologue, when it was produced at Court in 1671/2. See note to no. XXXVII. *126–8* These three lines occur on pp. 9, 10 of E.M. (Act 2, sc. i), but they are not consecutive. *l.* 126 is *l.* 10 of E.M. slightly misquoted. The line in the quarto of 1673 reads

> Their lofty Bulks the foaming Billows bear

It is part of Hamethalhaz's speech describing the fleet of Muley Hamet. The other two lines (127, 128) are *ll.* 61 and 62 of Act 2, sc. i, of the play appearing on p. 10 as part of the speech of Abdelcador, when he boasts of the towns taken by Muley Hamet. In the quarto they read as follows:

> *Saphee* and *Salli*, *Mugadore*, *Oran*,
> The fam'd *Arzille*, *Alcazer*, *Tituan*.

130 Crown] See above, note to LIV, *l.* 11. Crowne's romance was *Pandion and Amphigenia; or the Coy Lady of Thessalia*, published in 1665 when (according to the dedication) the author was 'scarce twenty years'. *The History of Charles VIII, Or the Invasion of Naples by the French* was acted in 1671 and published in 1672. *136–8* These lines are from Crowne's *The History of Charles VIII*, Act I, sc. 2. (*ll.* 85–7), where they are spoken by Ferdinand, Prince of Naples. *143, 144* These are the third and fourth lines of Act I, sc. 1, of Dryden's *The Indian Emperour*, where they are spoken by Cortez. *150 Souches*] Ludwig Raduit de Souches, an Austrian general, who commanded the Imperial forces for a short time in 1674. Harold F. Brookes in the article in N. and Q. quoted above has shown that Souches was confronting Turenne's French army in the spring of 1674, between March and May, when this poem must have been written. *151 Turene*] Henri de Latour D'Auvergne, Vicomte de Turenne (1611–75), the famous Marshal of France. *175 Hectors*]

This word was used in the second half of the seventeenth century for 'a set of disorderly young men who infested the streets of London' (O.E.D.).

LVII. *A Session of the Poets*: 1680, pp. 111–14; 1685, MS. 623F; MS. 636F; Osborn MS., Chest II, no. 14. It also appears in *The Miscellaneous Works Written by his Grace George, Late Duke of Buckingham, London, 1704*, and in the first vol. of *The Works of His Grace, George Villiers, late Duke of Buckingham, London, 1715*. In both these Collections it is attributed to Buckingham and Rochester. It appears without attribution in MS. 623F and MS. 636F. In Osborn MS., Chest II, no. 14, the poem is headed 'The Sessions of the Poetts: 167-$\frac{9}{7}$', but no author's name is appended.

This poem is one of a number of similar English works written in the seventeenth and early eighteenth centuries. The fashion was probably due to the popularity of Boccalini's *De' Ragguagli di Parnaso*, printed at Venice in 1612 and englished by Henry Carey, Earl of Monmouth, whose version appeared in 1656. A useful account of the various English 'Sessions of the Poets', 'Trials for the Bays' and poems and pamphlets of a similar nature is to be found in the Introduction to *A Journal from Parnassus*, edited by Hugh Macdonald (P. J. Dobell, London, 1937). The earliest English 'Session of the Poets' was probably that of Sir John Suckling, written about 1637 and first printed in his *Fragmenta Aurea* in 1646. There has been a good deal of discussion of the poem attributed to Rochester. R. G. Ham in his *Otway and Lee* (New Haven, 1931) and elsewhere argued that it was the work of Settle. J. H. Wilson in his important article on 'Rochester's "A Session of the Poets"' in R.E.S., xxii, 1946, summarized all the available evidence and concluded (1) that the poem could not be by Settle, (2) that Rochester was probably the author, (3) that the poem may well have been composed by a group of Court Wits under Rochester's leadership. He recommended that, until further evidence appeared, the poem should 'rest quietly in the Rochester canon'.

From the allusions in the poem, the date of its composition can be fixed as some time in the spring of 1676/7, and this is borne out by the date given in the Osborn MS. Most of the proper names appear only in the form of initials in 1680. They have been completed with the help of the other printed texts and MS. 636F. *14 R[eeve]*] Anne Reeve, an actress in Killigrew's company. She took the parts of Esperanza in Dryden's *The Conquest of Granada* and Philotis in *Marriage à-la-Mode*, and entered a nunnery about 1675. She was commonly reputed to be Dryden's mistress. *16 gentle George*] the usual nickname for Sir George Etherege among the Court Wits. *20 Seav'n years*] Etherege's second play *She Wou'd if She cou'd* was first staged in February 1667/8. About seven years elapsed till the production of his third and last comedy, *The Man of Mode* in March 1675/6. If we take 'Seav'n years' literally, *A Session of the Poets* could not have been written earlier than February 1675/6. *26 Tom S[hadwell] does wallow*] In the preface to his play *Ibrahim or the Illustrious Bassa* (1677) (see below, note to *l.* 47), Settle writes of Shadwell 'No sooner comes a play upon the Stage, but the first day 'tis Acted, he wallows into the Pit like a Porpoise before a Storm' (*Preface to Ibrahim*, ed. Macdonald, Luttrell Society, p. 18). *29 his Wife*] Mrs. Shadwell (formerly Ann Sibbs) was an actress in Davenant's company. *44 Ovid*] A reference to Lee's play *Gloriana or the Court of Augustus Caesar* (produced January 1675/6, published in 1676) in which Ovid appears as the

romantic lover of Julia, the daughter of Augustus.
47 Ibrahim] This is Elkanah Settle's play *Ibrahim or
the Illustrious Bassa*, staged in June 1676. These
lines must have been written shortly after its publication in the spring of 1676/7. *Ibrahim* contains a
polemical *Preface to the Reader* in which Settle
makes a violent attack on Shadwell. Most extant
copies of the play do not contain this preface, but it
appears in one of the copies in the British Museum
(c. 57, i. 50) in a gathering of four leaves inserted
after sig. A. It has been reprinted by the Luttrell
Society with an introduction by Hugh Macdonald
(Luttrell Society Reprints, no. 2, Oxford, 1947).
Macdonald expresses the opinion that the preface
was added to a few copies after the bulk of the
edition had been sold, but he seems to have overlooked this passage which suggests that Settle had
it removed after the publication of the play. *49
Newport*] This is presumably the 'young Newport'
mentioned by Pepys in his Diary, s.d. 30th May
1668, as an associate of Harry Killigrew and the
fast set called 'The Ballers'. He appears to have been
a son of Francis Newport, Lord Newport and Earl
of Bradford. *55 Don C[arlos]*] Otway's heroic tragedy, produced with Betterton as Philip II at Dorset
Gardens in June 1676 with great success. 'Certainly
one of the finest tragedies of the period' (J. C. Ghosh,
The Works of Thomas Otway, Oxford, 1932, I, 40).
61 C[rowne]] See above, note to no. LIV, *l.* 11.
73 Poetess Afra] The well-known writer Aphra
Behn (1640–89), who was about thirty-six at the
time when these lines were written. *79 ⟨her⟩...
⟨were⟩*] 1680 and the two editions of Buckingham's
works read

He told her were Conquests, and Charmes her
pretence.

81 ⟨At last Mamamouche⟩] 1680, 1685 and Buckingham's *Miscellaneous Works* (1704) and Works (1715) read the meaningless word 'Anababaluthu' here. This must be a mistake of the compositor confronted with a strange collection of syllables. MS. 623F gives the reading adopted in the text, which is obviously the correct one with the marginal note, 'Mr. Ravens'. The reference is certainly to Edward Ravenscroft (fl. 1671–97), author of an adaptation of Molière's *Le Bourgeois Gentilhomme*, published under the title *The Citizen Turn'd Gentleman* in 1672 and reissued in 1675 as *Mamamouchi*. 'Mamamouchi' is the imaginary Turkish title conferred on Monsieur Jourdain in Molière's play. 82 *Tom Essences* Author] MS. 623F has the marginal note 'Mr. Rawlins'. The reference is to Thomas Rawlins, author of *Tom Essence: or the Modish Wife*, produced in September 1676 and published early in the following year. 83–5 D[*urfey*]] Thomas Durfey (1653–1723), author of numerous plays and songs. His *Madam Fickle, or the Witty False One* was produced in November 1676 and published in 1677. 89 Tom B[*etterton*]] Thomas Betterton (1635–1710), the famous actor, author of several plays adapted from Shakespeare, Molière, Fletcher, Webster and Massinger. 97 In the version of the poem printed in Buckingham's *Miscellaneous Works* (1704), p. 46, this line appears with the word 'Made' in Gothic type. In Buckingham's *Works* (1715) it also appears in Gothic type and is spelt 'Maid'. Apparently a pun is intended with reference to Betterton's play adapted from Webster entitled *Appius and Virginia, Acted under the name of the Roman Virgin or the Unjust Judge*, produced in 1669 and published anonymously in 1679.

LVIII. *The History of Insipids*: SCNIP, pp. 9, 10;

POAS; 1707; 1709, etc.; Portland Miscellany. In 1707, p. 86, the title is 'The Restauration Or the History of Insipids; A. Lampoon'. The title in the Portland Miscellany is 'The Chronicle'. An edition of the poem was published by H. Hills in 1709 under the title *The History of Insipids, a Lampoon*, together with Rochester's *Farewell* and *Marvil's Ghost* by Mr. Ayloff. In the British Museum copy of SCNIP the words 'By John Earl of Rochester' are written in a neat late seventeenth-century hand below the title. The proper names and other words represented only by initial letters in the printed text are completed in the same hand and these MS. completions have been adopted in the text.

12 Grandsire Harry] Henry IV of France, father of Henrietta Maria, Charles II's mother. *13 Romish* Bondage breaker *Harry*] Henry VIII. *21 conscience tender*] the Declaration of Breda issued by Charles II just before his restoration promises an 'Indulgence to tender consciences'. On 26th December 1662 he issued a 'Declaration of Liberty to tender Consciences' and on 15th March 1672 a 'Declaration of Indulgence for tender consciences'. *23, 24.* These lines may possibly echo Charles's conversation. In December 1669 Sir Robert Moray in a letter to Lauderdale wrote of the King as follows: 'He is now beginning to declare himself more vigorously against persecution of people for their religion and says upon that subject things most pungent and unanswerable' (A. Bryant, *King Charles II* (1931), p. 209n.) *43 Blood*] Thomas Blood (? 1618–80), an Irish adventurer who tried to assassinate the Duke of Ormonde in 1670 and to steal the Crown jewels on 9th May 1671. With an accomplice he actually made off with crown and globe before he was caught and arrested. He was interrogated by Charles II in person, who was so pleased with his replies that he pardoned him and gave him back his Irish estates. The statement that Blood wore 'Treason in his Face' is borne out by the following passage in Evelyn's *Diary* (10th May 1671): 'The man had not only a daring but a villainous unmerciful looke, a false countenance, but very well spoken and dangerously insinuating' (*Diary*, ed. A. Dobson, II, 322). *49–60.* Cf. with these stanzas Trevelyan's description of the same Parliament (the 'Cavalier Long Parliament' of 1660–78): 'In the course of nineteen sessions, the members became habitual residents in London. Their persons and prices were well known at Whitehall. Neither George III nor Walpole, nor even Danby was the first to protect the position of ministers by the purchase of votes in the House. The system was introduced during the struggle over the accounts of the Dutch War of 1665–8 by statesmen of the new style. Clarendon indeed saw with anger and disdain the country members thronging Whitehall stairs, and going off with pensions and places to vote against their conscience' (G. M. Trevelyan, *England under the Stewarts*, p. 376). *67 the first Dutch* War] i.e. the war of 1665–8; this was the first Dutch war after the Restoration. Actually, the first war between England and Holland was Cromwell's war of 1651–4. This poem must have been written after the 'second' (i.e. the third) Dutch war of 1672–4. *69 Opdam*] Jacob Opdam or Obdam, Dutch admiral. He was defeated and killed in the naval action of 13th June 1665 when his ship blew up. *70 his Highness*] James, Duke of York. 'The duke, who had borne himself bravely in the fight, had gone to bed, leaving order that the fleet should keep its course. Henry Brouncker, a groom of his bedchamber afterwards delivered an order purporting to come from James, to slacken sail and thus allow the Dutch to escape'

(D.N.B., s.a. James II of England). *73 The Bergen Business*] the naval action off Bergen on 1st August 1665, in which Rochester took part. See Introduction, pp. xix, xx. *78 Skellum*] 'a rascal, scamp, scoundrel, villain' (O.E.D.). Applied here to the Dutch treasure fleet which escaped at Bergen. *79 choos'd*] probably for 'choused' from choase=to dupe, cheat, trick' (O.E.D.), a fairly common word in seventeenth-century English, apparently derived from a Turkish word. See note under 'chouse' in O.E.D. *83 Holms*] Sir Robert Holmes (1622–92), one of the chief English admirals of the period. In March 1672 he attacked the Dutch Smyrna Fleet off the Isle of Wight before war had been declared. This fleet was said to contain treasure worth a million and a half, and Holmes's attack was mere piracy. It was a failure, and, according to Andrew Marvell, 'all the Prize that was gotten sufficed not to pay the Chirurgeons and Carpenters' (*An Account of the Growth of Popery*, 1678). Marvell refers to the affair in *The Statue in the Stocks Market*, *ll.* 51, 52 (if that poem be his: See *The Poems and Letters of Andrew Marvell*, ed. H. M. Margoliouth, I, 180, 303). *80, 82.* All the printed editions read full stops after 'wise' and 'surprise'. To make sense of the passage it is obviously necessary to read a comma after 'wise' and a question mark after 'surprise'. The grammar is rather clumsy, but the meaning is clearly 'Would not Charles have scored off the States (i.e. the Dutch Republic) nicely (having learnt a lesson from the disaster at Bergen) and completely humiliated them by the surprise of their rich Smyrna Fleet? If only haughty Holms had called in Spragg, then indeed there would have been rich pickings.' *83 Spragg*] Sir Edward Spragg (killed in action 1673), one of the most brilliant English naval commanders of the period. Rochester served under him in the summer of 1666. Marvell in *An Account of the Growth of Popery* (1677) suggests that the failure of Spragg's squadron to support Holmes in the action against the Smyrna fleet 'proceeded partly from that jealousy (which is usuall to martiall spirits like *Sr. Roberts*) of admitting a Companion to share with him in the Spoile of Honour or Profit'. *89 Chattam*] An ironic allusion to De Ruyter's success of June 1667, when he sailed up the Medway and burnt part of an English fleet off Chatham. *91 Blackheath Host*] Cf. note to no. XX, *l*. 13. The reference is probably to the army which was raised for a landing in Holland in June 1673 when Charles II was allied with Louis XIV. *96 Maestricht*] Cf. note to no. XX, *l*. 12. *99 D'Etrees*] Jean d'Estrees, commander of the French squadron which was sent to co-operate with the English fleet against the Dutch in the summer of 1672. He was accused by the English of holding aloof from the battle of Southwold Bay. *100* To make the *French* of *Holland* Masters] the following Latin couplet with a burlesque translation ascribed to Rochester occurs in Tanner 89, f. 261:

Una dies Lotheros, Burgundos hebdomas una
    Una domat Batavos Luna: quid annus aget?

On Louis XIV burlesqued by the late E. of Rochester:

Lorrain he stole, by fraud he got Burgundy,
Holland he bought and I God He shall pay fort one
    day.

A slightly different version of the English couplet appears in Sancroft 53, p. 39, as Rochester's headed 'On ye French Ks Conquests ...' I owe this information to Dr. Percy Simpson. *101 Carewell*] A common English form of the name of Louise Rénée de Keroualle, Duchess of Portsmouth, the French mistress of Charles II and agent of Louis XIV. Brother *James*] James, Duke of York, who probably became a Catholic about 1670. *Teague*] A contemptuous name for an Irish Roman Catholic. *103–8 Robin Vyner*] Sir Robert Viner (1631–88), a goldsmith and Lord Mayor of London; he was an ardent royalist and erected a statue of Charles II in the Stocks Market or Woolchurch Market on the site of the present Mansion House. A report of the unveiling of this statue appeared in the *London Gazette* for 29th May 1672. It had originally been a statue for John Sobieski, King of Poland, which Viner bought and had altered to represent the English king. It was removed in 1736 and is now said to be at Newby Hall, Ripon. See the poem called *The Statue in the Stocks Market* attributed to Andrew Marvell and H. M. Margoliouth's note on it in his edition of Marvell's *Poems and Letters*, i, 300–3. *108* Bankrupt K[ing]] Viner was actually ruined by the closing of the Exchequer in January 1672, when the King is said to have owed him £416,724. *116* Freeman of *London*] The *London Gazette* of 17th–21st December 1674 gives an account of the presentation of the Freedom of the City of London to Charles II, when the Lord Mayor and Chamberlain were deputed to bring to the King 'the Copy of the Freedom of the City curiously written on Vellom, and adorned with Gilding after the best manner, in a large square Box of massy Gold'. See the satiric ballad *Upon his Majesties being made free of the Citty* attributed to Andrew Marvell and H. M. Margoliouth's notes on it in his edition of *The Poems and Letters of Andrew Marvell*, I, 303, 304. *118 French Jade*] The Duchess of Portsmouth. See above *l.* 101*n*. *120 Grocers*] Cf. *Upon his Majesties being made free of the City*, *ll.* 79–81 (*The Poems and Letters of Andrew Marvell,* ed. H. M. Margoliouth, I, p. 183):

> Then o London rejoice!
> In thy fortunate choyce
> To have made this Freeman of Spices;

Apparently Charles was made an honorary member of the Grocers' Company. *164* all Brutish] Portland Miscellany 'a Brittish'.

LIX. *A Ramble in St. James's Park*: 1680, pp. 14–19; 1685; MS. 636F; Portland Miscellany. The title in the Portland Miscellany is 'A Ramble in ye Park'. There seems no reason to doubt Rochester's authorship of this powerful and indecent poem. It is ascribed to him in MS. 636F, where it is entitled 'Upon ye Night walkers in St. James Park'. The table of contents of a MS miscellany in the Osborn MS. (Chest II, no. 3) includes 'A Sayter on St. Jameses Park by Ld Rochester'. The leaves containing the poem have been torn out, but it is fairly safe to assume that the title in the table of contents refers to this poem.

LX. *On Poet Ninny*: 1680, p. 143; 1685; Portland Miscellany. The name is taken from Shadwell's comedy *The Sullen Lovers: or the Impertinents,* where one of the characters is Ninny, described as 'A conceited Poet always troubling Men with impertinent Discourses of Poetry, and the repetition of his own Verses; in all his Discourse he uses such affected Words, that 'tis as bad as the Canting of a Gipsie'. It has been supposed that 'Poet Ninny' is the Hon. Edward Howard (see note to no. LIV, *l.* 10). *4* gentle *George*] Sir George Etherege (see above note to no. LVII, *l.* 16). *14 Nokes*] James Nokes, the well-known Restoration actor, famous for his success in 'character' parts. He created the part of Ninny in *The Sullen Lovers. 23 Romancy*] Obsolete form of 'romantic'. O.E.D. quotes from Anthony à Wood's *Life*: 'An old house situated in a romancy spot'.

LXI. *My Lord All Pride:* 1680, pp. 144, 145; 1685; Portland Miscellany. This poem is undoubtedly a satire on John Sheffield, Earl of Mulgrave (see Introduction, p. xxiii). It was printed in a broadside dated 1679 with no. XXXVI under the title 'Epigram on My lord All-Pride' (*Roxburghe Ballads*, ed. J. W. Ebsworth, IV, 3, 567).

18 Punchianello] Punchinello or Polichinello was the hero of a seventeenth-century Italian puppet show, the prototype of Punch, which appeared in London soon after the Restoration. Pepys saw 'Polichinello' at Moorfields on 22nd August 1666. See O.E.D., s.a. *Punchinello. 26 Lubbard*] Obsolete form of 'lubber'=a big, clumsy, stupid fellow, a lout (O.E.D.). *30 Knight, o' th' Burning Pestle*] An allusion to Beaumont and Fletcher's well-known burlesque. The name is doubtless applied to Sheffield because of his red nose.

LXII. ⟨*Draft of a Satire on Men*⟩: Portland MS., ff. 9, 10. In Rochester's autograph, written on both sides of one small sheet and one side of another. Corrections in ink and pencil are also in Rochester's hand. Passages enclosed in brackets in the text are crossed out in the MS. I have not attempted to punctuate the draft. The only punctuation in the MS. consists of commas at the ends of *ll.* 7 and 22 and after 'practice' in *l.* 49.

2 'Why wee can' is crossed out in pencil and 'How well we' written above also in pencil. *8–10* These lines are crossed out in pencil. *8* and] substituted in pencil for 'nay'. *21* Above this line there are the following words crossed out in ink:

E're I'de endure this scorne, I live

22 bee] this word is inserted above the line in ink.
28 The line should obviously be completed with the
word 'where'. *31* (Then)] Crossed out in pencil. *33,
34* These lines are crossed out in pencil. Two illegible
words are written in ink above 'wee dayly' in
l. 33. *36* The edge of the paper is clipped and 'sue'
is written above 'next'. It is possible that some such
word as 'do' followed 'next'. *38* Cloath⟨s⟩] The
clipping of the paper is probably responsible for the
disappearance of the 's'. *44* hardly] This word is
crossed out in pencil and an illegible word written
above it. *46* Rollo] The well-known play by Beaumont and Fletcher first published in 1639, with the
title *The Bloody Brother*. It was one of the plays
allotted to Killigrew's company at the Restoration
and was frequently revived by them in the reign of
Charles II. Hart] Charles Hart (d. 1683), great
nephew of Shakespeare and a famous Restoration
actor. He was one of the chief members of Killigrew's company and was Nell Gwyn's 'Charles the
First'. *48* worshipt] Written in pencil above 'hon-
oured', which is crossed out in ink. *53, 54* These
lines are crossed out in pencil. *55* Both are a] These
words are written in pencil.

LXIII. *To forme a Plott*: Portland MS., f. 8. In Rochester's autograph, written on one side of what is
apparently a scrap of a letter with part of the
address on the verso:

'To the Right
the Earle of'.

There is no punctuation in the MS. A full stop has
been inserted at the end of *l.* 5. It is not clear to
whom this fragment refers. The 'Ilustrius Bard' may
be Nat Lee (cf. no. LV, *ll.* 37–40) or Dryden, whose
All for Love (1678) certainly does not follow Plu-

tarch's *Life of Anthony* very closely. The 'Plott' may be Dryden's alliance with Mulgrave, Rochester's enemy, and the last two lines may refer to *An Essay on Satyr*, the lampoon which was circulating in November 1679. Rochester was attacked both in the Preface to *All for Love* and in the *Essay on Satyr*. See Letter XXXIII in *The Rochester–Savile Letters*, ed. J. H. Wilson (Illinois, 1941), and Wilson's notes.

LXIV. *A Satyr against Mankind*: 1680, pp. 6–13; 1685; 1691, etc.; 1709, etc.; MS. 636F; Rawl. Poet. 123; Portland Miscellany. This is the most celebrated of Rochester's poems. John Verney in a letter to Sir Ralph Verney dated 23rd March 1675/6 wrote that he would 'next week send the verses (said to be by Rochester) much after the manner of his satyr against man' (H.M.C. Appendix to Seventh Report, p. 467). If Verney is alluding here to this poem, it must have been written and in circulation before the date of his letter. It was apparently first printed in an undated broadside of four folio pages, where it is ascribed to 'A Person of Honour'. According to Anthony à Wood, the broadside appeared in June 1679 (*Athenae Oxonienses*, ed. Bliss, III, 269). An 'Answer' to the poem also appeared in an undated broadside, where it is ascribed to 'The Reverend Mr. Griffith'. Wood states that the 'Answer' appeared a month after the broadside of Rochester's poem. It is printed after the 'Satyr' in 1714 and elsewhere, and is sometimes attributed to 'Dr. Pocock'. Another answer by Thomas Lessey of Wadham appears in Harl. MS. 2607, f. 60 and is printed in *Poetical Recreations*.

The 'Satyr' exists in two forms, one consisting of 173 lines, and the other an extended version with an additional 51 (or in some versions 49) lines, sometimes headed 'Postscript'. 1707 (pp. 1–4) prints the postscript alone under the title 'An Addition to the

Satyr against Man'. The version printed in the broadside is the shorter one and this suggests that the 'Postscript' may have been added as a rejoinder to the answer by Griffith (or Pocock). Tonson's editions of 1691, 1696 and 1701 all print the shorter version, but the 'Postscript' in a slightly abbreviated form appears in 1714. 1680 (the text adopted in this edition), 1685, MS. 636F and the Portland Miscellany all print the extended version. The transcript in Rawl. Poet. 123 (ff. 110–17), like that of *A Letter from Artemisa*, is in Oldham's hand (see note to no. LII). It is incomplete and only includes *ll.* 1–165. There are a few marginal corrections, which seem to be in Oldham's hand except for two scrawls near the end, which are in a hand that appears to be neither Oldham's nor Rochester's. The title in Oldham's transcript is 'Satyr upon Man', in 1680 'Satyr', in 1691 etc., 'a Satyr against Mankind'.

A valuable study of 'Certain Aspects of the Background' of the poem by S. F. Crocker was published in *West Virginia University Studies*, III, *Philological Papers*, Vol. 2, May 1937. The 'Satyr' has usually been regarded as, in some measure, an 'imitation' of Boileau's Eighth Satire. Crocker, while admitting that Rochester had probably read Boileau's poem and retained certain passages in his mind, argues with great cogency and copious illustration that his chief indebtedness was to Montaigne (especially to the *Apologie de Raimond Sébond*) and to La Rochefoucauld. 'There is scarcely an idea of major or minor importance', he writes, 'in Rochester that is not present in Montaigne.' I am indebted to Crocker's article for some quotations in the following notes. I think he underestimates Rochester's indebtedness to Hobbes.

4 Case] 1691, etc., sort. 8 The senses are too gross] Cf. Montaigne, *Essais*, II, xii (*Ap. de R. Sébond*):

'Nous avons formé une verité par la consultation & concurrence de nos cinq sens, mais à l'avanture falloit il l'accord de huict ou de dix sens & leur contribution pour l'appercevoir certainement en son essence.' *12–28* W. E. H. Lecky, quoted by Hallam Tennyson in *Alfred Lord Tennyson A Memoir* (1898), II, 201, states that this passage was greatly admired by Tennyson and recalls 'the almost terrible force' with which he used to declaim it. *23 ⟨dazled⟩*] This is the reading of Rawl. Poet. 123 and 1691. All the 1680 editions read 'dazling', which is almost certainly a printer's error. *24 to Eternal*] Rawl. Poet. has this reading, but 'to' is corrected in the margin to 'in'. *25* Rawl. Poet. 123 reads:

'Lead him to Death, make him to understand'

but corrects in margin to reading in the text. *25–8* Cf. Montaigne, *op. cit.*: 'Ie croy qu'il me confessera, s'il parle en conscience, que tout l'acquest qu'il a retiré d'une si longue poursuite, c'est d'avoir appris à reconnoistre sa foiblesse.' Goethe quotes these four lines of Rochester in his *Dichtung und Wahrheit*, III, xiii, but does not give the name of the author. *29 the*] 1691 this; Rawl. Poet. 123 y^e. reas'ning *Engine*] a significant phrase expressing the new view of man as a mechanism. Robert Boyle calls men 'engines endowed with will' (*Works*, ed. Birch, 1772, V, 143). *32 Bubbles*] Rawl. Poet. 123 Cullies, corrected in margin to 'Bubbles'. *45 least*] Rawl. Poet. 123 lest; 1691 etc. heart. *46 Band*] i.e. the Geneva band worn by parsons at this period. *50 you*] 1691 you'l. Rawl. Poet. 123 reads:

'Likes me extremely but you must take care.'

51 this] Rawl. Poet. 123 that, corrected in margin to 'this'. *58 ferments*] Rawl. Poet. 123 corrects in margin to 'foments'. *69* This line is obviously a reniniscence of Lucretius, I, 73; 'flammantia mœnia mundi'. Rawl. Poet. 123 reads:

'The Limits of yᵉ Boundless Universe'.

'Boundless' is corrected in the margin to 'utmost'. *73 Ingello*] Nathaniel Ingelo (? 1621–83), graduate of Edinburgh and Cambridge and musician, to whom Andrew Marvell addressed a complimentary poem. He published in 1660 an allegorical romance called *Bentivolio and Urania*, to which Rochester is doubtless referring here. Sir W. Raleigh in *The English Novel* (1894) describes this work as 'marking the lowest depth to which English romance-writing sank'. *74 P⟨atrick's⟩ Pilgrim*] *The Parable of the Pilgrim*, a religious allegory by Simon Patrick, Bishop of Ely, published in 1664. *S⟨ibbs'⟩*] Richard Sibbes (1577–1635), Puritan divine and author of numerous religious works. ⟨Soliloquies⟩] The Folger and other issues of 1680 read 'replys', which must be a mistake. 1691, etc., The Portland Miscellany and Rawl. Poet. 123 read 'Soliloquies'. None of Sibbes's works actually bears this title, but the reference is doubtless to his longwinded lucubrations in general. *76, 77* Cf. Montaigne, *op. cit.*: 'Est il possible de rien imaginer si ridicule, que cette miserable & chestifve creature, qui n'est pas seulement maistresse de soy, exposee aux offences de toutes choses, se die maistresse & emperiere de l'univers, duquel il n'est pas en sa puissance de cognoistre la moindre partie, tant s'en faut de la commander?' *92* modern *Cloystered Coxcombs*] 1691 many modern coxcombs; Rawl. Poet. 123 modern Coxcombs also, corrected in margin to reading in the text. *115, 116* Cf. Montaigne, *op. cit.* (of animals): 'leur stupidite brutale surpasse en toutes commodites tout ce que peult nostre *divine intelligence*'. *120 M⟨eres⟩*] Sir Thomas Meres or

Meeres (1635–1715), M.P. for Lincoln in the Parliaments of Charles II, Commissioner for the Admiralty, 1679–84. *128* basest] Rawl. Poet. 123 corrects in margin to 'baser'. *133* hunt] Rawl. Poet. 123 haunt, corrected in margin to 'hunt'. *140–56* Cf. La Rochefoucauld, *les Maximes*, no. CCXIII: 'L'amour de la gloire, la crainte de la honte, le dessein de faire fortune, le désír de rendre notre vie commode et agréable, et l'envie d'abaisser les autres sont souvent les causes de cette valeur si célèbre parmi les hommes.' Rochester probably read La Rochefoucauld's *Maximes* (*Réflexions Morales*) in one of the five editions that appeared between 1665 and 1678. Cf. note to no. L, *ll.* 44, 45. *143* passion⟨s⟩] 1680 passion, 1691, etc., passions. *153* opposite this line in Oldham's transcript (Rawl. Poet. 123) there is an illegible correction in a different hand from that of the text. *165* Opposite this line in Rawl. Poet. 123 the following words appear in the same hand as that of the marginal scrawl opposite *l.* 153: 'Cowards if'. *166* Wrong'd, etc.] There seems an obvious connection between this line of thought and nos. LXV and LXVI as well as with the circumstances of Rochester's 'conversion'; see Introduction, pp. xxxvi, xxxvii. *173* The shorter version of the poem which appears in the broadside, 1691, etc., stops at this point. The remainder is headed 'Postscript' in 1714. In 1707 it appears as 'An Addition to the Satyr against Mankind'. *189, 190* 1714 omits. The text of these lines is obviously corrupt. One of the 1680 issues reads 'sly' for 'aureal' in *l.* 190. *191* Church-Man] 1714 Mortal. *193* Prelatique] 1714 aspiring. *195* his obstrep'rous] 1714 omits. *200* get drunk] 1714 drink free. *207* Pulpit proudly] 1714 stage of Honour. *209* B——] This is the reading of 1680 and the Portland Miscellany. 1714 leaves a blank. The only bishop of the period with a dissyllabic name whose character seems to fit Rochester's description is Thomas Barlow, Bishop of Lincoln (1607–91). He was a kind of Vicar of Bray who was 'one of the first to declare his loyalty to James II and turned Whig at William III's accession'. If the 'Postscript' was written in 1678 or 1679 Barlow would be some years short of 'Fourscore' at the time of its composition. *222 Rabble World,*] 1714 thinking World. *224* Cf. Montaigne, *Essais*, I, xlii: 'il y a plus de distance de tel à tel homme, qu'il n'y a de tel homme à tel beste'. He has just quoted a saying of Plutarch's 'qu'il ne trouve point si grande distance de beste à beste, comme il treuve d'homme à homme'.

LXV. *On Rome's Pardons*: 1680, p. 151; 1685; RRR; 1707; SCNIP; Sloane 1731a.
18 Devil] Sloane 1731a Jesuist [sic].

LXVI. *Plain Dealings Downfall*: 1685, p. 54; 1701; Rawl. Poet. 173. The transcript in Rawl. Poet. 173 is headed 'Plain Dealing abandon'd'. No author's name is appended to it. For this and the following poem, see Introduction, p. xxxvii.

LXVII. *Consideratus Considerandus*: 1685, pp. 66, 67; 1701.

APPENDIX

LXVIII. *As Concerning Man*: 1701, pp. 110, 111. This poem was also published in an undated, anonymous broadside. A note in the copy belonging to Mr. John Hayward attributes it to 'L⁴ Rochester'. It is also printed in Capt. Alexander Radcliffe's *The Ramble* (London, 1682), pp. 9, 10. Nevertheless I am inclined to believe that it is by Rochester. It may well have been a preliminary sketch for *A Satyr Against Mankind*.

J.W.   219   T

LXIX. *To His Mistress*: 1707, pp. 32–5; 1709, etc. This curious and beautiful poem is actually a kind of cento formed by combining lines from two poems of Francis Quarles (*The Divine Emblemes*, 1635, Book III, nos. VII and XII) and slightly altering the wording so as to transform them into a love poem. Most of the lines (Stanzas I–XIV) come from Book III, Emblem no. VII, a poem suggested by the words of the Book of Job (xiii, 24): 'Wherefore hidest thou thy face, and holdest me for thy enemie?' Stanza XV is the last stanza of another of Quarles's poems (no. XII, Book III). The word 'Love' is substituted for 'God' and 'Lord' in Quarles's poem and in stanza IX, *l.* 25 Quarles's 'Great shepherd' becomes 'dear Lover'. Much absurd moral indignation has been displayed by critics in connection with this poem and Rochester has been accused of plagiarism and irreverence. Actually the poem is only attributed to him on the very unreliable authority of the 1707 and 1709 editions. If it be his, it is probably a rough draft of a *pastiche* made for his own amusement, which it is very unlikely that he intended for publication. It might be entitled 'Variations on a Theme by Francis Quarles'.

22 The word omitted at the end of this line is the obsolete word 'tine' (=to kindle). The stanza in Quarles's Emblem VII, Book III, reads as follows:

> If my puff'd life be out, give leave to tine
> My flameless snuff at that bright lamp of thine:
> O what's thy light the less for lighting mine?

LXX. *A Satyr*: 1707, pp. 100–2; SPC; 1709. I have printed the version of this poem that appears in 1707 rather than that in SPC, because, although the latter is the earlier edition, the 1707 version is the fuller, containing six additional lines to which the editor calls attention by a single pair of inverted commas at the beginning of each of them, apparently to show that they appear in this collection for the first time. Some of the proper names have been completed with the help of the 1709 version. Title in 1709 is 'The First Satyr of Juvenal Imitated Semper ego Auditor Tantum &c.' The poem is obviously suggested by the opening lines of Juvenal's First Satire. It is difficult to date. If my identification of 'Henningham' with Sir W. Heveningham is correct in *l.* 5, it must have been written before October 1674, and, if 'Shrewsbury' in *l.* 33 is Francis Talbot, the eleventh Earl, before January 1668. On the other hand, *l.* 35 obviously refers to the cudgelling of Dryden in Rose Alley, Covent Garden, on 16th December 1679 (unless he was cudgelled on a previous unrecorded occasion). Possibly the last couplet was added after the 'Rose Alley ambuscade'.

5 Henningham] This is probably Sir William Heveningham of Kettering, son of William Heveningham, one of the regicides, and Lady Mary Heveningham. According to the D.N.B. he was knighted on 19th May 1674 and was buried on 14th October in the same year. *6 Arp*] This person is probably identical with the 'Mr. Arp: Orpe' mentioned in the key to *In Defence of Satyr* in the Portland Miscellany, see note to no. LXXIII, *l.* 28. *Arran*] This may be either the Scottish James, Earl of Arran, son of the Duke of Hamilton or the Irish Richard Butler, Earl of Arran. *Frank*] Possibly Frank Newport, see note to no. LVII, *l.* 49. *7 H[ewet]* Sir George Hewitt (1652–89), afterwards Viscount Hewytt of Goran, Co. Kilkenny, known as Beau Hewitt and said to be the person on whom Etherege based the character of Sir Fopling Flutter (see 'Sir Fopling Flutter and Beau Hewitt', by

A. Sherbo, N. and Q., 9th July 1949). *8 Villers]* Sir
Edward Villiers (1620–89). He was associated with
Sir George Hewitt and the Earl of Dorset in 1683
as a trustee for Nell Gwyn in respect of Burford
House at New Windsor (see Sherbo, *op. cit.*). *9
How]* John Grubham How (1657–1722), courtier
and politician known as 'Jack How'. *Brandon]*
Charles Gerard, Baron Brandon, First Earl of
Macclesfield (d. 1694). *10 S[outherlan]d]* George
Gordon, fourteenth (or fifteenth) Earl of Suther-
land. *11 Dencourt]* I am unable to identify this
person. The name is probably a seventeenth-century
spelling of the French name Dancourt. *12 Lumley]*
Richard Lumley, First Earl of Scarborough, d.
1721, Master of the Horse of Queen Catherine.
Savage] Thomas Savage, Earl Rivers (? 1628–1694).
21 R[anelagh]] Richard Jones, third Viscount Rane-
lagh (? 1636–1712). *26 N[ell]]* Nell Gwyn (1650–
87). *O[glethorp]]* This is either Sir Theophilus
Oglethorpe (1650–1702), an officer in Charles II's
lifeguards, or his brother Sutton Oglethorpe, one of
the king's pages. *27 S[outhampton]]*. This must be
Charles Fitzroy, son of Charles II and Barbara
Palmer (1662–1730). The allusion helps to date the
poem as Fitzroy was created Earl of Southampton
in 1670 and Duke of Southampton in 1675.

28 Y——] Probably Sir Robert Paston, First Earl of
Yarmouth (1631–83). *31 S[underland]]* Robert
Spencer, Second Earl of Sunderland (1640–1702).
32 Hallifax] George Savile, Marquis of Halifax
(1633–95). *Pembrook]* Philip Herbert, Seventh Earl
of Pembroke (1653–83), see Introduction, p. xxv. *33
Bardash]* 'a catamite, "cinaedus" ' (O.E.D) *S[hrews-
bury]]* This must be Francis Talbot Earl of Shrewsbury, husband of the notorious Anna Maria Brude-
nell, Countess of Shrewsbury, mistress of the Duke
of Buckingham. Shrewsbury was killed in a duel

with Buckingham in January 1668. *34 F—— ...
M——*] I conjecture that this stands for 'Fubbs's
chattering Monkey'. Fubbs was Charles II's nickname for Louise de Keroualle, Duchess of Portsmouth. *35 Dryden's cudgel'd Skin*] Obviously a
reference to the 'Rose Alley ambuscade' of 16th
December 1679. See Introduction, pp. xxiv, xxv. *36
Tom Thinn*] Thomas Thynne of Longleat (1648–82),
one of the wealthiest landowners of the period,
the Issachar of Dryden's *Absalom and Achitophel*.

LXXI. *Pindarick*: SPC, p. 239; 1707; 1709. Title in
1707, 'Lais Senior'; in 1709 'Lais Senior: A Pindarick.' Only parts of some of the proper names are
printed in SPC, but they are completed in 1707.
This amusing burlesque ode almost certainly refers
to Barbara Palmer, Duchess of Cleveland.
23 Ca⟨ndis⟩h] William Cavendish (1640–1707), son
of the Earl of Devonshire and afterwards First
Duke of Devonshire. *24 Henning⟨ha⟩m*] See above,
note to no. LXX, *l*. 5. *Scrope*] Sir Car Scroope. See
above note to no. LV *l*. 12. *25 Ned*] probably Sir
Edward Villiers, see above note to no. LXX, *l*. 8.
26 Frank] see above note to no. LXX, *l*. 6.

LXXII. *On King Charles by the Earl of Rochester*, etc.
POAS, p. 181; 1707; 1709.
25 Carewell] Louise de Keroualle, Duchess of Portsmouth. See note to No. LVIII, *l*. 101.

LXXIII, LXXIIIA, LXXIIIB: 1680, pp. 45–51; 1685;
1707, etc.; 1714; MS. 636F; MS. 623F; Portland
Miscellany. This group of poems, constituting
apparently a 'flyting' between two authors, presents
difficult problems to the editor. The traditional view
is that *In Defence of Satyr* (no. LXXIII) was written
by Sir Car Scroope in reply to the satiric reference to
him by Rochester in *An Allusion to the Tenth Satyr
of the First Book of Horace* (no. LV, II, 113–15),

that no. LXXIIIA ('On the supposed Author of a late Poem in defence of Satyr') was a reply by Rochester, and no. LXXIIIB ('The Answer') a rejoinder by Scroope. In Tonson's edition of 1714 *In Defence of Satyr* is preceded by the following note: 'The following verses were written by Sir Car Scroope on being reflected upon at the latter end of the foregoing Copy', i.e. Rochester's *Allusion to the Tenth Satyr of the First Book of Horace*. It appears without attribution in MS. 636F but is ascribed to 'Scroop' in MS. 623F and the Portland Miscellany. The poem is also ascribed to 'Scroope' in Osborn MS., Chest II, no. 14, and by Anthony à Wood in his *Fasti* (ed. Bliss, II, 294), where he states that he obtained his information from a 'MS in Mr. Sheldon's Library'. On the other hand, there is a tradition that *In Defence of Satyr* is by Rochester. It is ascribed to him by Sir Thomas Pope Blount in *De Re Poetica*, 1694, p. 44, and by Giles Jacob in his Poetical Register, 1723, pp. 232–3. In a very interesting transcript of the poem in a late seventeenth-century hand in the Folger Library, the name 'Rochester' is written in the margin against *l*. 46, obviously in the belief that the poem is Rochester's, while the person satirized in *l*. 25 is identified as 'Scroop'. However, in MS. 623F the name 'Rochester' appears beside *l*. 48 and 'Capt. Downes' beside *l*. 53. Actually the poem is very much in Rochester's manner and contains a number of phrases used by him in his authentic poems. The thought and movement of the verse in *ll*. 22–7 especially seem to me to be characteristic of Rochester. I am inclined to think that the poem was attributed to Scroope because the allusion to a street brawl in *ll*. 51–5 was taken to refer to the affair at Epsom in June 1676 when Downes was killed, which was constantly used to blacken Rochester's reputation. There were, how-

ever, many other street brawls in the reign of
Charles II and these lines may refer to some entirely
different affair. It seems strange that Scroope, when
satirized by Rochester, should have replied by writing a 'Defence' of Satire. In the 1715 edition of
Buckingham's *Works* the poem is said to be '*By the
Duke of Buckingham.* Ascrib'd falsly to the Earl of
R.' I suggest that *In Defence of Satyr* may have
been an anonymous lampoon written by Rochester
possibly in collaboration with Buckingham. A copy
of it may have fallen into the hands of some
collector of Rochesteriana like the editor of 1680,
who noticed *ll.* 51–5 and jumped to the conclusion
that they were an allusion to the brawl at Epsom
and that therefore the poem must be a satire on
Rochester. It would then be an easy step to ascribe
it to Sir Car Scroope, who was known to have
written lampoons and might be supposed to have
replied to the attack on the 'Purblind Knight' in
Rochester's *Allusion to the Tenth Satire of the First
Book of Horace*. It would probably not have been
beyond the power of such a person to have written
the two pieces of doggerel which form the rest of
the 'flyting'—thus creating a piquant addition to
the Rochester legend. Finally, of course, it is by no
means impossible that Rochester himself with his
love of impersonations and disguises may have
written the whole of the 'flyting'. On. p. 49 of the
Portland Miscellany there is a key to the interpretation of some of the personal allusions in no. LXXIII
Other interpretations are given in marginal notes in
the Folger MS., MS. 623F and MS. 636F. These
interpretations (together with one from 1714) are
recorded in the following notes, the letters PMK
being used to denote the key in the Portland
Miscellany.

28 vain Fop] PMK Mr. Arp: Orpe; Folger MS.

Hinch; MS. 623F Sir John Fenwick. Mr. Arp: Orpe is probably the person referred to in no. LXX, *l.* 6. I am unable to identify him. 'Hinch' must be Viscount Hinchingbrooke, son of Pepys's Earl of Sandwich and once Rochester's rival for the hand of Miss Malet; if this interpretation is correct the poem must have been written before Hinchingbrooke succeeded his father as Second Earl of Sandwich in 1672. Sir John Fenwick (1645–97) was a Colonel of Foot and M.P. for Northumberland. *32* Here one whom] PMK Sir Geo: Hewitt MS. 623F Captain Aston. For Sir G. Hewit; see note to no. LXX, *l.* 7. Aston is probably Col. Edmund Ashton, a friend of the Wits. *35* Folger MS. Scroop. *46* Folger MS. Rochester; *48* He that can rail at] MS. 623F Earl of Rochester. MS. 636F Ld Roch; PMK Rochester. *53* brave *Companion*] MS. 623F Captain Downes; MS. 636F Capt. Downes; footnote in 1714 Col. Dounes. The reference (if these interpretations are accepted) is to the brawl at Epsom in June 1676 when Downes (promoted to the rank of Colonel by the editor of 1714) lost his life, see Pinto, *Rochester, Portrait of a Restoration Poet*, p. 185. *61* Booby *Sotus*] PMK, Folger MS. Griffin; MS. 623F, MS. 636F Mr. Griffin. This is probably Col. Edward Griffin (d. 1710), created Baron Griffin of Braybrooke by James II (see G.E.C. Peerage, VI, 202–3). Provoe] a spelling of Provost in the sense of an officer of military police. *62* chatt'ring *Porus*] MS. 623F chattering Dorus. PMK Barbeck; Folger MS. Rash. MS. 623F Sir R. Bovy 'Burbeck' is probably Robert Villiers or Danvers (1656–84) styled Viscount Purbeck (see G.E.C. Peerage). I cannot identify 'Rash.'; Sir R. Bovy may be a mistake for James Bovey, see note to LII, *l.* 70. *77 Simius*, the *Buffoon*] PMK Arson; MS. 623F Newport; MS. 636F ffran. Newpo: I am unable to identify 'Arson'. 'ffran. Newpo:'

stands for Francis Newport (see note to no. LVII,
l. 49). Cully *Bash*] PMK Bask; MS. 623F Sir E.
Bash. The reference is probably to Sir E. Bache, a
Somersetshire baronet. *78 Alidores*] PMK, MS.
623F Ld Culpepper; MS. 636F Culpeper. This must
be Thomas Colepeper, Baron Colepeper of Thores-
way (1635–89), see G.E.C. Peerage, III, 364. *88
Milo*] PMK Savile; MS. 623F Mr. S[?avile] (the
rest of the word is erased). The reference is certainly
to Rochester's friend Henry Savile, see note to no.
LVI, *l*. 32. *90 Heroe Paris*] PMK, Monmouth MS.
623F D. of Mon. These lines obviously refer to
Monmouth's exploits at the mimic battle of Windsor in the Summer of 1674, see note to no. XX, *l*. 12.
92 Cornus] PMK Loftus; MS. 623F Mr. Loftus. This
may be the learned orientalist Dudley Loftus (1619–
95). *96 Grandio*] PMK Mulgrave; MS. 623F E. of
Mulgrave; Folger MS. Gar.; MS. 636F Ld Gerard.
97 MS. 636F Mulgrave. For Mulgrave, see Introduction, p. xxiii. 'Ld Gerard' can hardly be Baron
Gerard of Gerard's Bromley who died in 1667, or
his son who was born in 1662. It is probably Charles
Gerard, Baron Brandon, First Earl of Macclesfield,
see no. LXX, *l*. 9 n. *98* Folger MS. Moulg. *104
Albanus*] PMK St. Albans; MS. 623F E. of St.
Albans; Folger MS. St. Al. This is certainly the
doughty old courtier and *bon vivant* Henry Jermyn,
Earl of St. Albans (d. 1684). *105 florid Roscius*]
PMK, MS. 623F Ld Chancellor; MS. 636F Ld
Chanclr; Folger MS. Chan. This must be Anthony
Ashley Cooper, First Earl of Shaftesbury (1621–83),
who became Lord Chancellor in 1672.

LXXIV. *The Platonick Lady*: Bodl. Add. MS. A 301,
pp. 24, 25. First printed in Hayward, p. 142. This
poem, as far as is known, only occurs in a MS.
miscellany in a late seventeenth-century hand in the

Bodleian, where the title is followed by the words 'By lord Rochester'. The lines were probably suggested by the well-known poem of Petronius (*Poetae Latini Minores*, ed. Baehrens, no. 101) beginning 'Foeda est in coitu et brevis voluptas'.

14 'She'd' is written over the word 'will' in the MS. in a different hand from that of the text of the poem. *24, 25* These lines are possibly an echo of Marlowe's famous song:

> Come live with mee, and be my love,
> And we will all the pleasures prove,...

LXXV. *Song*: Portland MS., f. 14. Draft in Lady Rochester's hand on one side of a folded sheet of paper. This and the four following poems may be either by Rochester or by Lady Rochester. On f. 15 there is another version of this poem also in lady Rochester's hand, which is almost identical with that which occurs on f. 14 but has the name 'Phillis' in the first line crossed out and 'Cloris' substituted. It is also written on one side of a folded sheet of paper, on the inside of which is another poem in a different hand printed here as no, LXXVI.

LXXVI. *Your glory Phillis*, etc.: Portland MS., f. 15. See note to preceding poem. This poem is in a hand which is neither Rochester's nor Lady Rochester's.

LXXVII. *Song*: Portland MS., ff. 16, 17. Draft in Lady Rochester's hand on two scraps of paper. *9* 'though' is substituted for the word 'blinded' crossed out in the MS.

LXXVIII. *Corrina vainly*, etc.: Portland MS., f. 18. Draft in Lady Rochester's hand on one side of a small sheet of paper. The last couplet is written on the back of the sheet. Words enclosed in brackets are crossed out in the MS.

LXXIX. *Dearest Armilla*, etc.: Portland MS., f. 18. Draft in Lady Rochester's hand on one side of a single sheet of paper. Words enclosed in brackets are crossed out on the MS. On f. 21 there is another slightly different draft of the same poem also in Lady Rochester's hand.

LXXX. *Some Impromptus ascribed to Rochester*:

(1) The Earle of Rochester's Conference with a Post-boy, 1674: The text is from a MS. miscellany carrying the bookplate of Thos. Wentworth, Baron of Raby, etc., a folio of 325 pages containing poems in two late seventeenth-century hands, now in the Library of the Department of English of Ohio State University, Columbus, Ohio, where I was allowed to examine it by the kindness of Professor J. H. Wilson. The poem was first printed in full by Professor Wilson in a short article called 'Rochester's "Buffoon Conceit"' in MLN, May 1951, pp. 372, 373. A version of the first six lines entitled 'Spoken to a Post-boy, 1674' was printed by J. Prinz on p. 56 of his *Rochesteriana* (1926), where he states that he took them from an old manuscript entry in his copy of *The Poetical Works of the Earls of Rochester*, etc., 1739. Wilson suggests in his article that this poem may be the 'buffoon conceit' referred to by Sir Car Scroope in *l.* 55 of *In Defence of Satyr* (no. LXXIII), if that poem be by him.

(2) *My Lord Rochester attempting to kiss the Duchess of Cleveland*, etc.: 1707, p. 135; 1709, etc.

(3) *Spoken Extempore to a Country Clerk*, etc.: 1709, p. 75. According to Thomas Longueville (*Rochester and Other Literary Rates of the Restoration*, 1902, p. 273), Rochester extemporised these lines on a psalm-singing clerk at Bodicot, near Adderbury. Longueville quotes no authority to support this statement.

(4) *Extempore to his Lady*, etc.: First printed apparently in *The Literary Magazine: Or the Universal
Review from January to August, 1758* (London
1758). Reprinted by Prinz in his *Rochesteriana*,
pp. 55, 56.

(5) *Trust not that thing*, etc.: These lines, which may
perhaps be fairly classed as an impromptu, are from
a MS. commonplace book belonging to Thomas
Watson (*fl. c.* 1680) in the Library of Merton
College, Oxford. They occur on the verso of the first
leaf and the name 'Rochester' is appended to them.
I am indebted for them to Dr. H. W. Garrod, who
first drew my attention to the book.

LXXXI. *Rochester's Farewel*: TPCP, pp. 26–30;
POAS; 1707; 1709, etc.; MS. 624F. It was also
printed by H. Hills in 1709 with *The History of
Insynds*, etc. See note to no. L. This vigorous and
interesting poem was apparently first printed in
TPCP, which I have used as the copy text of the
present edition. The version in MS. 624F is slightly
fuller, containing 216 lines as against 211 in TPCP.
The proper names have been filled in for the most
part from MS. annotations in the British Museum
copy. The external evidence for attributing the
poem to Rochester is not very strong. However, the
powerful style and the allusions to Court life,
obviously the work of someone who knew it from
the inside, point to Rochester's authorship of at
least parts of the poem. It has been objected that the
lines on the embarkation of the expedition to Tangier must have been written after 13th June 1680
when that event took place and when Rochester
was on his death-bed and not in a condition to
write satiric poetry. Samuel Woodforde in his *Ode
to the Memory of the Right Honourable John Lord
Wilmot Earl of Rochester* (printed by Prinz in his

Rochesteriana, p. 67) seems to deny Rochester's authorship of the 'Farewel':

But still as they were wont before
With Farwells, Droll, and Shredds of Verse
They vex his Happy Ghost, and miserably disguise
    his Herse.
Yet Farwels such as those He never took
Nor would a Wise man howsoever mov'd ...

However, it must be remembered that Woodforde was a pious writer who wished to make all the capital he could out of Rochester's conversion. I am inclined to think that Rochester sketched a 'Farewell to the Court' in the spring of 1680. According to Luttrell's Diary (I, 46) the 'troops designed for Tangier' were ready and 'commanders appointed' on 26th May 1680. Rochester would doubtless have had access to sources of information which enabled him to know all about the plans for the Tangier expedition even before that date. According to Burnet he left London for the last time 'about the beginning of April' and 'he had not been long in the Country when he thought he was so well' that he decided to ride to his wife's estates in Somerset. He may have sketched his 'Farewell to the Court' in May just before he rode to Somerset and was attacked by his last fatal illness. The version printed in TPCP is probably a considerably edited version of Rochester's draft and the slightly extended version in MS. 624F may represent another attempt to give it coherence.

2 Part] MS. 624F past. *11* will] MS. 624F stil. *13* ⟨then⟩] POAS and MS. 624F insert this word, probably omitted in error from TPCP. *20* Goggling] MS. 624F Hosa: ing. *24* Sir C[ar]] marginal note in B.M. copy of TPCP 'Sir Car Scroop'. For Sir George Hewitt, see note to no. LXX, *l.* 7. *32*

S[alisbur]y MS. 624F, POAS *Shrewsbury*. Shrewsbury is probably the correct reading. The reference would then be to the young Charles Talbot, Earl of Shrewsbury (1660–1718). *42* ⟨*Frazier*⟩] TPCP has the obviously mistaken reading *Torrezer*; Frazier is the reading of POAS, (MS. 624F 'frazer'). The reference is to Sir Alexander Fraser the well-known court physician; see note to no. XXXII (1). *50* Chit] 'A person considered as no better than a child' (O.E.D.), 'Generally used of young persons in contempt' (Johnson's Dictionary). The ministry of young men formed by Charles II in 1679 was nicknamed the Ministry of Chits. These are the 'Chits of Stale' of *ll*. 48–50. *S[underlan]d*] Robert Spencer, Second Earl of Sunderland (1640–1702). *L[ory]*] 'Lory Hyde', marginal note in B.M. copy of TPCP. This is Laurence Hyde (1641–1711), created Earl of Rochester on the death of the boy Charles Wilmot, 3rd Earl of Rochester in 1681. *51* *P[limouth]*] Charles Fitzcharles, Earl of Plymouth (1657–80), natural son of Charles II by Catherine Pegge. *53* *R[ichmon]d*] Charles Lennox, another of Charles's bastard sons. His mother was the Duchess of Portsmouth. Born in 1672, he was created Duke of Richmond in 1675 and would be eight years old when this poem was written. *63* Little *W[rot]h*] This person, according to Hayward (note, ad loc.), was one of Monmouth's six Life Guards. He was probably a son of Thomas Wroth, M.P., who sat in the Long Parliament and the first Restoration parliament. After *63* MS. 624F has the following lines:

butt now they are all unbarqued & curse their fate
curse Charles y^t gave them leave but chiefly Kate
who then Tangier to England and ye King,
besides her self no greater plague could bring

and wish ye Moors since now their hand is in
as they have got yᵉ porcõn had ye Queen

67 Mastrich] See note to no. XX, *l.* 12. *68* 'D. Mon-
mouth', marginal note in TPCP. *76 A[rmstron]g*]
Sir Thomas Armstrong (? 1624–84), an officer in the
Guards and adherent of Monmouth, was implicated
in the Rye House Plot and executed in 1684.
V[erno]n] James Vernon (1646–1727), secretary to
Monmouth, later Secretary of State under
William III. *81 R[oss]*] Thomas Ross, tutor to the
Duke of Monmouth. *84* P[roger]s] 'P[almer]s' is
written in text of B.M. copy and 'Progers' substituted in margin. Edward Progers was groom of
the Bedchamber to Charles II and confidant of his
intrigues. It was rumoured that he was the father of
the Duke of Monmouth. *85* B[uckingha]m] See note
to no. LV, *l.* 118. POAS and MS. 624F read 'Brandon'. This is Charles Gerard, Baron Brandon and
Earl of Macclesfield (d. 1694), one of Monmouth's
adherents. *110 S[hrewsbur]y to Le M[arr]*] Sh[rews-
bur]y refers to Buckingham's notorious intrigue
with the Countess of Shrewsbury, whose husband he
killed in a duel in 1668. Le M[arr]] I am unable to
identify this person. According to Hayward (note,
ad loc.) the allusion is to Buckingham's unsuccessful
negotiations with William of Orange. POAS reads
Le Meer, MS. 624F Lemar. *114 M[azarin]e*] Hortense Mancini (1646–9), favourite niece of Cardinal
Mazarin, married to Lorenzo Mancini (created Duc
Mazarin) at the age of sixteen, separated from her
husband after six years of married life, spent
another eight in convents and small Italian courts
and arrived in London in the winter of 1675/6,
where she soon became a prominent figure at the
court of Charles II and a rival to his mistresses.
124 S[usse]x] Anne Fitzroy, illegitimate daughter of

Charles II by Barbara Palmer, born in 1661. She married Thomas Lennard, Earl of Sussex. *B[roghi]ll]* This must be Mary, wife of Roger Boyle, Earl of Orrery, 'styled Lord Broghill 1660–1679' according to the G.E.C. Peerage. Her title when this poem was written was Countess of Orrery, as her husband succeeded to the earldom in 1679. *Betty F[elto]n]* This is Lady Betty Howard, wife of Thomas Felton, see note to no. XLII. *130 Pedalian]* MS. 624F reads Pelean. Both readings are probably mistakes for 'Pellean', i.e. native of Pella, capital of Macedonia, reputed birthplace of Alexander the Great. *138 Messaline]* Messalina, wife of the Emperor Claudius notorious for profligacy. *158 D——s]* This name is not filled up in the B.M. copy of TPCP. In POAS the word is printed as 'Dutchess'. In MS. 624F the reading is 'My Lady Harriot.' *D——s* might stand for 'Dacres'. One of the titles of Thomas Lennard Earl of Sussex was Lord Dacre, often spelt 'Dacres' in the seventeenth century. His wife (see note to *l.* 124 above) could be known as 'Lady Dacres'. *181 B——y]* This name is not completed in the B.M. copy of TPCP, In POAS it is printed as 'Bromley'. MS. 624F reads

> to send her Bromley, Hide and Mazareen

Bromley is probably Jane, wife of Charles Baron Gerard of Gerard's Bromley, a gentleman of the Bedchamber to Charles II who died in 1667. His wife survived him and died in 1703. Hide must be Henrietta, wife of Laurence Hyde. *182 M[onmout]h]* Anne Scott (1651–1732), Countess of Buccleuch and wife of James Scott, Duke of Monmouth, whom she married in 1663. *185* This seems to be unjust to Mazarin, who, whatever her faults may have been, was a woman of culture and the friend of men of letters like Saint-Evrémond and Saint-Réal. *200*

P[ortsmout]h See note to no. LVIII, *l.* 101. *201*
S[underlan]d See note to no. LXX, *l.* 31. MS. 624F
reads 'ye great faction'. *205 S[haftesbur]y* Anthony
Ashley Cooper, First Earl of Shaftesbury (1621–83),
the famous Whig leader, Dryden's Achitophel.

INDEX TO FIRST LINES
AND TITLES

Titles are printed in italics

INDEX TO FIRST LINES AND TITLES